微观中国
1-MINUTE CHINA

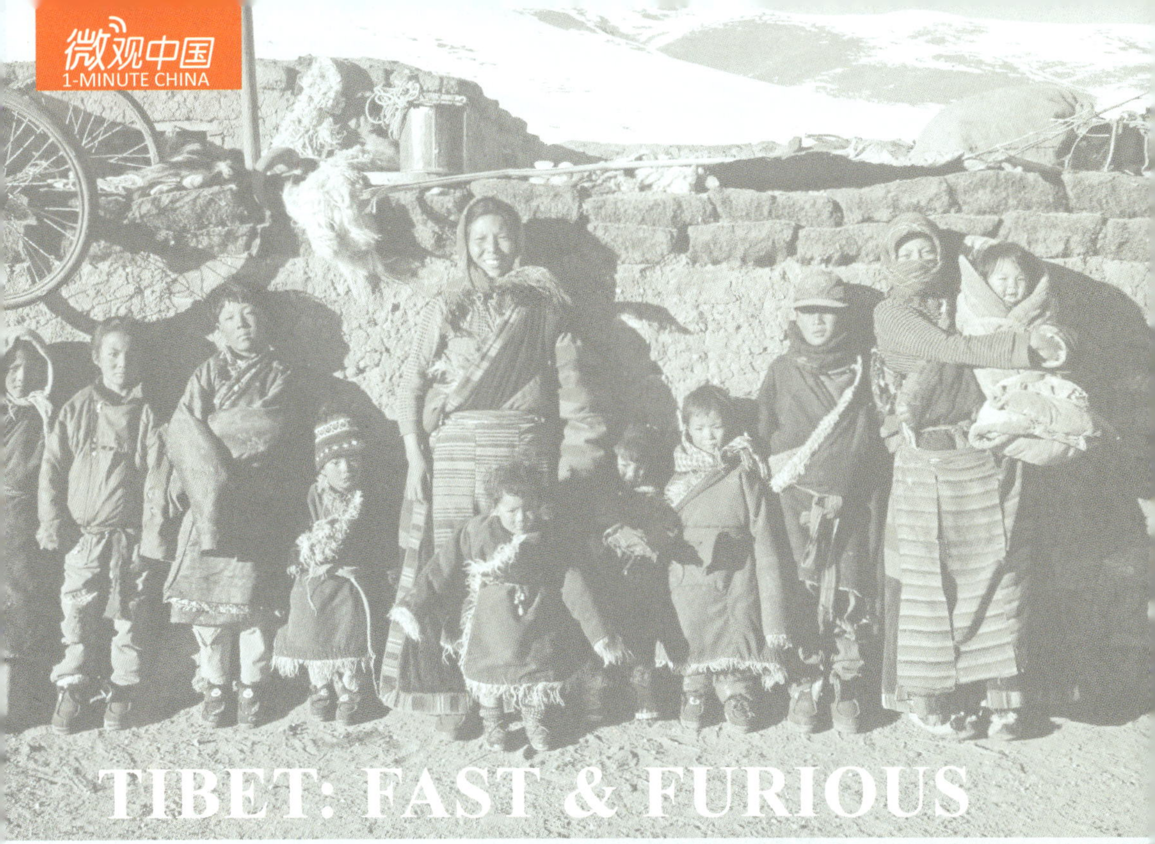

TIBET: FAST & FURIOUS

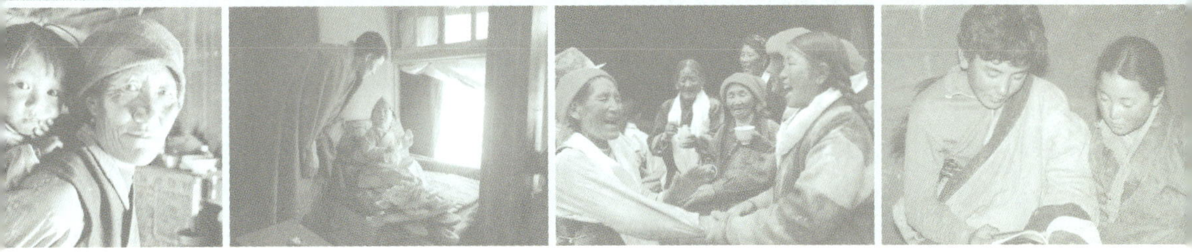

微观西藏

（汉英版）

聂晓阳 主编

SINCE 1897
商务印书馆
The Commercial Press
2018年·北京

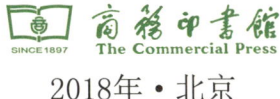

主　　编	聂晓阳
编　　写	聂晓阳　肖淼晨　胡逸君
	胡继平　吕海春　蔡长虹
	储丹丹　何毓玲　倪咏娟
审　　订	旦增伦珠　廉湘民
英文翻译	周驰（加）　陈博玚　胡逸君
	梅皓（美）　董怡（美）　许舒园
英文审订	师鲁道（澳）　张永青　丁逸旻
	赵守辉（澳）
英文编辑	钱厚生
责任编辑	储丹丹
装帧设计	东方美迪
统筹策划	《汉语世界》杂志社

Chief Compiler	Nie Xiaoyang
Compilers	Nie Xiaoyang　Xiao Miaochen　Hu Yijun
	Hu Jiping　Lü Haichun　Cai Changhong
	Chu Dandan　He Yuling　Ni Yongjuan
Reviewers	Tenzin Lhundrup　Lian Xiangmin
English Translators	Chris Zhou (CAN)　Chen Boyang　Hu Yijun
	Mei Hao (USA)　Elizabeth Tung (USA)
	Xu Shuyuan
English Reviewers	Rudolf Salzlechner (AUS)　Zhang Yongqing
	Ding Yimin　Zhao Shouhui (AUS)
English Editor	Qian Housheng
Executive Editor	Chu Dandan
Art Design	EmDesign
Project Coordinator	THE WORLD OF CHINESE

| 前 言 |

真实西藏的心灵之旅

应商务印书馆之约构思这本书的时候,我最先想到的是好友嵇永强生前说过的一句话。这位温文尔雅的援藏记者说,有些人,到趟西藏就说经历了回生死,爬了个雪山就写文章说过了次鬼门关……嵇兄说:请不要向人民撒娇。

一晃永强兄殉职已经12年了。但是,不要用读者赋予的话语权向读者撒娇,这一信念已经永远地留在了我的心底。有人说,西藏是行者的不老情人。但对我来说,差不多每年都去一两次的西藏,更像是一块神奇的布,每次都把我的心擦拭得更加干净。这片土地改变了我,让我的内心更加平和柔软。所以,我对西藏除了热爱之外,总有一种亏欠之心。怀着这种亏欠之心做事,唯一能让我有所慰藉的就是:如何更好呈现一个真实的、深刻的、不矫情的西藏?

那就是相信真实的力量。对于敬畏文字的人来说,哪怕是真实的瑕疵,也胜过虚假的完美。我曾好几遍细读书云女士的《西藏一年》,给我印象最深的是乡村医生拉姆的故事。她在一间简陋的卫生院负责全乡5000多人的医疗。因为积劳成疾,拉姆医生患有严重的胃病,但身为医生的她却相信自己的病是"前世的孽障"造成的,因此首先求助于法师,而不是比自己更高明的医生。这个听起来匪夷所思的例子其实在西藏并不稀奇,这就是普通西藏人的故事。这个故事也许无法充当正面传播西藏的绝佳素材,却散发着原汁原味、真实的西藏乡土气息。

所以,这本书从一开始的定位就是一个"真"字。我们要用真诚的心态,找到尽可能多的真正了解和理解西藏的人,挖掘和呈现那个超越了走马观花、一惊一乍和非黑即白的西藏真容。

这本书在形式上的一个创新,是采用了所谓的"微博体"。个中原因,不仅是因为越来越多的人开始习惯这种更方便浏览、转发和扩散的"段子阅读",更是因为这种体裁更加能够见微知著,更有利于发掘和呈现有关西藏的点点滴滴,并且通过大量有血有肉的细节,拼接出一个有喜乐有忧愁有希望也面临挑战的西藏。我深信,一个真实的西藏是更美的西藏,而这种美丽,蕴含于大量的、鲜活的、一手的细节中,蕴含于大量的、深入的、中肯的言论中,也蕴含于大量的、有趣的、独到的小故事中。

一座雪山远远就能看到,可是要真切地看到西藏人日常生活中能够拨动人心弦的细微之处,却需要长期的浸润和近距离的凝视,需要对这方水土丰沛的

微观西藏
TIBET: FAST & FURIOUS

感情和持久的热爱。作为一本在新媒体环境下追求最佳阅读体验的、试图用最短的文字还原那些最了解西藏的人心中最真实的西藏的书，书名《微观西藏》中的"微"字，正是"微博"的"微"，也是"细微"的"微"，还是"微妙"的"微"。我希望书中每一条"微博"，都能够像一把钥匙，打开一扇被想象和偏见阻隔的厚门，帮助人们登堂入室，一窥西藏的容颜。

实际上，《微观西藏》这样一本书的构思，最早可以追溯到我的西藏妈妈（阿妈拉）、著名藏族民间文学专家德门·德庆卓嘎。两年前的一个晚上，在拉萨大昭寺旁她的家中，她给我讲了两个她从刚刚探亲回来的保姆那里听来的故事。当时我就想，如果能够搜集到足够多这样的故事，编成一本带领读者走入西藏人内心深处的书，该是一件多好的事啊。

那天76岁的阿妈拉陪我喝青稞酒，吃风干牦牛肉，还兴致勃勃地载歌载舞，用藏语唱了几首她从小就会唱的六世达赖喇嘛仓央嘉措情歌。等到一直安静地坐在一旁编织金刚结的保姆曲珍来收拾桌子的时候，天已经很晚了。这时，阿妈拉忽然对我说："你不是要了解藏族人吗，我给你说两个最新鲜、最真实的故事，是曲珍昨天刚对我讲的。"

"曲珍村里有个十来岁的女孩去镇上买东西，路上被一位邻居的车撞死了。小女孩的妈妈很伤心，整整三天没有出门，那位肇事者很内疚，也有些担心。没想到第四天早上，小女孩的妈妈来到他家，不是为了要赔偿，而是安慰他，请他不要自责。"

"小女孩的妈妈怎么安慰那个闯祸的人呢？那位妈妈说：每个人都有自己的因果，我女儿出了事不仅仅是因为你的过错，更是因为她前世和今生所造的业。车祸只是一个表面的现象，我女儿去世前每分每秒的念头和行为，汇集起来才是导致这个后果的因。所以，让我们都接受这个事实，只有生者不再悔恨难过，死者才能更安心地往生。"

阿妈拉的讲述立刻深深地震撼了我。但她还有一个同样震撼的故事在等着我。

"曲珍这次回家，正好她们家一头牛摔到悬崖下受了伤，很重的伤，被救上来已经奄奄一息了。怎么办？按照有些人的想法，养牛就是为了吃肉，现在既然这样了，干脆杀了吃肉吧。可是她家的人想法不一样，她们认为牛既然还有生命就应该找兽医来看病，结果花了比一头牛还贵的钱把牛治好了。这就是西藏牧民，他们的想法到现在还跟过去一样，那就是一头牛的生命和人没有什么区别。这辈子是头牛，也许下辈子就是一个人呢。"

那天晚上从阿妈拉家出来，八廓街格外安静，屋顶的经幡在柔和的月光下清晰可见。那一刻，我恍然行走在儿时的故乡，内心深处有一种熟悉、亲切和

前言
Preface

温暖的东西在流动。

当时的我怎么也不会想到,两年之后的 2012 年 6 月 23 日,我抵达拉萨的第二天,阿妈拉在自治区人民医院永远闭上了她豁达了一辈子的眼睛。在陪阿妈拉的遗体最后一次走过八廓街的那个雨夜,我觉得一种只有母亲才有的气息一直萦绕着我。

阿妈拉有次跟我说,现在仍有很多人觉得西藏很"神秘"。"为什么呢?你不了解的东西就会觉得神秘。当你了解了之后,还有什么可神秘的呢?对于西藏如果只看到表面的形式,那就只能看到神秘,别的什么也看不见。所以,我觉得你要把很多表面的东西弄清楚,这样才能把西藏人的心看透。"

阿妈拉去世后,家人为她供请了七七四十九天的酥油灯。在我寻访西藏的精神之旅中,阿妈拉正是一盏不灭的明灯。

在和商务印书馆副总编辑周洪波先生共同带队到西藏的调研中,我印象最深的,是"西藏画派"两位代表人物的谈话。他们一位是旅居西藏 30 年的前西藏文联副主席余友心先生,一位是进藏 40 年的现任西藏美协主席韩书力先生。

余友心先生称西藏是一个可以"让心安驻"和"不再火烧火燎"的地方。他说,要发现和理解真正的西藏,就要撇开一切偏见,摆正心态,把自己当作小学生,忘记那些条条框框的成见,把心打开。

"西藏人有他们自己的生存状态和生活方式,对这些不能机械地用外来者的标准去衡量,也不需要用过分的辞藻来包装。能让人看到一个真实的西藏和西藏人,这就是最大的价值。"他说。

韩书力先生讲了这样一个故事:"有年冬天我下乡采风,坐在冰冷的石头上画画,当地的藏民就把小木板放在太阳下晒热了悄悄递给我,还生怕打扰我画画。"在两个语言不通、生长环境迥异的人之间,一个无所欲求的、真诚的举动,就使一块小小的木板温暖了另一个人的心,即使过了很多年。

他在谈到对待西藏的心态时,给了我们三点建议:第一,用平视的眼光看西藏,平视就是不怀偏见的注视;第二,用平常心看西藏,不要一惊一乍;第三,用包容的心态看西藏,不要带着救世主的心态和优越感。

和余、韩两位前辈文人的谈话让我想起来有一次在北大,我参与的与 CNN、《华盛顿邮报》、《时代周刊》驻北京首席记者以及美国一位华裔女大使进行座谈的情形。记得座谈中有人提出,同是在北京工作的记者,外国记者的自由度和采访的活动空间要小得多,比如外国记者就很难有机会去西藏,即使去了,也往往受到种种限制。

当时在座的听众大都是北大国际政治专业的研究生。其中一个学生站起来质疑说:西方记者对西藏的报道是不是过于片面?为什么你们总把镜头对准那

微观西藏
TIBET: FAST & FURIOUS

些负面的非主流的东西？你们去西藏是为了发现什么，还是为了证明你们早已存在的偏见？

在争论中，一位中国资深记者感慨道：其实作为记者，受到个人背景、语言、经历等等的制约，我们都是受到种种限制的，这些限制很大程度上来自我们自身而并非外界。他说：我们都是在一个笼子里，有时候我们在一个比较大的笼子里，有时候你们在一个比较大的笼子里。

这让我产生了这样的联想：两只青蛙分别蹲在两口井底，同时望着蓝天，同时觉得蓝天就是它们看到的样子。从某种意义上说，我们每一个人都是这样的青蛙。所不同的是，那限制了我们视野的"井底"，往往正是我们内心的成见——在需要打开窗户以便看得更清的时候，我们往往连门都关上了。

是的，当人们在你的窗前众声喧哗的时候，明智的做法不是连门带窗都关严，更不是赶走人群，而是把窗户开得更大，或者擦亮玻璃，让他们看得更清楚。

为什么不呢？一个立体的、有阴影但更有亮点的真相就在那里，我们要做的，只不过是让更多的人更好地看见。

聂晓阳
2012 年 9 月

| Preface |

A Spiritual Journey to Tibet

The idea of creating this book, I should say, was first conceived through my interactions with my Tibetan mother 'Amala' Demen Dechen Drolkar, a renowned expert on Tibetan folk literature. One night two years ago, at her home near the Jokhang Temple in Lhasa, she told me a story that she had heard from her maid, who had just come back from visiting her family.

That day, the 76-year-old Amala kept me company in drinking barley wine and eating dried yak meat. She performed local dances and songs, and the songs she sang were the love songs she had known from her childhood, written by the sixth Dalai Lama Tsangyang Gyatso. When her maid Chodron, who had been sitting at the side and knitting a *vajra* knot, came over to clean up the table, it was already quite late. At that moment, Amala suddenly said to me, 'Didn't you say that you wanted to understand Tibetans? I'll tell you a fresh and true story that Chodron just told me yesterday.

'There was a teenage girl in Chodron's village who was killed on her way to town after being hit by a neighbor's car. Her mother was heart-broken and stayed home for three days. The driver felt very guilty and worried. Unexpectedly, on the morning of the fourth day, the girl's mother went to his house, not to retaliate, but to comfort him, and urge him not to blame himself.

'Can you guess how the girl's mother comforted the man who had killed her daughter? She said, "Everyone has their own destiny. My daughter died not merely because of your actions, but more from the karma she had accumulated from her deeds in her previous life and this life. The accident was just a visible result, but it was caused by the fusion of karma she had accumulated from her thoughts and actions every second before she died. Hence, we should all accept this as a fact. Only after we stop being remorseful and upset can she go into her next reincarnation with more ease".'

Amala's words moved me deeply and I thought how nice it would be if we could collect more of these stories and assemble them into a book that would lead readers to a true appreciation of Tibetans' mindsets. So I decided to find as many people as possible who truly understand Tibet, to unpack and present the real Tibet that surpasses cursory glimpses, startling conjectures, and misleading right-or-wrong perceptions.

This book is now in your hands. It isn't perfect, and not all of the stories are as wonderful as Amala's. However, I believe that the result is overall very valuable and the effort is worthwhile. I hope that through the 'microscopes' hidden among the words and between the lines of the book, readers can find the doorway to the real Tibet, instead of merely being onlookers, skimming over the surface buzz concerning this snowy plateau.

Nie Xiaoyang
September, 2012

目录 Contents

文化·传承	1	Culture and Traditions
记忆·回望	41	Memories and Recollections
风土·管窥	69	Sights and Sounds
圣城·拉萨	115	Lhasa, a Mystical City
行旅·品味	127	Travel and Taste
印象·讲述	167	Impressions and Expositions
精神·信仰	203	Spirituality and Faith
逸闻·趣谈	243	Cool Stories
参考文献	280	References
后记	282	Afterword

文化·传承
Culture and Traditions

微观西藏
TIBET: FAST & FURIOUS

西藏的中心
Center of Tibet

拉萨有三条古老的转经路，分别是环绕大昭寺主殿的"囊廓"（内圈之意），环绕大昭寺的"八廓"（中圈），以及环绕拉萨老城的"林廓"（外圈）。这三条转经路基本形成同心圆，其核心是大昭寺主殿内的释迦牟尼12岁等身像。这尊文成公主带去的佛像，是大昭寺的中心，是拉萨的中心，也是整个西藏的中心。

Lhasa has three old circumambulation paths. They are 'Nangkhor' (meaning the inner circle), embracing the main shrine of Jokhang Temple, 'Barkhor' (middle circle), embracing the whole of Jokhang Temple, and 'Lingkhor' (outer circle), embracing which circles old Lhasa. These three paths form three concentric circles, and their core is the life-sized statue of twelve-year-old Sakyamuni. This figure of Buddha was brought to Tibet by Princess Wencheng. It is the center of Jokhang, of Lhasa, and of the whole Tibet.

给自来水管献哈达
Presenting *Hada* to the Water Tap

藏历新年初一的清晨，最重要的仪式就是取新年的第一道水。按惯例，打水是女人的活儿。过去，新年的第一天，井边会有不少身着新装的妇女，背着水桶取水。现在，自来水入户也没有阻挡这一习俗的传承：家庭主妇要为水龙头献上一条哈达，还要燃起桑烟，虔诚祭拜，然后才打开水龙头。

The most important ritual on Tibetan New Year's Day is to collect water. According to the traditional practice, Tibetan women are supposed to be responsible for doing this task. In the past, there would be many newly-dressed women beside wells on this day, fetching water and carrying the buckets on their backs. Today, this traditional ritual still exists, even though most families have water piped into their homes. Nowadays, on New Year's Day, the housewife will first present a *hada** to the faucet, light incense, and worship piously before she turns it on.

* A traditional ceremonial scarf made of white silk, presented at weddings, funerals, births, graduations, and during arrivals and departures of guests.

文化·传承
Culture and Traditions

向神致敬
Saluting Deities

在西藏，人们外出旅行，每路过一个山口，就要脱掉帽子向山神致敬。在山坡上，人们还要"撒风马"，即撒印着骏马图案的五色纸，表示向山神奉献坐骑，同时高喊"拉加罗"，意思是神胜利了，表达对山神的安慰和友好。人们认为每座大山都是一个神灵，都有决定自己命运的法力。

When people travel in Tibet, they need to take off their hats to show respect to the gods of mountains every time they go through a mountain pass. On the hillside, they need to 'spread wind horses', which means scattering five-colored drawings of fine horses, in order to offer them to the mountain gods. At the same time, they shout, 'Lhagyalo!' (meaning 'victory') to express their comfort and respect toward the mountain gods. Tibetans believe that there is a god for every mountain who determines their destiny.

摄影：车刚

评论

微观西藏
TIBET: FAST & FURIOUS

陌生人的信任
Trust for Strangers

有一个故事说,在西藏某地,一位姑娘拦住了一辆汽车,托陌生的司机给在前方镇子打工的哥哥捎1000块钱,却问也没问司机的名字。为了人和人之间这份纯粹的信任,很多人希望这个故事是真的。作为佐证,有位上海的女编导说她就碰到过类似的事,"在西藏,人的确会这么信任一个陌生人"。

There's one story that goes like this: somewhere in Tibet, a girl stopped a car and asked the unknown driver to take 1,000 yuan to her elder brother who was working in the town ahead, but she did not even ask the driver's name. In a world where such pure trust is rare, many hope this is a true story. As supporting evidence, a female director from Shanghai remarked she had encountered something similar: 'In Tibet, people will definitely give such trust to strangers.'

西藏的"吉普赛人"
Tibetan 'Gypsies'

西藏作家扎西达娃的祖先是康巴人,他说:"他们彪悍好斗,爱憎分明,幽默并喜爱流浪,是西藏的'吉普赛人'。直到今天,西藏各地还能看到他们流浪的身影。他们在寻找什么?千百年沿袭下的集体无意识,使得他们似乎永远找不到。"

Tibetan writer Tashi Dawa is a descendant of the Khampas. He said, 'The Khampas are tough and competitive and know clearly what to love or hate. With a great sense of humor and a love for rambling, they are the Tibetan "Gypsies". Up to now, you can still see them roaming throughout Tibet. What are they looking for? The collective unconsciousness, which has been passed down for hundreds of years, seems to have resulted in their failure to find anything.'

评论

文化·传承
Culture and Traditions

摄影：聂晓阳

在甜茶馆里付账
Paying in Sweet Tea Houses

有一句俗语形容西藏人的生活：早上是甜的（因为喝甜茶），午后是酸的（午饭要饮青稞酒）。在西藏甜茶馆里，围坐一桌的茶友谁到座就会从兜里掏出几元钱放在桌上，倒茶的姑娘每倒一次茶就从桌上拿一次钱。茶友之间不计较谁付的钱多，最后剩在桌上的钱总是互相谦让。

As a proverb goes, the life of Tibetans is sweet in the morning (because they drink sweet tea) and sour in the afternoon (as barley wine is a must for lunch). In the sweet tea houses of Tibet, friends sitting around a table will fish out some money and put it on the table as soon as they arrive. The waitress will then collect money each time she adds more tea. The drinkers don't fuss over who pays more. Before they leave, every person always asks others to take the leftover money on the table.

尊老重老
Respect for Elders

老人是藏族人家中的精神核心，是最受尊敬的。有人回忆说，小时候，他跟同学一起拿弹弓打鸟或打架斗殴，有时被一些根本不认识的老人看到，就会被当场训斥。而他们这些挨了训的孩子们也老老实实，从不敢顶嘴。

The elderly are the spiritual core of a Tibetan family and they are the most respected. One person remembers that in his childhood, when he was shooting birds with a slingshot or fighting with his classmates, an elder, who did not know him at all, would sometimes scold him on the spot. When children were scolded by elders, they would stand there and accept it, never daring to talk back.

微观西藏
TIBET: FAST & FURIOUS

从不生气的母亲

No Angry Mothers

西藏作协主席扎西达娃感叹:"西藏的母亲是最好的母亲。她们从不打骂孩子,也不以所谓理性的方式约束和管教孩子,任孩子自由成长,调皮的孩子哪怕把家里折腾得一片狼藉,母亲也只是并无怒气地提高声调嚷一声,然后又忙自己的事去了。"西藏的孩子也许没有时尚的玩具,却有更快乐的童年。

Tashi Dawa, president of the Tibet Writers' Association, once said with emotion: 'Tibetan mothers are the best in the world. They never beat their children, nor do they restrict or discipline their children in a so-called rational manner. They let their children grow at their own pace. Even if a naughty child messes up the home, the mother will only call out at the child without anger, and go back to the work she has on hand.' Tibetan children may not have fashionable toys, but they do have happy childhoods.

摄影:车刚

文化・传承
Culture and Traditions

都记在心里呢
Grateful Hearts

演员姜昆曾帮助在西藏建了一所希望小学。他讲了这样一个故事:"有一次,我带着一些外国朋友去学校参观。孩子们事先准备了很多哈达,我让孩子们把哈达献给外国朋友。可孩子们不肯,把哈达全部都献给了我。我数了数,脖子上足足挂了有七八十条哈达。我只不过做了一点点事情,可孩子们都记在心里呢。"

Cross-talk actor Jiang Kun once helped to build a Hope School in Tibet, and he recounted an incident he encountered, 'Once I took some foreign friends to visit that school. The children prepared a lot of *hadas* in advance. I asked the children to present them to my foreign friends, but they refused to do so. Instead, they gave all of them to me. I counted, and there were about eighty of them on my neck. I only did a little thing, but the children held the memory in their hearts.'

耍猴人的故事
The Story of a Monkey-Trick Performer

有作家讲过这样一个故事:有个耍猴人来到拉萨,让猴子表演杂耍赚钱,没想到围观的人们一边要求耍猴人停止虐猴,一边朝耍猴人脸上吐唾沫,耍猴人仓皇而逃。后来,他带着猴子装作相依为命的样子在拉萨乞讨,竟得到了双倍布施。

A writer tells this story: 'A long time ago, a monkey-trick performer came to Lhasa and tried to earn money by making a monkey juggle. Contrary to his expectations, the audience there spat on him and demanded he stop abusing the monkey. The performer fled in panic. However, when he came back later, pretending to be poor and lonely with the monkey, he was surprised to be given donations that were double of what he got previously.'

评论

微观西藏
TIBET: FAST & FURIOUS

《格萨尔王》
King Gesar

《格萨尔王》是世界上最长的史诗，堪称世界文学巨著。除故事的散文部分，仅史诗部分就有 100 多万行，上千万字。有趣的是，西藏的不少艺人尽管目不识丁，是地地道道的文盲，可是却能凭借惊人的记忆力，终生以说唱这部史诗为生。

As the longest epic poem in the world, *King Gesar* has been called a masterpiece of world literature. In addition to the prose section of the story, the poem comprises more than a million lines, resulting in tens of millions of characters. Interestingly, even though a large number of Tibetan bards are totally illiterate, they can recite this epic poem and make a living, depending only on their amazing memories.

不知道自己名字的化缘者
An Almsman Who Doesn't Know His Own Name

《中国国家地理》曾提及一位步行来拉萨的藏族大叔，他不知道自己的名字、年龄，这个世界上大概只有佛知道他的存在。他每天都坚持环绕着布达拉宫转三圈，靠化缘活着。如果哪天化缘得来的东西超过了自己的需要，他会接济别的乞丐或者供奉给佛。

Chinese National Geography magazine once mentioned a Tibetan man who came to Lhasa on foot. He didn't know his own name or age; perhaps only the Buddha knew about his existence in the world. He persisted circumambulating the Potala Palace three times a day and lived on alms others gave him. If he got more than he needed from alms one day, he would give the rest to beggars or offer it to the Buddha as tribute.

摄影：聂晓阳

文化·传承
Culture and Traditions

骷髅舞
Skeleton Dance

骷髅舞是萨嘎达瓦节跳神的一个项目。两位舞者戴骷髅面具，装扮有些狰狞。有位20世纪40年代就在寺庙中跳骷髅舞的老先生介绍说，舞蹈的主角是守护天葬场的精灵，虽然样子可怕，但心地善良。他们说："骷髅舞是为了让人们了解佛所说的无常。""死亡是必然的，应把它看作另一种存在的开始。"

The skeleton dance is one of the festive events on the Saga Dawa Festival (the Tibetan Vesak, a celebration of the Buddha's birthday). Wearing skeleton masks, two dancers dress ferociously. Two old men who performed the skeleton dance in the 1940s say the leading role in the dance is a spirit who is the guardian of celestial burials. Although he looks frightening, he is kind-hearted. 'The skeleton dance encourages people to understand the impermanence mentioned in Buddhism,' they say. 'Death is inevitable. It should be seen as the start of another existence.'

共处而相安
Coexisting in Peace

西藏有些地区原始苯教与藏传佛教相融相续，同一座城，一早一晚，你右向绕圈，我左向转经，共处而相安。所以，走进西藏，就要带着藏民般的包容心和平常心，撇开一切偏见来观察和思考这片土地。

In some areas of Tibet, the traditional Bon (an indigenous Tibetan belief, which dominated the region before Buddhism was introduced) and Tibetan Buddhism mingle and develop in harmony. So in the same city, one group does the same thing in the morning that the other does in the evening: you circle clockwise and I circle counterclockwise, all in peaceful coexistence. Hence, when you enter Tibet, you should take with you a humble and tolerant heart like that of a Tibetan, observing and pondering this land without any prejudices.

评论

摄影：车刚

快乐最重要
Happiness Is Most Important

在西藏，家长和学校很少会过分逼迫孩子读书。作家白玛娜珍说，这要归功于古训：不要执着于世间万事万物，而要观照内心。西藏的孩子虽不一定在考试中出类拔萃，但他们往往拥有更多快乐的能力，笑容总是很容易写在他们脸上。

In Tibet, parents and schools seldom force their children to study excessively. Writer Pema Nadron attributes this to an ancient saying: 'Don't be so persistent with things in the world.' One should concern oneself more with inner feelings. Tibetan children may not be at the top in examinations, but they usually know how to find happiness. Smiles are always come easily to their faces.

藏文化摇篮
The Cradle of Tibetan Culture

有趣的是，西藏历史上的第一座宫殿、第一座佛堂、第一块农田、第一座寺庙、第一部经书、第一部藏戏等都诞生在同一个地方，这就是山南地区。这里被公认为"西藏民族文化的摇篮"。

Interestingly, in Tibetan history, the first palace, the first prayer hall, the first agricultural field, the first temple, the first scripture, and the first Tibetan opera all appeared in the same place — Lhoka (Shannan), which has become widely known as 'the cradle of Tibetan culture'.

文化·传承
Culture and Traditions

老人与老鼠
The Elder and the Mouse

作家白玛娜珍忆起自己的外婆时说:"外婆和小老鼠都是朋友,外婆给它们每个起了名字,每晚一招呼,它们就会从房梁上窜下来,等着外婆爱怜地训斥或是送给它们一顿美餐。"西藏官员德吉女士也回忆说,她奶奶过去住在八廓街的时候,家里的老鼠一个个都能叫得上名字,老鼠们只吃喂食,从不乱咬东西。

Writer Pema Nadron says this of her grandmother: 'My grandmother made friends with mice, and she gave names to every one of them. Every night when she called them, they would scurry down from the beams, waiting for my grandmother's affectionate reprimand or delicious food.' Female Tibetan official Dekyi shares similar memories: when her grandmother lived at Barkhor Street, she knew all the names of the mice. They only ate what they were fed and would never gnaw on other things.

敬畏文字
Revering Writings

一位喇嘛曾说,他年轻时有一次急着上厕所,抽了一张旧报纸当手纸,师父知道后,罚他面壁省悔。作家次仁罗布说,藏族人绝对不会把经文、报纸等有文字的东西踩在脚下或坐在屁股下面。在他们看来,即使明天就要离世,今天也要追求知识,因为知识让人更容易托生为人。

A lama says that when he was young, once he had to relieve himself urgently and tore a piece off a newspaper. His master learned about it and punished him; he had to face a wall for introspection. Writer Tsering Norbu says, 'Tibetans absolutely won't step nor sit on scriptures, newspapers or other writings. In their eyes, even if you die tomorrow, you need to pursue knowledge today, because they believe knowledge will give them a greater chance of recarnating as a human.'

评论

微观西藏
TIBET: FAST & FURIOUS

拉萨踢踏舞
Lhasa Tap Dance

"见到六弦琴,腿脚痒几分,演唱堆谐歌,手指自然跳。"堆谐最初是由六弦琴乐器伴奏的舞蹈,后来逐渐演变成踢踏舞形式,被称为"拉萨踢踏舞"。

'When one sees a *vielle**, both the legs and feet itch to dance, and when one sings *Duixie* songs, one's fingers cannot help tapping to the melody.' The origins of *Duixie* are a kind of dancing, usually as an accompaniment to the music of the *vielle*. It later gradually evolved into a style of tap dancing, known as 'Lhasa tap dancing'.

* A *vielle* is a six-stringed instrument.

藏戏的起源
The Origin of Tibetan Opera

唐东杰布被誉为"藏戏的开山祖师"。相传,当年为了召集更多的人参与架桥,也为了筹集更多的资金,他请来琼结七姐妹,组成专业演出队,并编排了很多新鲜的剧目,吸引观众,最后竟攒出50多两黄金来架桥。而藏戏也得以发端,成为藏族人喜闻乐见的艺术形式。

Thangtong Gyalpo has been honored as 'the founder of Tibetan opera'. According to legend, in order to draw together more people to get involved with bridge construction and gather funds for the project, he assembled seven sisters from the Qonggyai family into a performing troupe, and penned a number of new operas, which in the end drew large audiences and raised over fifty taels of gold for the construction of the bridge. This was the origin of the popular art form Tibetan opera.

摄影:车刚

文化·传承
Culture and Traditions

笑看变故
Smiling on Misfortune

有人说，藏民家如果失窃，这家人在短暂的懊恼之后便会释然，他们认为这是前世所欠的债，现在还了债，未来就会有更多的机会得到更好的报应。实际上，因为笃信因果报应，藏族人对自己所遭遇的各种变故的确更能"看得开"，也更能接受人生的各种苦难。

Some people say that if a Tibetan family is visited by a thief, after a short period of annoyance, they will be happy again, because they believe that such an experience is a debt from their previous life. If you pay off your debts now, you will have more chances of receiving a good reward in the future. Since Tibetans have such faith in karma, they are more 'tolerant' of misfortune or suffering in life than people of other cultures.

牛角特权
Cow Horn Privilege

虽然高寒缺氧的环境使得西藏一些地区农作物生长期短，但乐观的藏民还是会在丰收时节感恩并庆祝。有作家说："在割麦子时有一项娱乐：谁偶尔捡到一只牛角，他就有了特权，可以用牛角敲打在场所有人的脑袋。于是田野上顿时大笑大闹——这里有个典故：藏族人把吝啬的人、暴躁的人都称作'牛角'。"

Although the oxygen-deficient atmosphere results in a shorter growth period for crops in Tibet, the optimistic Tibetans still appreciate and celebrate at the time of a plentiful harvest. One writer says, 'They play a game when harvesting barley: whoever finds a cow horn has the privilege of hitting everyone else's head with it. Hence, you can often find people laughing and having fun in the fields. There is actually an allusion in this game — Tibetans call stingy and irritable people "cow horns".'

评论

微观西藏
TIBET: FAST & FURIOUS

塔葬
Pagoda Burial

对藏传佛教顶级活佛来说，葬礼的最高规格是肉身灵塔，即把遗体做防腐处理并风干，再用丝绸缠起来，祀奉在包金的佛塔里。在遗体处理时，人们会把遗体滴下来的盐水和黏土混在一起，制作成小佛像。据说这样的佛像具有非凡的"加持力"。

For the greatest living Buddha in Tibetan Buddhism, the highest standard for a funeral is the pagoda burial. That is to embalm and dry the body first, then wrap it with silk, and finally enshrine it in a golden pagoda. While disposing of the body, people mix drops of saline fluid from the corpse with clay to make a small Buddha statue. It is said that this statue has extraordinary powers of blessing.

"天生的"尼姑
A 'Born' Nun

拉萨仓姑寺尼姑次成拉姆曾对来访者说："在我出生前，妈妈还生了三个孩子，但都相继夭折。我们那里有风俗，家里孩子去世多，下面生的孩子就要送去寺庙，这样才会给家里带来吉祥。所以我没出生就被决定出家。出家之前，我最向往的是能到拉萨大昭寺磕头。"

Tsultrim Lhamo, a nun of the Tsanggu Temple in Lhasa, once told a visitor, 'Before I was born, my mother had three children, but they all died. My hometown had a custom: when many children die in a family, the next child will be sent to a temple. Only in this way can the child bring good fortune to the family. Thus, even before I was born, I was destined to become a nun, and before I came to the temple, what I longed for most was to worship at Jokhang Temple.'

评论

文化·传承
Culture and Traditions

藏语新词汇
Tibetan Vocabulary

藏文具有1300多年的历史。《汉藏对照词典》里面收录的藏语词汇有8万多条。据说"非典"流行的时候，有四五种藏语版本的"非典"译名，后来西藏编译局专门组织研讨，才最后统一了一个规范的藏语表述。

Tibetan script has a history of more than 1,300 years. In *The Chinese-Tibetan Dictionary*, more than 80,000 Tibetan words are listed. When 'SARS' became rampant, four or five different translations of the word into Tibetan from Chinese were used. Then the Tibetan Translation Bureau convened a special discussion and finally chose one standard translation.

超度被捕杀的动物
Releasing the Souls of Poached Animals

记者刘沙笔下记载过一个故事：在喜马拉雅山脚的定日，有一对夫妻，丈夫是迁居至此的康巴人，为保护当地的动物被偷猎者枪杀。妻子在丈夫死后，每星期带着三个孩子一起赶着羊群穿过荒原到绒布寺点香叩拜，不是超度她的丈夫，而是超度那些被捕杀的动物，并替天堂里的丈夫为荒原上的动物祈祷平安。

Reporter Liu Sha once recorded this story: in Tingri County, at the foothills of the Himalayas, there lived a couple. The husband was a Khampa who had immigrated from elsewhere. While performing his duty of protecting wild animals, he was killed by a poacher. After his death, his wife took their three children and drove their flock of sheep across the wilderness to Rongbuk Monastery every week. Once there, they would light incense and worship — praying not for her husband, but on behalf of her husband, for the liberation of the souls of those slaughtered animals, and for their peaceful life in the wilderness.

摄影：蒋越

藏装
Tibetan Costumes

时装设计师马艳丽：我最强烈的感受就是西藏服饰带来的感染力——它是一种很有力度的服饰，尤其是藏族女装，色彩丰富，同时运用了很多石头配饰，具有非常强的视觉冲击力。藏装蕴涵了藏族文化，能带给人更多的精神享受。藏装是穿在身上的文化。

Ma Yanli, a fashion designer, says, 'The most intense feeling I ever had was attraction to Tibetan costumes — they were a kind of powerful dress, especially those of the women. The female clothing used rich colors and many stone-made accessories, providing a very strong visual impact. Tibetan costumes crystallize the culture of Tibet, giving people a kind of mental enjoyment. It is a kind of culture you can wear.'

摄影：车刚

方便投胎
Convenient for Reincarnation

天葬藏语叫"恰托",意思就是喂鸟。人死之后一般停放三天,然后把亡者身体对折,头颅纳入两膝间,用白布包好,像是婴儿出生前在母体里的姿势,据说这是为了下一世投胎方便。亡者被送到天葬台分解成碎块并用糌粑拌匀后,燃起桑烟,引来秃鹫。人们相信一个人的遗体被吃得越干净,就越有利于灵魂转世。

Celestial burial is called *qatog* in Tibetan, which means 'feeding the birds'. Three days after a man dies, his body is folded with his head between his knees and wrapped in a piece of white cloth in the same posture as that of a fetus inside the mother. It is said to be more convenient for reincarnation. Dead people are sent to a celestial burial ground, where they are dismembered and mixed with *tsampa*[*]. People then light incense to attract vultures. They believe the more completely a body is eaten, the better it is for the soul to reincarnate.

* *Tsampa* is roasted barley or wheat flour, a staple Tibetan food.

不能灭的精神之灯
Don't Put Out the Light of the Spirits

一位藏族老阿妈将远来的客人安顿在经堂过夜,第二天早上发现堂内的酥油灯竟然灭了,感到十分难过。原来是醉酒的客人半夜抄起酥油灯出门上厕所,回来再睡时随口吹灭了灯。对藏族人来说,酥油灯可谓精神之灯,要恭敬相待,不能熄灭。

An old woman in Tibet housed a traveler from far away in a prayer hall, and the next day she discovered the butter lamp in the hall had unexpectedly gone out. She felt very sad. It turned out that the drunken guest had taken the lamp out with him in the middle of the night to go to the toilet, and had thoughtlessly blown it out when he returned to the hall. For Tibetans, butter lamps are spiritual lights. They should be respected and never extinguished.

评论

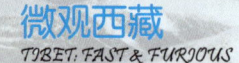

西藏首座佛寺
The First Tibetan Buddhist Temple

桑耶寺是西藏第一座藏传佛教寺庙，据说这座由莲花生大师亲自主持修建的寺庙得名于一位赞普（国王）的惊呼"桑耶"（出乎意料的意思）。有人形容，在西藏，从寺庙里传出的喇嘛们的念经声悠远飘荡，如同从岁月深处浸润而出的清流，恍然间，仿佛时光缓缓回到从前。

Samye Monastery is the first temple connected to Tibetan Buddhism, and its construction is said to have been directed by Padmasambhava (the earliest preacher of Tibetan Buddhism). This temple took its name from a Tibetan king's exclamation: *Samye* (meaning 'out of expectation'). As some people describe, the sounds of lamas' recitation of scriptures drift out of the temple like a clear stream flowing from past years. All of a sudden, you felt as if time is drifting slowly back to the past.

民间故事一则
A Folk Story

有一个广为流传的西藏民间故事说，俄曲河边住着牧马少年蒙白吉武和恋人琼青尼玛，但姑娘的母亲却将姑娘嫁给了一个商人。姑娘十分想念蒙白，小伙子也是茶不思、饭不想。此事被她婆婆发现，全家一商量，就邀请小伙子加入这个家庭，和商人一起拥有琼青尼玛做妻子，日子过得十分美满。

There is a widespread Tibetan folk tale: a young herdsman named Mobai Gyiwu and his lover Qongchen Nyima lived by the Equ River. The girl's mother, however, married her to a businessman. The girl missed Mobai very much, while the young man had no appetite for any food or drink. When the merchant's mother found this out, she held a family discussion, and invited this young man into the family to share Qongchen Nyima with the businessman and all of them lived happily from then on.

[评论]

文化·传承
Culture and Traditions

《西藏度亡经》

The Tibetan Book of the Dead

在西藏，为亡灵超度时，最常念的经文是莲花生大师所著的《西藏度亡经》：尊贵的某某，所谓死亡这件事已经来临，你已经脱离尘世，但你不是唯一的一个。有生必有死，人人都如此。不要执着于这个今生，纵令你不舍，你也不能长留人间。除了在轮回中继续生命，别无办法。不要依恋了，不要怯懦。

In Tibet, the most common scripture recited for releasing souls of the dead is *The Tibetan Book of the Dead*, written by Padmasambhava (the first preacher of Tibetan Buddhism), which reads like this: 'To the honored departed, the so-called death incident has come, and you are no longer in the human realm. However, you are not the only one — everyone experiences life and death. Do not be obsessed with this life. Maybe you are reluctant to go, but you cannot stay here forever. There is no way other than resuming your life in *samsara* (the endless cycle of birth, suffering, death and rebirth). Do not be reluctant, and do not be a coward.'

跟自己的影子玩

Playing with His Own Shadow

藏族画家边巴曾这样回忆儿时的放牧生活：一整天在山里与羊为伴，时间过得很慢、很慢。有时会站在山口等待一两个过路的人，与他们说说话。偶尔也在太阳下看看自己的影子，然后摆出各种身姿与自己逗着玩……"我时常觉得自己与大山里的一草一木或一虫一鸟没什么区别，自己也养成了与自然对话的习惯。"

Penpa, a Tibetan painter, recalls the herding life of his childhood: 'I usually spent an entire day in the mountains with sheep, and I felt that time passed very, very slowly. Sometimes, I would stand at a mountain pass to wait for one or two passers-by and chat with them for a while. Sometimes, I would watch my shadow under the sun and assume various poses to amuse myself... I often felt that there wasn't any difference between me and other creatures in the mountains. I could be a tree, a blade of grass, an insect or a bird. I got into the habit of talking with nature.'

微观西藏
TIBET: FAST & FURIOUS

站在人类的高地看世界
Viewing the World from the Height of Human Development

西藏作协主席扎西达娃在谈到西藏文学的未来时说:"我只能算是藏族新文学的开拓者,最多只是堆积成了一个土丘,远不是一座高峰。真正的藏族文学大家,应该站在人类的高地俯瞰世界,应该是掌握了几种语言文字,能用母语书写出最奇幻最优美的文字。"

Tashi Dawa, president of the Tibet Writers' Association, talked about the future of Tibetan literature, 'I can only be taken as one of the pioneers of new Tibetan literature. My achievement, at most, is piling up a mound, which is far from building a high mountain. The really great Tibetan writers should view the world from the height of human development. They should master several languages, and create the most fantastic and exquisite pieces of writing in their mother tongue.'

超越宗教
Beyond Religion

说起西藏,人们总是想起一个个转经的身影,也总是把它跟藏传佛教等同起来。但作家阿来说:"其实西藏文化内部可能更丰富,绝非一个宗教就可以把它全部覆盖。我所写过的东西,包括格萨尔王,为什么要寻找口头传统?因为口头传统包括很多非宗教的、民间的因素。"

When talking about Tibet, people often think of circumambulating figures, or else they equate Tibet with Tibetan Buddhism. However, the writer Alai says, 'Tibetan culture is much richer and can never be covered by just one religion. The works I have written, including those about King Gesar, are based on oral accounts. Why? Because oral traditions contain lots of secular folk elements.'

评论

文化·传承
Culture and Traditions

摄影：车刚

精神之灯
Lamp of the Spirits

酥油灯在西藏人生活中占据着重要的位置。无论是在寺庙还是在普通藏族人家中，都能看到长明不灭的酥油灯。藏族人家做法事或祭祀逝者时，有的甚至要点上几百盏酥油灯。当地人把它视为精神之灯，他们相信生命终结时如果没有酥油灯的陪伴，灵魂将在黑暗中迷失。

The butter lamp plays an important role in Tibetan life. In temples and ordinary Tibetan homes, you can always see burning butter lamps. When Tibetan families perform religious rituals or mourn the dead, some will even light hundreds of butter lamps. The locals regard butter lamps as the lamps of the spirits, and they believe if they don't end life in the company of butter lamps, their souls will lose their way in the darkness.

依然独特
Stay Unique

美国背包客 David：西藏的文化就扎根于茶馆这样的地方以及窗外的街头、小巷和寺庙里。尽管从内地来的生意人和西方游客随处可见，但你仍能看到出家人、朝圣者和当地人按照古老和传统的方式在生活。对我来说，拉萨不管怎么变，始终是个独特的所在。

An American backpacker named David says, 'Tibetan culture is rooted in its tea houses, and in the alleys, streets, and temples outside their windows. Although businessmen from other parts of China and visitors from the West can be seen everywhere, you can still witness the ancient and traditional lifestyle of monks, pilgrims, and locals. No matter how Lhasa changes, this city will always be a unique place for me.'

微观西藏
TIBET: FAST & FURIOUS

生命的意义
The Meaning of Life

西藏社科院前院长平措次仁:西藏有一个传统,在你活着的时候一定要去天葬台一次,这样当你看到肢解尸体时,就可以明白生命的意义,明白什么才是生命中最重要的东西。有句谚语说,乞丐一袋糌粑饱兮兮,国王一座金山饿兮兮。

Phuntsok Tsering, the former president of the Tibetan Academy of Social Science, remarks, 'Tibet has a tradition that says it's important to visit celestial burial sites at least once. When you see the dismemberment of a corpse, you can understand the meaning of life and what the most important thing in life is. As an old saying goes, a bag of *tsampa* can fill the stomach of a beggar, while a mountain of gold keeps a king hungry.'

摄影:车刚

文化·传承
Culture and Traditions

闭关静修
Closed Retreats

藏传佛教讲究"闭关静修",这是一个人佛法修为上升的必经之路。在闭关期间,修行者只摄取最基本的饮食,远离尘世的干扰,摒弃自己的各种欲望,除短暂的睡眠外,其余时间全部用来观想、体验自己的心性。有人甚至认为,严格说来,闭关才是真正的修行。

Tibetan Buddhism stresses the importance of 'closed retreats', which is the only way for a Buddhist to further his or her cultivation. During the retreat, practioners only take in a minimum of food and drink. They try to stay away from earthly interference, dump their personal desires, and spend all their time meditating and experiencing their inner world, except for a short sleep every now and then. Some even believe that closed retreats are the only real way to practice Buddhism.

神灵无处不在
Gods Are Everywhere

藏传佛教在传教初期把苯教诸神吸收进来,作为佛教的护法。至今在西藏,很多人仍然相信人们的肩上有护法神,身体的各个部位也有神灵栖息。所以打招呼时手不能搭在对方肩上,不能拍对方的脑袋,也不能跨过或踩在别人的衣服上。

Tibetan Buddhism, in its early stage, took gods from the Bon religion as guardians of the Buddha. Even now, many Tibetans believe that there are guardians are on their shoulders and that different gods dwell in every part of their bodies. So when you greet others, you cannot put your hand on their shoulders, pat their heads, step on their clothes, or step over their bodies.

评论

微观西藏
TIBET: FAST & FURIOUS

尸语故事
The Corpse's Stories

西藏流传着一个饶有趣味的故事集叫《尸语故事》。据说在某个神秘的地方有个尸体，如果能一路不说话把它背回家，它就会变成金子，但是在背的过程中尸体会不停地讲有趣的故事，背的人会不由自主地发出赞叹，尸体就会重新回到墓地。这个尸体每次所讲的故事，就汇集成了《尸语故事》。

In Tibet there is a very interesting story collection called *The Corpse's Stories*. It is said that hidden someplace is a corpse that will turn into gold if one can carry it home on his or her back without saying a word. However, during the transportation the corpse will keep telling interesting stories, and people carrying it cannot help gasping and exclaiming. In such cases the corpse will return to its burial site. The stories the corpse tells every time are collected in *The Corpse's Stories*.

最辉煌的灵塔
Most Magnificent Stupa

在西藏，顶级活佛的灵塔按传统应该用纯金打造，其中以布达拉宫里五世达赖喇嘛的灵塔最为金碧辉煌。这是一座修建在大殿里上下贯通3层楼的大金塔，高14.85米，从上到下所用黄金约有3721千克，塔外还镶有无数宝石。

In Tibet, the stupas of the highest living Buddha should be built with pure gold, and the most magnificent among them is that of the fifth Dalai Lama in the Potala Palace. It is a huge gold tower three stories tall inside the Buddha Hall, with a height of 14.85 meters. Approximately 3,721 kilograms of gold was used in building this stupa, and countless gemstones cover its surface.

评论

文化·传承
Culture and Traditions

摄影：车刚

朝圣者不孤单
Pilgrims Are Not Alone

在西藏随处可见刻着六字真言和神佛形象的石头堆成的玛尼堆，朝圣者路过的时候，都要顺时针绕转几周，往上面添加一块石头，表达对佛的敬意。有人说，这种先辈朝圣者们留下的痕迹，会把一种精神传递给后来者，给他们力量，告诉他们并不孤单，告诉他们这里曾有先行者，未来还会有后来者。

Across Tibet you can see *mani* stone (prayer stone) piles composed of stones inscribed with the six-syllable mantra '*om mani padme hum*' and images of Buddha. When pilgrims pass one of these stone piles, they circle it clockwise several times and add one stone to show their respect toward the Buddha. Such traces left by predecessors can pass on a certain spirit to successors, giving them power and telling them that they are not alone — there have been pioneers and there will also be newcomers in the future.

微观西藏
TIBET: FAST & FURIOUS

下辈子还做亲人
Wishing to Be in the Same Family in the Afterlife

藏医丹增塔克：汉族人喜欢把死者的灵魂召唤回来，藏族却不是，他们喜欢把灵魂赶出去，好让死者不要留恋今生，顺利转世。藏族人死后做法事，其中一个重要目的，是为了亲人下一辈子能够再回到这个家庭。如果有人发现邻居家新出生的小孩在某方面像自己的母亲，就会对那个孩子很好。

Tibetan doctor Tenzin Take says, 'Han people like to summon dead people's souls back, while Tibetans don't. They prefer to expel those souls to prevent the dead from looking back, so they can have smooth reincarnations. One of the most important purposes of the ceremonies Tibetans hold after people die is to enable their relatives to come back to the same family again in their next reincarnation. If someone finds that the newborn baby in the neighbor's family looks like his or her mother in some way, he or she will be very nice to that baby.'

观音泪滴中诞生的女神
The Goddess Born from Avalokitesvara's Tears

在西藏，老百姓遇到困难，会以手加额，请求度母保佑。据说度母是诞生于观音泪滴中的女神。相传，当年观音菩萨发现自己救度的受苦众生并未减少，流下热泪，那泪滴化作莲花，莲花又变身度母，发愿协助观音实现救度众生的宏愿，于是便有了21位美丽的度母女神。西藏民间认为文成公主就是度母的化身。

When Tibetans run into difficulties, they often place their hands on their foreheads and ask Tara for protection. Tara is said to be the goddess born from Avalokitesvara's tears. It is said that when Avalokitesvara discovered that the number of suffering people didn't decrease, she burst into tears. The tears turned into lotus flowers, and then into Taras, who vowed to fulfill Avalokitesvara's aspiration to help people. Hence, twenty-one beautiful Tara goddesses came into being, and Tibetans believe Princess Wencheng is an incarnation of one of them.

文化·传承
Culture and Traditions

总把旧幡换新幡
Renewing Prayer Flags

每到藏历新年，西藏家家户户都会迎请新的经幡，随后全家集中到屋顶的平台，大家一起将已经破旧的五彩经幡换下，再换上新请的经幡。这些破旧褪色的经幡会被送到附近的河边，人们认为，挂了一年的旧经幡也不可以随意丢弃，而是必须放到干净的地方。

When the Tibetan New Year arrives, every Tibetan family welcomes it with new prayer flags. The whole family gathers on a platform on the roof of the house, takes off the worn flags, and ties new flags around their house. Afterward, people take the old and faded flags to a nearby river, because they believe the prayer flags, which have been hung for a year, cannot be discarded carelessly. Instead, they should be put in a clean place.

园林中的文化交流
Horticultural Exchange

西藏不少园林的设计，都有汉文化的痕迹。据载，十三世达赖喇嘛曾派工匠到北京学习，达赖喇嘛夏宫园内建筑的槅窗、窗棂的形制与纹样等，很多都采用了内地的装饰手法。这些窗棂的雕饰，还保留有八仙过海、福禄寿喜、龙凤呈祥等主题。

The design of many gardens in Tibet bears the traces of Han culture. Records show that the thirteenth Dalai Lama dispatched craftsmen to Beijing to study, therefore the shapes and patterns of the partitioned windows in the Dalai Lama's summer palace express the decorative skills of the mainland. Decorative themes include the Eight Immortals, the Gods of Fortune and Longevity, and the Dragon and Phoenix.

评论

微观西藏
TIBET: FAST & FURIOUS

天葬师的歌
Singing Celestial Burial Masters

在西藏，时常有喇嘛选天葬台这样的地方修行，以帮助他们克服恐惧，体会人生的短暂和无常。在天葬台，有的天葬师还一边工作一边唱歌，像劳动号子一样。这是对人生无常的了悟，更是对死亡的看破。

In Tibet, lamas often choose places like celestial burial sites for meditation, in order to help them get over fear and realize how transient and changeable life is. At celestial burial sites, some burial masters even sing as they work. This shows their understanding of the impermanence of life and their comprehension of death.

藏香
Tibetan Incense

很多人去西藏都要带点藏香回来，却不知藏香是怎么制作的，其实很简单：将柏木块泡水并磨成木浆，做成泥砖晾干，与藏药按一定的比例和水搅拌，然后用前部钻眼的牛角将香挤制成细长条晾干即可。最有名的藏香出自尼木县的吞巴乡，所以好的藏香都打着尼木藏香或吞巴藏香的旗号。

Many visitors bring incense back home from Tibet without knowing how it is made. Actually, it is quite simple: cypress wood chunks are soaked in water, ground into a pulp, mixed with Tibetan medicine to form a paste, and then let dry. In the end, it is pushed through the hole of a horn into a long stick, which is then left to dry. The best known Tibetan incense is from Tunba Township in Nimu County, and thus many varieties claim to originate from this place.

摄影：觉果

文化·传承
Culture and Traditions

彻底忘却
Forgetting Completely

西藏传统观念认为，尸体本不属于自己。从丧事办完那天，全家人都不能提亡者的名字，而是要说"去世的那位"。因为亡者真正的生命已经彻底离开，不再是家里的人，必须放手，让亡者彻底没有牵挂地离开。

According to traditional Tibetan thought, a corpse doesn't belong to anyone. After the funeral, all family members can only refer to the dead as 'the one that passed away' instead of using his or her name, because the real life of the dead person has gone completely, and he or she is not a family member any more. The family must let the dead leave without any worries.

为青稞招魂
Recalling the Spirit of Barley

藏族人认为万物都有"央"（有灵魂之义），要想得到某物，必须得到"央"，否则会得而复失。过去拉萨地区秋收时，要举行召回"青稞魂"的仪式，由老人领唱，众人附和，随着最后一句唱诵词，同时收割下最后一束青稞，而后毛驴驮着青稞捆，载着"青稞魂"，随着人们欢欢喜喜地回到家中。

Tibetans believe that all things have souls. When they desire something, they must acquire its soul, or else they will later lose what they have obtained. In the past, when the farmers of Lhasa conducted their autumn harvest, they would perform a ritual to recall the spirit of barley, with the elders chanting and the crowd echoing. As soon as the last line had ended and the last plant was harvested, a donkey would be laden with the barley bundle, merrily following people home with the soul of the barley it carried.

评论

微观西藏
TIBET: FAST & FURIOUS

藏纸
Tibetan Paper

许多西藏的经书历千年而不烂，不遭虫蛀，其秘密就在于用狼毒草制作的藏纸。狼毒草也叫断肠草，根部有剧毒。做纸之前用铁锤砸碎草根，使皮肉分离，用小刀取出外皮与肉间的纤维晾干水煮，再将纸浆均匀地浇在纱布框上晾干，一张精美耐用的藏纸就制成了。

Many Tibetan scripts have lasted for centuries without falling apart or being attacked by worms. The secret lies in the paper-making ingredients, which contain natural pesticides from the root of *gelsemium elegans*, or 'heartbreak grass'. When making paper, the roots are hammered, the bark and contents separated, and then the fibers extracted and boiled. The pulp is then dried on a gauze frame. In the end, a piece of enduring fine Tibetan paper is produced.

看病
Treating Illness

西藏人生病以后，有的会去找医生，有的会去找法师。在西藏，不论医生还是法师，最重要的不是医术高明或法力高超，而是怀有善心。信仰令西藏人看淡生死。即便重病不治，也看作是解脱今生、投奔来世。因而西藏是个很少有医疗纠纷的地方。

When Tibetans fall ill, some go to see a doctor, while some consult a soothsayer or shaman. In Tibet, the most important thing for a doctor or a soothsayer is not having superb medical skills or *mana* (supernatural power), but having a benevolent heart. Faith makes Tibetans take birth and death lightly. Even if an illness cannot be cured, it is seen as a release of this life to the afterlife. Hence, Tibet is a place with few medical disputes.

评论

文化·传承
Culture and Traditions

引导灵魂出窍
Guiding the Soul Out of the Body

在西藏，一个人生命行将结束之时，家人并不是手忙脚乱地哭天抢地，而是赶忙请僧人诵经，引导其即将出窍的灵魂不致盲目飘荡。家人对逝者的悼念以一年为限，一年后逝者已矣，家人则不会再举行悼念活动。

In Tibet, when a person's life is about to end, his or her family won't cry or scramble frantically, but instead quickly invite a monk to chant scriptures to help liberate the soul from purgatory and guide it so that it won't drift around blindly. The family's mourning is limited to only one year. After a year, the deceased has gone forever, and the family will not hold any more mourning activies.

幸运的天葬者
The Luck of Celestial Burials

作家白玛娜珍的家附近有一处天葬台，她父亲有天早起散步回来告诉她说，今天飞去的秃鹫很多，天葬的那个人真是幸运，因为秃鹫会使那个人的肉身在这个世界上不留痕迹，没有什么可以再执着。

There is a celestial burial site not far from Tibetan writer Pema Nadron's home. One morning, her father came back from a walk and told her there were a lot of vultures flying to that site, so people who had celestial burials today were lucky, since the vultures would leave no traces of their bodies in this world, and they would have nothing on earth to stick to anymore.

摄影：车刚

微观西藏
TIBET: FAST & FURIOUS

摄影：觉果

骷髅墙

The Skeleton Wall

曾居西藏27年的资深记者刘伟说：对生命的体悟，最深刻的莫过于对死亡的豁达。在西藏比如县热西乡的达木寺天葬台，那里的人们用几百个骷髅砌了两堵墙。为什么用骷髅砌墙呢？这无非是为了告诉活着的人，要珍惜生命，多行善事，少有俗念，因为无论贵贱，死后不过是一堆白骨。

Liu Wei, a senior journalist who lived in Tibet for 27 years, says, 'There is no deeper understanding and feeling about life than Tibetans' open-mindedness toward death. At the celestial burial ground of Dam Temple in Rakshi Township of Biru County, people built two walls with hundreds of skeletons. Why did they use skeletons to build walls? They just wanted to remind those alive to cherish life, do more charity and have less desire, because no matter who you are, nothing more than a skeleton remains after death.'

评论

文化·传承
Culture and Traditions

猫的一个哈欠
The Yawn of a Cat

西藏有个谚语：人生之短好比猫打一个哈欠。旅居西藏40年的韩书力在参加了多次葬礼之后，最大的感受便是藏民面对死亡的隐忍和理智，以及对逝者获得理想轮回的期待。

There is a saying in Tibet: 'Life is as short as a cat's yawn.' Painter Han Shuli has been sojourning in Tibet for forty years, and his deepest impression after attending several Tibetan funerals was the rational mood of endurance Tibetans held toward death, and their expectation of the departed to find an ideal reincarnation.

去世前最重要的事
Foremost Matter Before Death

有位朋友讲过一个故事：他父亲千辛万苦到拉萨朝佛，将家传的一颗稀世绿松石献给了大昭寺，才心满意足地离开人世。对西藏人来说，出生不用特别欣喜，死亡也不必过度悲伤。他们认为，去世之前最重要的事情就是舍弃家产。

A friend of mine once told me this story: his father overcame enormous hardships on a pilgrimage to Lhasa, presented an inherited rare turquoise to the Jokhang Temple, and then passed away contentedly. For Tibetans, there is no need to rejoice over birth or to grieve over death. They see offering family property as the foremost thing before death.

生死如搬家
Death and Birth Are Like Moving House

藏族人把生死看作搬家，所以今生的身世、家财、遭遇都只是暂时性的，他们不过分追求物质满足。就像你去住旅店，难道还会把旅店房间重新装潢一下吗？

Tibetans consider birth and death as a change of residence, so they believe their backgrounds, wealth, and life experiences are temporary. They don't pursue excessive material satisfaction. Just think: if you stay at a hotel, are you going to redecorate your room?

微观西藏
TIBET: FAST & FURIOUS

临终遗愿
Last Wishes

有人讲了这样一个故事，他的一位藏族朋友得了重病，弥留之际他问朋友在想什么，这位朋友说："我得这个病一定是因为什么前缘，但我现在想全世界的人都不要得这种病，我把这个病带走。"

Someone told a story about one of his Tibetan friends who became seriously ill. During his friend's final moments, he asked him what he was thinking. His friend replied, 'There must be some karma for me to get this disease, but now I just wish everyone in the world won't suffer from this disease any more. Let me take this disease away with me.'

选择天葬
Choosing Celestial Burial

有画家曾问一位 64 岁的藏族司机朋友："你百年以后会选择火葬吗？"他回答道："我信了一辈子佛，念了一辈子经，只是自己能力有限，现在对别人还帮不上什么忙，死后能将身体分给神鹰吃，也算是这辈子最后的奉献了，我只会选择天葬。"

A painter once asked his Tibetan friend, a 64-year-old driver, 'Will you choose cremation when you pass away?' The driver answered, 'I have been a Buddhist all my life, and I have also chanted sutras for a lifetime. I only have limited abilities, so I can not be any big help for others at present. Letting the eagles eat my body is my last tribute, so I will choose celestial burial.'

摄影：车刚

文化·传承
Culture and Traditions

灵魂超度
Releasing the Soul

纪录片导演书云讲过这样一个故事：有人本想去吊唁一位去世的藏族老妈妈，却被拦在了门外。一位好心的藏族老人轻声告知，逝者的灵魂还在体内，陌生人打扰会影响他转世。这人才明白，一直以来西藏的葬礼谢绝外人参与，也是为了帮助逝者的灵魂得以超度。

Documentary director Shu Yun once told a story about condolences. A person wanted to console an old Tibetan mother, but he was stopped outside the door. A kind old Tibetan quietly informed him, 'The soul of the dead is still in the body and is silently searching for a reincarnation. Please don't bother him.' He then understood that the reason strangers are turned away from Tibetan funerals is to help release the dead's soul from purgatory.

央宗的婚礼
Polyandry

西藏的某些地区仍有保留一妻多夫传统制度的家庭。书云在江孜采访时，听到女主人公央宗说："我17岁就到了婆家，婚礼那天连新郎是谁都没记住，反正不是洛嘎就是顿旦，也不知道后来还要给那时才13岁的次旦做老婆。不过我现在的日子过得挺好。"淡淡地说完，央宗抿嘴一笑。

In some areas of Tibet, there are still families that keep the traditional polyandric system. Film producer Shu Yun once interviewed a female Tibetan named Yangzom in Gyangze, who lived under such a system. She said, 'I came to my husband's family when I was seventeen. I didn't even remember who the groom was in the wedding, but it seemed to be either Lokar or Donden; I didn't know either that I would also become the wife of the then thirteen-year-old Tseten. But my life is pretty good now.' Finishing her story calmly, Yangzom gave a gentle smile.

评论

微观西藏
TIBET: FAST & FURIOUS

定亲
Engagement

定亲前，一些传统家庭的父母会拿着孩子和家庭所有成员的生辰属相，请法师算算两家孩子能否成婚。书云在《西藏一年》一书中感慨：找个志同道合的伴侣已经够难了，要找个八字相合，而且与全家人都相合的伴侣，不比登天还难？

Before engagement, parents often take the eight birth horoscopes of their children and family members to a fortune-teller and ask him which two children can marry each other. Shu Yun sighs in her book *A Year in Tibet*, 'finding an ideal partner is already hard enough; isn't it murder trying to find a partner whose birth horoscope matches those of all family members?'

团结族
The United Ethnic Group

汉藏通婚的后代被称作"团结族"。《紫青稞》作者尼玛潘多说："一位与汉族丈夫育有一儿一女的藏族同事希望儿子找藏族媳妇，女儿找汉族老公，因为汉族男人更体贴，藏族女孩更会干家务。"

The children of mixed Han-Tibetan marriages are called 'the united ethnic group'. Nyima Phentok, the author of *Purple Barley*, says, 'A Tibetan colleague whose husband is Han ethnicity has a son and a daughter. She wants her son to marry a Tibetan woman, and her daughter to marry a Han man, as Han men are more considerate and Tibetan women are better at house work.'

摄影：车刚

站着就是一幅画
Just Standing There Forms a Painting

画家陈丹青谈到他著名的《西藏组画》时说："我想让人看看在遥远的高原上有着如此强悍粗犷的生命。如果你看见过康巴一带的牧人，你一定会感到那才叫真正的汉子……他们浑身上下都是绘画的对象，我找到一种单刀直入的语言：他们站着，这就是一幅画。"

When Chen Danqing, a famous Chinese painter, talked about his work, *Tibet Series*, he said, 'I wanted people to see that there were such vigorous and tough lives on that faraway plateau. If you had seen the herdsmen around Kham, you would definitely feel they were real men. Every part of their body could become a subject of painting. I found a straightforward expression to describe them: "They stand there, and that forms a painting".'

不再惶恐
No More Fear of Death

导演陆川：在拍摄电影过程中，我所接触到的西藏人的生死观感染了我。他们有信仰，他们觉得很平静，他们给你很有力量的感觉。先前每天拍戏都有被死亡笼罩的感觉，惶惶不可终日，然而和他们一起，突然觉得对生死有很轻松的感觉……拍电影的过程把我净化了。

Film director Lu Chuan says, 'During the process of filming, I was deeply moved by Tibetans' outlook on life and death. They had beliefs, they felt calm, and they gave you a powerful feeling. Previously, I was shrouded in the fear of death from day to day, and felt nervous all day long, but when I stayed with Tibetans, I started to have an easy feeling toward death. The shooting had purified me.'

评论

微观西藏
TIBET: FAST & FURIOUS

摄影：觉果

西藏女人
Tibetan Women

作家扎西达娃说，西藏女人敏感而乐观，大胆而温柔。对于弱者，即使是个恶棍，她们也会发出怜悯的轻叹，但针头线脑的小事她们从不放在心上。

As writer Tashi Dawa once said, Tibetan women are sensitive but optimistic, brave but gentle. When they face the weak, they sigh in sympathy even if that person is a villain. But they never bother about trifles.

转生之前
Previous Life

藏传佛教认为，人离开肉体后栖身在今生和来世的中间状态有49天，期间只依靠烟和气味生存。在这期间，一定要请喇嘛念诵经文，为灵魂进入下一轮回扫清障碍。有时喇嘛也会写符咒放在尸体上，以防止灵魂回到肉身捣乱。

Tibetan Buddhism believes that after a soul leaves the body and dwells between the past life and the future life, it can live for as many as 49 days on smoke and odor. During this period, a lama must be invited to recite scriptures to prepare the way for the soul to its next reincarnation. Sometimes a lama puts written spells on the corpse to make sure that the soul does not come back to desecrate the body.

文化·传承
Culture and Traditions

澜沧江边的请茶会
Tea Parties by the Lantsang River

在藏区澜沧江怒江流域盛兴一种"请茶会"的风俗：少男少女相邀相聚，喝茶对歌，在展示才艺的同时相互心生爱意，留下了一段段缠绵悱恻的爱情佳话。这样的请茶会经常是天色亮了，少男少女们还意犹未尽……

A custom called 'invitation to a tea party' prevails among the Tibetans living along the Lantsang River and the Nujiang River. Young boys and girls invite each other to meet, drink tea and sing songs to each other. While demonstrating their talents at the party, the seed of love is also planted in their hearts, giving birth to all kinds of tender and romantic love stories. The party often lasts all night, yet the boys and girls are still reluctant to say goodbye...

天葬师的职业要求
Qualifications of Celestial Burial Masters

民俗学家廖东凡曾听一位僧人天葬师说："做天葬师这行，有两条最重要：一是要有佛心、怜悯心、同情心，整个葬礼中间，心里要想着神佛，口里要念着经文，这样才具有加持力，帮助死者灵魂超生；二是要技术娴熟、手脚麻利，要让尸体干净利落、一点不剩地让神鹰吃光，这样死者家属才放心。"

Folklorist Liao Dongfan once heard a celestial burial master say, 'To become a celestial burial master, two things are most important. One is that you must have a compassionate and sympathetic Buddhist heart. Throughout the burial ceremony, you must keep the Buddhas and bodhisattvas in mind and recite the scriptures out loud. Only then will the ceremony generate the power of blessing to help the spirit of the deceased go into rebirth. The second is to be adept in your technique and swift with your actions. You should let the vultures finish every bit of the corpse neatly, then the family of the deceased can rest their hearts.'

评论

微观西藏
TIBET: FAST & FURIOUS

摄影：觉果

葬礼
Funerals

在藏语里尸体的意思是"剩下来的东西"，即肉体不过是生命暂时的寓所，本不属于自己，所以在葬礼之后要把亡者留下的痕迹都烧掉。在种种葬礼中，塔葬和火葬最为尊贵，只有高僧大德才能拥有。一般藏民用天葬，他们认为遗体被处理得越干净，就越有利于灵魂的转世。

Corpse means 'leftover' in Tibetan. That is to say the body is merely a temporary residence for life. It doesn't belong to the self, thus the traces left by the dead are burned after the funeral. The most respected funerals are pagoda burials and cremation, but they are only used for eminent monks or people with great virtues. For common Tibetans, celestial burials are used. They believe the more cleanly their remains are disposed of, the better for their souls' reincarnation.

记忆·回望
Memories and Recollections

微观西藏
TIBET: FAST & FURIOUS

友情
Friendship

有人讲了这样一个故事：一位西藏朋友忽然失去了一切，但过年时他怕内地去的朋友寂寞，仍邀请大家到他家做客。朋友们到了他家才发现，他家已家徒四壁，仅有两件奢侈品：一个是泡沫软坐垫，另一个是收音机。真正的友情就是这样，即使一无所有也惦记着别人。

Someone told a story about his Tibetan friend, who suddenly lost everything. When the new year came, this friend was afraid that his visiting mainland friends might feel lonely, so he still invited them to his home. It was only after they had arrived at his house that they found how destitute his home was. The only two luxuries were a soft bubble cushion and a radio. A true friendship is like this: still thinking of friends even when you haven't a penny to your name.

简单生活
Simple Life

藏学家王尧先生曾借住在山南一对老人家中，老汉每天赶羊上山，老太太给他准备干粮。老汉到了半山，放羊吃草，自己架火煮茶，诵经，非常虔诚，怡然自得。他们的物质生活很贫乏，精神生活却非常富有。

Wang Yao, an expert in Tibetan studies, once stayed at a Tibetan old couple's home. The old man herded sheep up the mountain every day. His wife prepared dry food for him. When the old man was halfway up the mountain, he pastured the sheep, started a fire to brew tea, and chanted Buddhist sutras very devoutly. He was happy and satisfied. The Tibetans' material life was very simple, but their spiritual life was very rich.

摄影：车刚

记忆·回望
Memories and Recollections

信则灵
True if You Believe

卡麦乡卫生所的女医生拉姆去江孜医院看病，被诊断为胃溃疡，吃了一段时间药没见效果，家人就帮她找了村里的法师。法师开出的处方是：到五十里开外的山洞朝圣，用肚子触碰洞壁，据说这样可以洗刷前世孽缘。有人问：有用吗？拉姆说：信则灵。

A female doctor named Lhamo in the clinic of Karmai Village once went to Gyangze Hospital for a severe stomachache. She was diagnosed with stomach ulcers. She took some medicine for a while, all to no avail. Then her family found the village's shaman for her, and the prescription he gave her was to make a pilgrimage to a cave 25 kilometers away and touch the cave walls with her belly, then her past sins could be brushed away. Somebody asked, 'Does it work?' Lhamo said, 'Yes, if you believe.'

通电视
Television Access

1998年，茶巴朗村第一次能接收到电视信号时，由于村里唯一的一台电视转播车依靠太阳能发电的能力有限，村长规定每天晚上7点到10点是看电视的时间。这3个小时便成为村民们一天中最有乐趣的时光。28岁的穷达回忆起当时仍然兴趣盎然："晚上有时候我都舍不得回家吃饭，就等着7点钟在村委会看电视。"

In 1998, Carbanang Village received TV signals for the first time. Due to the limited solar power storage of the village's only TV broadcast relay van, the head of the village prescribed seven to ten every evening as the time for watching TV. These three hours then became the most entertaining time for villagers. When twenty-eight-year-old Qungda recalls that time, he is immersed in high spirits: 'Sometimes I was even reluctant to go home for supper, because I was waiting to watch TV in the village committee at seven o'clock.'

评论

微观西藏
TIBET: FAST & FURIOUS

送别一匹马
Farewell to a Horse

作家凌仕江在去墨脱途中，曾看到马队中一匹负重的马踉跄前行，牧马人却在它身上左拍右打，令人费解。后来，马滑落山坡，牧马人也冲下去，抱着奄奄一息的马与它告别。凌仕江才发现，原来之前牧马人一直在为受伤的马拍打蚂蟥，最后即使知道马要死了，也对它不离不弃。

Once when writer Ling Shijiang was on his way to Mêdog County, he saw a horse staggering under a heavy load as it walked alongside its driver, who was constantly slapping it. This sight was beyond Ling's comprehension. Later on, the horse fell down a slope. Its driver rushed to the dying horse to bid farewell to it. Then Ling discovered that the owner had been flicking leeches off the horse. When he knew the horse was dying, he could hardly tear himself away from it.

石锅也有宿命
Stone Pots Also Have a Fate

"驴友"小湖夫妇在林芝吃石锅鸡，饭店老板说石锅是由特殊材质制成的，市场价1000多元钱一个。但他们偏偏碰翻了一个石锅，掉地上摔碎了，心想可能要赔一笔巨款。但老板过来只关心人烫伤没，说石锅的生命到头了，去了它该去的地方，不用心痛，也不用赔了。

When backpacker Xiaohu and his wife ate stone-pot chicken in Nyingchi, the restaurateur told them that the stone pot was made of special materials and worth over 1,000 yuan. Unfortunately, they accidentally knocked the pot to the ground and broke it. They were ready to pay a large sum of money for breaking the pot. However, when the restaurant owner came over he was only concerned about whether anyone was hurt. He said that the life of the pot had reached its end, and it would go to the place it was supposed to go. He told them there was no need to feel sorry or pay for the damage.

评论

记忆·回望
Memories and Recollections

牦牛的关心
Yaks Care

赔光了全部家产的背包客阿山，不堪面对老婆无休止的抱怨，逃到了西藏。在堆龙德庆县的一个山坡上，他近距离观察一群可爱的牦牛时，突然头晕目眩呼吸困难，倒在了草地上。醒来发现几头牦牛围着他，好像在关心他的生死。那一瞬间他明白了，除了生命，其他一切都不重要。

A backpacker named Ashan ran off to Tibet after he had gone broke and could not tolerate his wife's endless complaints. At a hillside in Doilungdêqên County, when he was observing a herd of yaks at close range, he suddenly felt dizzy, had trouble breathing, and fell to the ground. When he awoke, he found himself surrounded by a few yaks, who seemed to be concerned about his life. At that instant, he realized that nothing mattered more than life.

摄影：觉果

微观西藏
TIBET: FAST & FURIOUS

知足
Contentment

藏族有句谚语：当一个人懂得知足时他才算是富有。有游客在某寺院前被人要求施舍："给一毛钱吧。"这游客给了他两块钱。那人举着钱看了半天，发现竟然不是一毛钱而是两块钱，一毛钱的二十倍啊，他开心地"噌"地跳起来，"嗖"地就跑走了。"今天够花了，不用再要了！"

Tibetans have a saying: 'When a person knows how to be content, then he has true wealth.' In front of a temple, a beggar asked a tourist, 'Please give me a dime.' He gave him two yuan. The beggar held up the money and stared at it a while, then he realized it was not a dime but two yuan, twenty times a dime. He jumped up happily and 'whoosh', he disappeared. 'That is enough for today. Now off I go.'

招手上车
Beckon to Board

有人讲了这样一个故事：一次他在纳木错徒步旅行，走到十点多，周围漆黑，这时一位骑摩托车的牧民在他身边停下，招呼他："上车吧，太晚了，你不安全。"他便上车，这位牧民载他回到了驻地。也许只有这里的天和地才塑造了这样的人性，他敢招手，你也敢上车。

Once someone was hiking at Lake Namtso. It was ten at night, and the sky had turned dark. At that time a Tibetan riding a motorcycle stopped beside him and said, 'Get on. It's too late. You aren't safe.' He got on, and the Tibetan took him back to the station where he lived. Perhaps only the sky and earth there could shape such humanity. One dares to beckon, and you dare to respond.

评论

摄影：觉果

优越感不再
An End to Feelings of Superiority

作家马丽华说，在西藏会看到各样的女人，最初她还会有点朦胧的优越感，直到那次借住藏民家，当家主妇一边给她收拾床铺，一边啧啧连声："宁吉（意指'可怜见的'）！宁吉！"原来那主妇诚恳地认为一个四处奔波的女人太可怜了。那一刻，马丽华才感觉自己其实也很可笑。

Author Ma Lihua explains that she saw all kinds of women in Tibet. At first she had a vague sense of superiority, until she stayed at a local's house, where she overheard her host murmuring to herself earnestly, while doing her bed, 'Nyingje! Nyingje!' (meaning 'poor soul'). Ma understood the Tibetan women sincerely pitied a woman running all over the place. Hearing that comment, Ma felt a bit pathetic herself.

女婿的最佳人选
Ideal Son-in-Laws

作家平措扎西记载说，在上世纪六七十年代，司机是西藏最受欢迎的女婿人选。那时候物资缺乏，他们却可以走南闯北，买回来不少稀罕货。有民谣唱道："方向盘往右转，给爸爸带来了烟叶；方向盘往左转，给妈妈带来头巾。"

Tibetan writer Phuntsok Tashi records that during the 1960s and '70s, the most popular choice for son-in-laws in Tibet was drivers. At that time, material supplies were not abundant, so drivers had the advantage of traveling extensively and bringing back many rare goods. A folk song sings, 'Turning the steering wheel to the right brings father tobacco; turning the steering wheel to the left brings mother a headscarf.'

微观西藏
TIBET: FAST & FURIOUS

被陌生人拉去喝酒

Invited by a Stranger to Drink

摄影师十一郎：1997年，我挎着自己的第一台相机，第一次走进了布达拉宫。然而，那一次我并没有游览这座宫殿，而是刚进门，就被一位当地人拉去喝酒了，原因是他家的女孩考上了大学。我们彼此是陌生的，听不懂对方的语言；但我们又是熟悉的——我们过着同样的平凡生活，感受同样的欢喜悲伤。

Photographer Juichiro says, 'In 1997, equipped with my first camera, I set foot in the Potala Palace for the first time, but I failed to see the palace, because the moment I stepped in, a local man dragged me off to have a drink, for his daughter had just been accepted to a university. We were strangers and couldn't understand each others' language, but we felt very close since we led the same kind of simple life and shared common passion.'

文成公主的甘露

Manna from Princess Wencheng

画家余友心先生一次到拉萨郊区的一个村子里，那里很久没有下雨，青稞都快要死了，他到的第二天就下雨了，村民们觉得是他带来了吉祥，于是到他门口唱："你就是文成公主啊，给我们带来了甘露。"帮助过他们的人，西藏人不会忘记，即使过了一千多年。

Painter Yu Youxin once went to a village near the suburbs of Lhasa. There hadn't been any rain for a long time in that village, and the barley was going to die. However, it rained the second day Yu arrived. Hence, the villagers thought Yu brought auspiciousness and sang at his door, 'You are the Princess Wencheng, bringing us the *manna* (a life-sustaining gift).' Tibetans will never forget those who have helped them, even after a thousand years.

评论

记忆·回望
Memories and Recollections

色拉寺辩经
Sutra Debate at Sera Monastery

有人回忆说，上世纪80年代，色拉寺喇嘛辩经刚刚恢复时，每天下午，几乎所有的年轻僧人都会聚集在色拉寺大殿一旁小院里，他们两人一组，一人站立，一人席地而坐，一问一答煞是热烈。外人虽然听不懂，但他们那种追求知识和真理的激情着实让人钦佩。

One person recalls that when sutra debate at the Sera Monastery was resumed in the 1980s, almost all the young monks would gather every afternoon in the yard beside the monastery. They appeared in pairs, one standing and the other sitting, as they carried out heated debates in a question-and-answer manner. Although it was hard for visitors to understand what they were arguing about, their passion for knowledge and truth was truly admirable.

摄影：觉果

微观西藏
TIBET: FAST & FURIOUS

开个会都不易
Not Easy to Hold Meetings

有人这样形容西藏：拉萨最好、山南最近、日喀则最大、林芝最美、那曲最高、阿里最远、昌都最险。一位援藏干部回忆说：西藏每年确定大型会议时间时，都要考虑到阿里、昌都等偏远高寒地区的特殊情况。会议得在秋天或初冬召开，初冬时节开会也不能太晚，否则大雪封山，不是出不来，就是回不去。

Tibet has been described in this way: Lhasa is the best, Lhoka is the nearest, Xigaze is the largest, Nyinchi is the most beautiful, Nagqu is the highest, Ngari is the farthest, and Qamdo is the steepest. An official sent to work in Tibet recalls, 'When arranging large meetings every year, people had to consider the special weather conditions of remote and high-altitude areas such as Ngari and Qamdo. It's better to hold large meetings in autumn or early winter. The mountains will be blocked by heavy snow in winter, and the participants will either be unable to come out or unable to go back.'

互助组织
An Organization for Mutual Assistance

有人注意到，如果几位藏族老太太畅谈，她们也许不是姐妹，不是亲戚，也不是一般意义上的朋友，而同属一个"吉都"（藏语里的意思是同甘共苦的小集体）。一个"吉都"一般由十个家庭组成，每年都会有两个总管，负责小团体中其他家庭的婚丧嫁娶等大事，平时也会时常聚会，唱歌、跳舞以解忧愁。

Some have noticed that if a couple of elder Tibetan ladies are having a great talk, they are probably neither sisters nor relatives, and they might not even be 'friends' in the general sense. Instead, they perhaps belong to the same *gyido*, which in Tibetan means a small group sharing joys and sorrows. A *gyido* is usually composed of ten families, and each year two families act as the group's executives, who are responsible for major events in the families, such as weddings and funerals. They also organize singing and dancing parties for sharing and easing worries.

记忆·回望
Memories and Recollections

牦牛的泪
A Yak's Tears

作家凌仕江有次在去江孜的路上，看到一个黯然神伤的小姑娘和一头低头吃草的牦牛。询问之下，才知道小姑娘为要上学而不得不与牦牛分开而伤心。凌仕江对孩子说："总有一天你的生活不再需要牦牛为伴。"言罢，他看到的是小姑娘慌张而无言的神情，而那头牦牛似乎在流泪。

Once on his way to Gyangze, author Ling Shijiang saw a sad little girl and a yak, with its head lowered, eating grass. Upon asking, he came to know that the girl was sorrowful because she had to part with the yak and go to school. He said to the child, 'Sooner or later in your life, you won't need this yak to accompany you.' Having finished this consolation, he saw the panicked and speechless look in the girl's eyes, and even the yak seemed to be weeping.

西藏的诱惑
Lure of Tibet

艺术家巴荒在《阳光与荒野的诱惑》一书中这样描述她的西藏："十年之际，回首西藏，西藏之行在我的人生旅途中匆匆而过。我在那个充满诱惑的土地上停留的时间真是太短了，我不曾想过要走遍她的每一个角落，但我却因为她的诱惑而走遍了我自身的每一个角落。"

In her book *Temptations of Sunshine and Wildness*, artist Ba Huang described what Tibet is like in her mind: 'After ten years, when I look back, I find the trip to Tibet has been very short. I have spent too little time in that land full of lures. I haven't thought of traveling to every corner of Tibet, but, because of its temptation, I did walk over many parts myself.'

评论

微观西藏
TIBET: FAST & FURIOUS

服务员的歌声
Waitresses' Singing

在拉萨的一个青年旅社,每个清晨,人们坐在庭院里看书喝茶,藏族服务员边收拾房间边唱歌。她们的歌声优美嘹亮,穿过三层高的楼,传到庭院里,那是五星级酒店都没有的服务。正如有位作家所说的:"劳动的快乐像一首史诗,使这个民族拥有高贵的精神。"

There is a youth hostel in Lhasa. Every morning, when travelers sit in the yard reading and drinking tea, the waitresses of the hostel sing as they clean the rooms. Their beautiful and resonant singing passes from the third floor to the yard. This is a service that even a five-star hotel cannot provide. Just as one writer wrote, 'The happiness of working is like an epic, endowing this ethnic group with a noble spirit.'

萨迦寺里皇家僧
Royal Monk in the Sagya Monastery

有作家曾描述:1288年冬十月,全副武装的蒙古军士护送一位神情落寞的汉僧远行。他正是南宋少帝赵㬎。此行就是发遣西藏萨迦寺出家。赵㬎得法名"合尊",即天神家族的出家人。黄仁宇曾感慨故事到此戛然而止。但在藏文典籍中,说他潜心修行,成为著名的译师。

A writer once described how, during the winter of 1288, heavily armed Mongolian troops escorted a lonely and saddened Han monk on a long journey. That monk was Zhao Xian, the young Emperor of Song. At that time he was sent to be a monk at the Sagya Monastery in Tibet. He was called 'Hezun', meaning 'the monk from the celestial family'. Historian Ray Huang once sighed that the story stopped abruptly there. However, records in Tibetan say that he cultivated himself with great concentration and became a famous translator thereafter.

评论

记忆·回望
Memories and Recollections

摄影：觉果

享受学习
Enjoying Learning

作家白玛娜珍讲了这样一个故事：一天，一个朋友接到了在内地中学上学的女儿打来的电话，她对女儿说："宝贝，妈妈明天去给你祈福考个好成绩，考不好也算了，开心就好。"挂了电话她还唠叨："我女儿是去享受教育和学习的，不是去考试的。"

Writer Pema Nadron tells this story: one day, a friend of hers received a phone call from her daughter who was studying at a mainland high school. She said to her daughter, 'Darling, tomorrow I will go pray that you get a good score on the exam. But don't worry. It's okay if you don't have a high score. I just want you to be happy.' After hanging up the phone, she muttered, 'My daughter went there to enjoy the education and learning, not just to take exams.'

一筐鸡蛋
A Basket of Eggs

30多年过去了，西藏的物质供应空前充沛，但画家余友心仍然记得，上世纪70年代末，他第一次进藏时千里迢迢运送过去的，是"一筐鸡蛋"；第二年他探亲回西藏，带给朋友们的珍贵礼物，是一筐"顶花带刺的新鲜黄瓜"。

These days material supplies are unprecedentedly abundant in Tibet. However, painter Yu Youxin still remembers that when he went to Tibet for the first time at the end of the 1970s, he brought a basket of eggs, which then were a rare delicacy. The second year he entered Tibet again to visit his friends, and this time he carried a basket of fresh cucumbers as a precious present.

微观西藏
TIBET: FAST & FURIOUS

人在碗在
A Bowl for Life (and Death)

在过去，藏民几乎是人手一木碗。父子不共碗，兄弟不共碗，夫妻不共碗，叫花子再穷也有一只破木碗。出门，要将木碗擦拭得干干净净，或者用舌头舔干净，用布包裹，揣在怀中。人在碗在，人死了碗也要送出门。

In the past, almost all Tibetans had their own wooden bowls. Fathers and sons never shared the same bowl, nor did brothers or couples. Even a beggar owned his broken wooden bowl, no matter how poor he was. Before a person left his home, he would wipe or lick his bowl clean, wrap it in a piece of cloth and tuck it in his shirt. As long as he was alive, the bowl would always be with him. When the person died, the bowl would stay with him too.

小童僧
Child Monks

在西藏，传统上如果一个家庭有一两个在寺庙生活的僧人，是一件值得骄傲的事情。因此，不少家长在孩子七八岁的时候就安排他们出家。60多岁的强久回忆他8岁那年随父母到格桑师父家，父母给师父献上哈达、一块羊腿肉、一陶壶茶和一些藏币，强久跪地给师父磕了头，他的童僧生活也就开始了。

According to Tibetan tradition, if someone in the family was a monk, it was something to be proud of. Therefore, many parents sent their children to become monks when they were only seven or eight years old. Chamgur, who is now over sixty years old, recalls that when he was only eight, his parents led him to the home of Master Gesang. His parents presented the master with a *hada*, a leg of lamb, a pottery teapot filled with tea, and some Tibetan coins. Chamgur knelt down and kowtowed to the master. Then his life as a child monk began.

摄影：车刚

记忆·回望
Memories and Recollections

秘密提亲

Secret Marriage Proposal

一位旅藏作家提到一个很特别的藏族习俗：提亲要背着结婚当事人进行。比如法师说宗嘎和嘉措适宜结婚，两家的父母就要秘密操办，直到正式婚礼的当天，男孩女孩才知道谁将成为自己的伴侣。在过去的西藏，"父母赐予我生命和一切，服从是我的义务"是很流行的观念。

A travel writer once mentioned a very unique old Tibetan custom: marriage proposals were done behind the backs of the future couple. For example, if a soothsayer said Zomkar and Gyatso matched each other very well, then the parents of the two youths would prepare for the wedding secretly. The couple could only know who they were marrying on the wedding day. In the past, 'Parents gave me life and everything; obeying is my duty' was a very popular sentiment in Tibet.

我的生日我做主

Choosing a Birthday

歌唱家才旦卓玛1937年出生在日喀则的一个农奴家。藏族普通老百姓对生日并不重视。才旦卓玛的母亲只记得她是藏历的老虎年出生的，大概是1937年。后来她到内地上学，填表时要求填写出生月日，实在是记不住日子了，才旦卓玛就选择了8月1日作为自己的生日。

Singer Tseten Drolma was born in to a serf family in Xigaze in 1937. Back then, most Tibetans didn't pay much attention to birthdays, so Drolma's mother only remembered that her daughter was probably born in the Year of the Tiger, which was 1937. Later Drolma went to a mainland school and was asked to write her birthdate on a form. She truly couldn't remember the exact date, so she chose August 1st as her birthdate.

评论

微观西藏
TIBET: FAST & FURIOUS

如此吃盐
Precious Salt

作家色波描写1976年西藏最偏僻的地方墨脱时说，那里没有任何形式的农贸市场，吃盐都是按年度计划好了的。当地人放盐时小心翼翼，几根指头搓磨半天，也不见有几粒盐掉进锅里。放完盐后，不管是否有剩余，都要把手重新伸回盐袋，弹几下指头。

When writer Sebo describes Mêdog County, the remotest area of Tibet, he says in 1976 there were no farmers' markets of any form. Even the salt they ate was allotted according to an annual plan. The locals always put salt into their dishes scrupulously. They rubbed with their fingers only a few grains of salt into the pot. After the salt was added, they would always reach into the salt bag and flick the remaining salt off their fingers, no matter how little was left on them.

红柳做燃料
Rose Willow as Fuel

作家毕淑敏回忆她40多年前在西藏阿里当兵时用红柳做燃料的情形。起初，她舍不得烧这种稀罕的植物，但炊事员说红柳的根是高原上最强大的燃料，一旦燃烧起来，它就好像要把自己汲取了千万年的光芒迸发出来似的。在火焰中，每一块红柳，直到烧尽之前，都傲然地保持着盘根错节的状态。

Writer Bi Shumin recalls using rose willow as fuel when she was a soldier in Tibet's Ngari forty years ago. At first, she pitied burning such a rare plant, but the cooks told her the root of rose willow is the most powerful fuel on the plateau. Once it burns, it seems to burst out the brilliant rays it has absorbed over millions of years. While burning, rose willow always maintains its unyielding knotty form till it burns out.

评论

记忆·回望
Memories and Recollections

"脏户"
'Dirty Households'

在西藏，逢年过节，最抢手的当属屠户，他们要去各家各户帮助屠宰牲畜。但是在过去，屠户被称为"脏户"，地位很低。哪怕他们很富有，一般人也不愿意和他们联姻，或和他们同桌共餐，甚至"喝酒或是喝茶的时候，屠夫身份的人会自觉地把自己的杯子放在远离他人的位置上"。

During Tibetan festivals, the most sought-after people are butchers, who need to help families slaughter livestock. In the past, however, households of butchers were called 'dirty households'. Their social standing was very low. Even if they were wealthy, ordinary people were still unwilling to marry them, or to eat with them at the same table. It went as far as 'when drinking wine or tea, butchers would consciously put their cups away from those of others.'

生孩子
Giving Birth

唐麦·贡觉白姆出身于西藏有名的贵族桑珠颇章家庭，她说："旧西藏女人生孩子只能在家生，老人用一个木棍一头缠上羊毛，蘸上菜籽油来消毒。对新生儿的处理是先把脐带打个结然后切断。产妇和新生儿死亡率很高。贵族产妇有佣人伺候，能休息，而一般家庭的妇女生完孩子就起来干活。"

Thangme Konjo Palmo, who was born in the famous Tibetan noble family Samdrup Phodrang, says, 'In old Tibet, women could only give birth at home. The elderly would wrap some wool on one end of a wood stick and dip it in canola oil for sterilization. As for the treatment of the baby, they would first knot the umbilical cord and then cut it off. The death rate of mothers and babies was very high. Those from noble families had servants who looked after them so that they could rest, but ordinary mothers had to get up and work shortly after giving birth.'

微观西藏
TIBET: FAST & FURIOUS

摄影：觉果

雪村
Shol Village

过去西藏的寺院总是建在高山上，而山脚下就需要一个世俗的村落，为寺院内的人员提供生活服务。这些山下的村落就被称为"雪村"，村民们被叫作"雪巴"。布达拉宫脚下的"雪村"是让人向往的住所，这里除了几户贵族外，其他都是经过严格筛查、遵纪守法的平民。

In the past, Tibetan temples were mostly built on high mountains, and the villagers at the foot of these mountains were needed to provide logistical services to those living in the temples. These villages were called '*shol* villages', and villagers were called *sholpa*. The *shol* village at the foot of the Potala Palace was a place where many people yearned to live. In this village, apart from some noble families, other villagers were strictly-chosen law-abiding citizens.

节省的贵族
A Frugal Nobleman

作家次仁罗布：我小时候见过一个贵族，叫宇拓厦，他过的一种什么生活呢？他每次吃饭只吃半碗，留另外半碗晚上吃。他很节制自己的欲望，精神满足是他更看重的追求。

Author Tsering Norbu recalls, 'I met a nobleman called Yuthoksha when I was young. Do you know what kind of life he lived? He only ate half a bowl of food at lunch, leaving the remaining half for supper. He strictly controlled his desires because spiritual fulfillment was the most important aspiration he pursued.'

记忆·回望
Memories and Recollections

农奴的孩子
Children of the Serfs

巴桑老人是旧西藏时农奴的女儿,因为父母分属不同的农奴主,巴桑姐妹两人归属了母亲的主人家,三个兄弟归属了父亲的主人家。后来母亲因病早逝,父亲带着五个孩子,给农奴主支差。其中,小弟弟后来夭折,剩下姐弟四人散布在各处,给不同的主人当奴隶,天各一方。

Pasang was the daughter of two serfs in old Tibet. Since her parents belonged to different serf owners, Pasang and her sister went to the home of their mother's owner, and their three brothers were sent to the home of their father's owner. Later Pasang's mother died from a disease, and her father looked after the five children while working for his master. Pasang's youngest brother died very young, and the rest of the siblings became serfs of different masters. Since then, the family was separated.

吐蕃的玄奘
The Xuanzang of Tibet

唐代的吐蕃僧人法成大师在敦煌潜心佛经翻译,曾将故事集《贤愚经》译成藏文,使佛法教理直达人心,《贤愚经》又成为唐卡、藏戏的故事蓝本,千年流传。而他去后,汉传佛教与藏传佛教各行其道,一个时代也就此终结。陈寅恪先生称他为吐蕃的玄奘,"一代文化所托命之人"。

Master Facheng, a monk of the Tibetan Kingdom during the Tang Dynasty, rendered the *Sutra of the Wise and the Fool*, a collection of stories into Tibetan when he dedicated himself to the translation of Buddhist texts in Dunhuang. He meant to bring the Buddhist teachings directly to people's hearts, and the sutra became the source of the themes of *thangkas** and Tibetan Operas over the next millennium. After he passed away, Han and Tibetan Buddhism pursued different courses, and an era came to an end. Chen Yinque called Facheng 'the Xuanzang of Tibet' and 'a trustee of an era's culture'.

* A *thangka* is a Tibetan silk painting with embroidery, usually depicting a Buddhist deity or scene.

评论

微观西藏
TIBET: FAST & FURIOUS

肢体语言
Body Language

过去，年轻藏族女子若将发辫铺在酒杯下面敬酒，会被认为是莫大的尊重，是心完全向你敞开之意。有关藏族人丰富的肢体语言的另外一个例子，是过去每当负责巡逻的铁棒喇嘛走过拉萨街头，所有僧俗百姓都要闪向两旁，而且要弯腰、吐舌，作惊恐敬畏状，嘴里发出一些哆哆嗦嗦的声音。

In the past, if young Tibetan ladies made toasts by putting their braids under their cups, this meant they had great respect for you and had opened their hearts completely to you. Another example of the sophistication of Tibetans' body language is when lamas on patrol walked through the streets of Lhasa with an iron rod, all pedestrians would stand aside, bend down, stick out their tongues, pretend to be terrified, and mumble frightened words.

20世纪40年代的八廓街
Barkhor Street in the 1940s

沈宗濂在《西藏与西藏人》中记载了20世纪40年代的八廓街：一条未经铺砌的土路，没有路灯，有点肮脏，还有不少护卫着自己地盘的狗……它不仅是拉萨的主要大道，也是全西藏唯一的一条真正的街道。然而，人们对它并不珍惜，他们随地扔垃圾，随地大小便。但无论如何，这都是他们的圣道。

In his book *Tibet and the Tibetans*, Shen Zonglian describes the Barkhor Street of the 1940s: 'As an unpaved dirt road, it had no street lights and was a bit dirty. There were also many dogs that guarded their territories... This street was not only the main avenue of Lhasa, but also the only real street in the whole of Tibet. Nevertheless, people did not cherish it. They dropped litter and defecated on the street casually, though this was their sacred avenue after all.'

摄影：佚名

西藏的城堡
Tibetan Fortresses

汉藏交流源远流长，在建筑方面尤其"有迹可循"。如萨迦寺中规模最大的整体建筑——萨迦南寺，其平面布局呈方形，便是效仿了内地城池建筑的格局。寺庙四周修有坚固的围墙，围墙外修有低矮的土城，土城外有一道石砌的堑壕，围墙之上还有四个角楼，这些都与当时内地城堡建筑无异。

There is a long history of exchange between Tibetan and Han cultures, with traceable patterns in architecture in particular. The square layout of the Southern Sakya Temple, the biggest structure at the Sakya Monastery, is an imitation of mainland fortresses. The temple is surrounded by a strong wall, with a low earth fortification around it and an extra stone trench. There is a turret at each corner of the wall. All these aspects resemble those of the mainland fortresses of the past.

第一个到拉萨的外国女人
The First Foreign Woman in Lhasa

据考证，第一个走进西藏的外国女人是法国的大卫·妮尔，她在1921年6月化装成一个乞丐，和义子一起抵达拉萨。她在《一个巴黎女子的拉萨历险记》一书中，记述了她拉萨之行的全过程。在98岁生日时，她还写下这样的文字："我应该死在羌塘，死在西藏的大湖畔或大草原上。"

According to research, the first foreign female to enter Tibet was Alexandra David-Neel, a French woman. In June 1921, she disguised herself as a beggar and arrived in Lhasa with her adopted son. She recorded the whole trip in her book *My Journey to Lhasa*. On her 98th birthday, she wrote, 'I should pass away in Changtang (a plateau in northwestern Tibet), by the shores of Tibet's big lakes or on its grassland.'

评论

微观西藏
TIBET: FAST & FURIOUS

江孜的英雄山
Heroic Mountain of Gyangze

江孜是拉萨到日喀则途中的一个普通县城，但那里的宗山城堡却值得缅怀。1904 年，近万人的英国武装由亚东侵入，江孜军民和白居寺僧侣在宗山上筑起炮台，用土制枪炮与入侵者展开血战，弹尽粮绝之后，这些从 16 岁到 60 岁的勇士们仍用石头拼死抵抗了三天三夜，最后全部阵亡或跳崖殉难。

Gyangze is an ordinary county town on the road between Lhasa and Xigaze. The Dzongri Castle in this county, however, ought to be remembered. In 1904, when nearly ten thousand British troops from Yadong County invaded, residents and soldiers in Gyangze, along with monks from Palcho Monastery, built a fort on Mt. Dzongri and bravely fought the invaders with self-made guns. After their supplies ran out, these warriors, aged sixteen to sixty, stood up before the enemy, throwing stones in resistance for three days and nights. In the end, all of them were killed or jumped off a cliff.

投宿在拉萨
Lodging in Lhasa

据当地老人回忆，过去拉萨没有现代意义上的客栈。地方政府接待官方客人都是给各贵族大户签发一种特殊的文告，不管情愿不情愿，文告贴在谁家的大门口，谁家就要承担接待任务。一般的商人和香客则要自己找房东投宿，或者就住在野外的帐篷里。如果长期住，除了房租，还要再为房东支应一定的劳动差役。

As old local people recall, in the past Lhasa had no inns in the modern sense. When the local government needed to accommodate official guests, it would issue a special edict to the aristocrats. Regardless of the host's will, the order came into force automatically if the edict was tacked on his door. Ordinary business people and pilgrims would have to find their own accommodation or set up a tent in a field. If they wanted to stay for long, they'd have to do some work for the landlord in addition to paying rent.

记忆·回望
Memories and Recollections

小喇嘛开拖拉机
Young Lamas Driving a Tractor

记者宁世群回忆说，扎什伦布寺里有了第一台拖拉机的时候，小喇嘛们十分喜爱，不少人背地里悄悄学着摆弄，居然能让拖拉机突突地冒着黑烟叫唤起来。终于有一天，一个小喇嘛把拖拉机开动了，却停不下来，以致撞到僧房的墙头上，不过还好小喇嘛没有受伤。

Reporter Ning Shiqun recalls when the Tashilhunpo Monastery acquired its first tractor, the young lamas loved it, and many of them secretly tried to figure out how to make it run. To their surprise, they eventually made the machine puff out black smoke, and one day, a young lama got it move at last. However, he could not stop it. He ended up driving the tractor into the wall of the monastery, but luckily he was not injured.

活在民间的公主
The People's Princess

文成公主至今仍扎实地活在西藏民间。山南的百姓说：他们吃的粮食，是公主带来的种子；他们用的盐巴和茶叶，是公主带来的；他们用的纺织、木工等技术是公主带来的匠人教会的……甚至民间传说她用过的锅灶，只要能摸一下，就能做出可口的饭菜。

Princess Wencheng still lives in Tibetan folklore. The people of Lhoka (Shannan) say the grain they eat grows from the seeds brought by the princess, and the salt and tea leaves they consume are brought by the princess too. The textile technology and carpentry are also taught by craftsmen brought along by the princess... Folk tales even say that if you can touch the ovens and pots she used, you will be able to cook delicious food.

评论

微观西藏
TIBET: FAST & FURIOUS

"疯喇嘛"的壮举

The Undertakings of the 'Crazy Lama'

在民间,最令西藏百姓感到亲近的高僧大概就是唐东杰布了。他被称为"铁桥活佛"。据载,他一生共主持修建了58座铁索桥。甚至在别人嘲笑他是"疯喇嘛"时,他也从不退缩,一如既往。据说,至今在他的家乡,还保存着相传是他晚年主持修建的铁索桥。

One of the most revered monks among the Tibetan people may be Thangtong Gyalpo. He has been called 'the Living Buddha of the Iron Bridges'. Records show that in his lifetime he constructed fifty-eight iron chain bridges. Even when he was ridiculed as 'Crazy Lama', he never withdrew but always moved on. It is said that the bridge in his hometown was constructed by him in his later years, and it still stands there.

加持坐骑

Blessing for Horses

西藏的宗教仪式很多,在过去有一项是专门用来加持坐骑的仪式。这个仪式上的主角是"护法神坐骑",也就是官员们和大喇嘛们的坐骑。它们常年在马厩里养精蓄锐,没人骑,也不用干活,一年之中最重要的事情就是:披戴着护法神的佩物,参加正月初一的加持仪式。

Among the many rituals in Tibet, there was one in the past meant especially for giving blessings to horses. The leading figures in this ritual were 'guardian deities' horses', i.e. the horses of officials and prominent lamas. These horses were kept in stables throughout the year. They were seldom ridden and didn't have to work. Their sole important task in a year was wearing the accessories of guardian deities and receiving blessings on Tibetan New Year's Day.

评论

记忆·回望
Memories and Recollections

不离不弃
Always by Your Side

作家马丽华在接受采访时坦言:"我是个重情义的人,西藏待我好,我以文字回报。不曾想它因此对我更好,我只好再回报。如此循环不已,我便不能离开它,不能不持续地赞美它。"

Writer Ma Lihua admitted in an interview: 'I cherish ties and friendship. Tibet was nice to me, so I wrote about it in return. But I did not realize that Tibet would show even more of its affection because of my writing, so I had to repay this again. After a few rounds, I felt that I could never tear myself away from it, and that I couldn't help praising it again and again.'

精神战胜一切
Spirit Overcomes All Difficulties

藏画大师尼玛泽仁回忆说:很多年前的一天,路上刮起大风沙,风能把一个躺在地上的人托起来。我看见远处几个妇女在风沙中奔忙,寻找丢失的牦牛。看见她们在这样恶劣的自然环境中表现出顽强的生命力,我感到自己领悟了某种东西,这就是藏民族的精神,而这种精神构成了藏民族所有的历史。

Nyima Tsering, a master of Tibetan painting, recalls: 'On a day many years ago, a raging sandstorm took place and the wind could easily raise a person lying on the ground. In the distance I saw several women rushing about in the sandstorm to look for their lost yaks. Seeing the power of their vitality under such an adverse natural circumstance, I felt that I learned something — a tenacious spirit runs through the entire history of the Tibetan ethnic group.'

摄影:车刚

微观西藏
TIBET: FAST & FURIOUS

劝人种痘碑
A Pillar for Persuading People to Vaccinate

大昭寺门前至今竖立着一块清乾隆年间刻制的"劝人种痘碑"。当时，西藏流行天花，为避免天花病人被赶到山野岩洞等死，清政府驻藏大臣在藏北草原上建造房屋，派人诊治，使不少病人痊愈生还。事后西藏官员在大昭寺前立碑称赞驻藏大臣，并宣传天花并非不治之症，劝人种痘以策防治。

A stele erected in the Qing Dynasty for the purpose of persuading people to vaccinate still stands in front of the Jokhang Temple. Before its construction, smallpox struck Tibet. To prevent people from driving the sick to wild mountains and caves, where they could only wait for death, the Qing minister for Tibet built houses on the grasslands of northern Tibet and sent doctors there to treat the patients, thus helping many of the sick to recover and survive. Afterward, Tibetan officials set up this pillar in front of the Jokhang to praise the minister, publicizing that smallpox was not incurable, and persuading people to vaccinate.

传奇法王
Legendary Dharmaraja

西藏最有名的历史人物也许要算六世达赖喇嘛仓央嘉措了，他的诗歌在西藏传唱了近300年。"入夜去会情人／破晓时大雪纷飞／足迹印在雪上／保密还有什么用处？"一代年轻的法王把自己私会情人的事情写成诗歌传唱，这不但需要才气，更需要超凡脱俗的豁达和通彻。

One of the best-known historical figures in Tibet is probably the sixth Dalai Lama, Tsangyang Gyatso, whose poems have spread all over Tibet for nearly 300 years. 'Meet my lover at nightfall / At dawn a big snowfall / Snow betrays my trail / How is confidentiality useful at all?' A young dharmaraja bravely wrote popular poems based on his story of secretly meeting a lover. It required not only talent, but also extraordinarily refined spiritual openness.

评论

记忆·回望
Memories and Recollections

摄影：聂晓阳

刻苦的学僧
Hardworking Monks

据历史文献记载，西藏僧人学习佛经大都非常刻苦，要求也非常严格。因为人们相信在夜晚或天未亮时背诵最有效果，所以秉烛夜读是家常便饭。有的僧人为了节省灯油，也为了不打扰别人，往往手拿一炷点着的香条，用香条的火光逐行扫描作为照明。

According to historical documents, most Tibetan monks studied Buddhist sutras very hard and exercised strict self-discipline. They believed the best time for recitation was at night, so staying up and reading by a candle was quite normal for them. Some monks held a piece of burning incense and read every line by its light, in order not to waste lamp oil or disturb others.

米拉日巴小故事
Story of Milarepa

西藏最著名的密宗大师米拉日巴曾在山洞修行，传说他后来不食人间烟火，只靠吃荨麻草为生。据说他修行的洞口有一丛荆棘，开始的时候他想把它砍掉，但每次都想到人生无常，自己每次出洞都不知道能不能回来，就不想浪费精力，所以过了很多年，那个荆棘丛一直都在。

The most famous Tibetan Esoteric Buddhist master Milarepa once meditated in a cave. According to legend, he didn't eat ordinary food but lived on nettle grass. There was a clump of brambles in front of his cave. He initially wanted to cut them off, but he gave up doing so because he thought it was a waste of energy, considering that life was unpredictable and he might not come back after he left the cave. After many years, the brambles were still there.

微观西藏
TIBET: FAST & FURIOUS

达观如此
Such Optimism

藏族作家扎西达娃曾讲过这样一个故事：有对老夫妇和两个女儿到拉萨朝圣，刚来没几天，两个女儿突然失踪了。像所有藏族人一样，老夫妇对此表现出超然与达观，他们相信女儿们一定是找到自己的意中人私奔了，他们很有耐心地等待着某天女儿们抱着刚出生的孩子，领着夫婿来见他们。

Tibetan author Tashi Dawa tells this story: an old couple went on a pilgrimage with their two daughters, but their daughters mysteriously disappeared after only a few days. Like all other Tibetans, the old couple showed detached optimism and believed that their daughters must have met their beloveds and went away with them. They would wait patiently for their daughters to come back with their husbands carrying their newborn babies.

专注的力量
Power of Concentration

很多西藏人都知道一个故事：五世达赖喇嘛有次经过一位不识字的老人身边，发现尽管他念诵的经文是错的，但总有吉祥天女（度母）出现在他的头顶。后来，当老人念诵正确的经文时，度母反而不见了。原来，当他念真经的时候，他的心灵都被经文占据了，心反而没有念错经时那么专注，所以度母就不再出现了。

There is a well-known story among Tibetans: the fifth Dalai Lama once went past an illiterate old man. Though the scriptures he recited weren't right, Pelden Lhamo (Tara, a bodhisattva representing the virtues of success in work and achievements) would always appear above his head. Later, when the old man started reciting the scriptures correctly, Tara disappeared unexpectedly. Why? Because when he was reading the scriptures correctly, his whole attention was attracted by the reading. As a result, he was no longer as concentrated as when he was reciting the scriptures wrongly, so Tara never appeared again.

评论

风土 · 管窥
Sights and Sounds

微观西藏
TIBET: FAST & FURIOUS

西藏的乞丐
Beggars in Tibet

到了西藏你会发现，西藏的乞丐大都是欢天喜地的，他们不装可怜，更不卑躬屈膝，因为在他们的观念里：富人布施给我，我帮他们上"天堂"。所以西藏人认为：布施不是施舍，它是一种互助。

When you arrive in Tibet, you will find that most of the beggars there are very cheerful. They don't present pitiful faces or bend their knees, because in their view, the rich give alms to them, and they help the rich get to 'heaven'. Hence according to Tibetan values, giving alms is not a charity, but an action of mutual assistance.

牦牛的死
Death of Yaks

西藏人视牦牛如亲人，牦牛的死亡自然也是一个庄严的时刻。旅藏美国人龙安志介绍，牦牛死后，藏民会取下它的头骨，供到玛尼堆上，或吊在门的上方祈求它的保护，同时也使牦牛得到永远的纪念。

Tibetans regard yaks as family members. Therefore, the death of a yak should be a solemn moment. Laurence Brahm, an American traveler, wrote of the following scene after a yak died: Tibetans would take its skull and enshrine it on *mani* stones or hang it above the door, praying that it would protect them. Yaks would also be commemorated forever in this way.

摄影：聂晓阳

风土·管窥
Sights and Sounds

坚毅的夏尔巴人
The Persistent Sherpas

珠穆朗玛峰下生活着强悍的夏尔巴人，他们以坚韧不拔和善于攀登冰封雪岭驰名于世。许多登山家和探险家都是因为夏尔巴人的护送和向导，才得以征服这座壮丽无比的第一高峰的。民俗学家廖东凡说：假如珠穆朗玛峰是人类登山的丰碑，那么这座丰碑上闪烁着许多夏尔巴人的光辉名字。

At the foot of Mount Qomolangma live some very tough people called Sherpas. They are well-known for their persistence and capability of climbing snowy peaks. Many mountaineers and explorers conquered the highest and most magnificent peak of the world only because they were escorted and guided by Sherpas. Folklorist Liao Dongfan states, 'If Mount Qomolangma is the monument of humans' mountain-climbing history, then the names of many brilliant Sherpas are engraved on this monument.'

门巴族人的背筐
Backpacks of the Monpa People

作家色波发现门巴族人不养马，一应物品全凭人力背运。他们的背筐系着三根带子，两根背带一根顶带。在村庄附近背运东西时，为了方便，他们往往只用一根顶带。因为很小就开始干活，等到长大成人，头上差不多都被顶带勒出一道沟槽，从一侧耳鬓到另一侧耳鬓，男人尤其明显。

Writer Sebo found that people of Monpa (an ethnic group living in Tibet's Cona County) don't breed horses, they carry everything on their own backs instead. Their backpacks have three straps: two braces and one headband. If they just carry things around the village, they only use the headband for convenience. Since Monpas start working at a very young age, after they grow up, the headband will leave them with a deep groove spreading from one ear to the other. This groove is particularly visible on men.

评论

微观西藏
TIBET: FAST & FURIOUS

圣母的面纱
Veil of the Virgin

天气晴朗时，在珠峰顶总有一些乳白色的烟云，因它总沿着山顶飘向一边，像一面白色的旗帜迎风招展，所以被称为"旗云"，堪称世界一大奇观。由于旗云的变换可以反映高空气流的变动，因此珠峰旗云又有"世界上最高的风向标"之称，外国探险家给它起了个更浪漫的名字："圣母的面纱"。

When the sky is clear, a few creamy white clouds often surround the top of Mt. Qomolangma. They usually drift along the peak to one side, like a white flag unfolding in the wind, so they have been dubbed 'flag clouds'. They are one of the most remarkable sights in the world. Because shifts of the flag clouds reflect changes in the high altitude air currents, they are also known as 'the world's highest weathervane'. Foreign explorers gave them an even more romantic name: 'the Veil of the Virgin'.

"冬天不睡春天睡"的湖
A Lake that 'Doesn't Sleep in Winter but Sleeps in Spring'

据说，三大圣湖之一的当惹雍错曾是魔鬼湖，被苯教祖师制服后成为神湖。但也说不清是神气还是魔气，这座湖每年到藏历元月十五日（公历近三月）才结冰，至藏历二月底、三月初，又在一天之内全部解冻，当地人称它"冬天不睡春天睡"。如果某年湖水不结冰，当地人还会认为必有灾难降临呢。

It is said that one of the three holy lakes, Tangra Yumtso, used to be called a 'devil's lake'. It was discovered and designated a holy lake by the founder of the Bon religion. However, it is unclear whether it is good or evil: the lake doesn't freeze until the fifteenth day of the first month of the Tibetan calendar (at the end of February), and at some point near the end of the second or start of the third month, it will thaw completely in one day. It has been said 'not to sleep during winter, but sleep in spring instead'. If the lake does not freeze any one year, the local people believe that disaster is imminent.

评论

风土·管窥
Sights and Sounds

摄影：聂晓阳

"阿嘎"地板
A-ga Floors

在西藏的宫殿、古城堡、大寺院和达官贵族的住宅里，往往都能看到一种特殊的地板或屋顶：阿嘎。这种材料类似水泥，但更加光滑环保，长期拖擦会呈现出斑斓而厚重的色彩，显现出古朴的魅力。据介绍，所谓阿嘎既不是石头也不是土，而是岩石深处形成的一种地下矿。由于阿嘎打夯程序复杂，一般人家是消受不起的。

In the palaces, fortresses, monasteries, and aristocratic residences of Tibet, you can always see a special floor or ceiling made of *a-ga*. This material is similar to concrete, but it is glossier and environmentally friendly. Continuous cleaning and polishing can bring out gorgeous, heavy colors of ancient glamor. This material is neither stone nor earth, but a kind of mineral from deep underground. Due to the complexity of mining *a-ga*, few common people can afford it.

水果首饰
Fruit Ornaments

藏历七月的日喀则有一个盛大的节日叫"嘎布节"。这一天人们只穿新装不戴首饰，因为人们会把桃子当成松石，玉米当成珍珠，豌豆荚当成玉石，穿成一串串食物项链，从远处看，几乎可以以假乱真。

The big 'Karpo Festival' takes place in the seventh month of the Tibetan calendar in Xigaze. People celebrate this day by wearing new clothes without ornaments, instead taking peaches as turquoise, corns as pearls, and pods as jade, and stringing them into fruit necklaces. Viewed from a distance, they can easily be taken for real jewelry.

微观西藏
TIBET: FAST & FURIOUS

冰山之父
The King of the Icy Mountains

在西藏众多的雪山中，有"冰山之父"之称的南迦巴瓦主峰高 7782 米，虽然不是最高，但因为攀登难度极大，长期以来一直是未被人类登上的最高一座"处女峰"，直到 1992 年中日联合登山队方登顶成功。相传天上众神时常降临其上聚会和煨桑，那高空风造成的"旗云"就是众神燃起的桑烟。

Among the snowy mountains of Tibet, there stands 'the King of the Icy Mountains', Namjagbarwa Peak, 7,782 meters high. Even though it is not the highest, it is the most difficult to climb, and had never been summitted by anyone until 1992, when a Sino-Japanese expedition team accomplished the feat. According to legend, gods often descend to the peak and light ritual fires, and the smoke becomes the 'flag clouds' that we see.

圣洁依旧
Keeping Pureness

有"驴友"形容西藏的湖时说，"两岸青山相对出"，却没有"孤帆一片日边来"，有的只是彻头彻尾、漫天卷地的蓝，在阳光下闪耀着。"这就是西藏的湖和江南的湖最大的不同，这里有水却不见游船，这些湖保存着它们原有的圣洁，岸上的人都不会高声言语，更别说会有游船打扰了。"

A backpacker used a line in Li Bai's poem to describe the lakes in Tibet: 'The mountains on both banks leap into the eye,' but he didn't mention the next line: 'A lonesome sail comes from the side of the sun.' In Tibet, there is only one complete color of blue glittering under the sunlight that pours into your eyes. He said, 'This is exactly the biggest difference between the lakes in Tibet and those in southeast China. In Tibet, there is only water but no boats. These lakes keep their natural pureness. People ashore won't even talk in a loud voice, let alone row a boat in the lake, so as not to disturb its pureness.'

世界的中心
World Center

冈底斯，藏语意为"大雪山"，其主峰冈仁波齐则为"雪山珍宝"之意。冈仁波齐神山同时被西藏原始宗教苯教、藏传佛教、印度教以及耆那教认为是"世界的中心"。有人形容它是"东方的奥林匹斯山"，对当地人来说，也许在地球上没有任何一座山峰能够比它更为神圣。

Gangdise means 'great snow mountain' in Tibetan. The main peak, Kangrinboqe, means 'the treasure of the snow mountain' and is regarded as 'the center of the world' in Tibetan Buddhism, Hinduism, Jainism, and Bon (the indigenous Tibetan religion). Mt. Kangrinboqe is also called 'the oriental Mt. Olympus' by some people. However, for the locals, perhaps no other mountain on earth is more sacred than it is.

观湖知前生
Seeing Past Lives in a Lake

山不在高，有仙则名；水不在深，有龙则灵。拉姆拉错正是这样一个充满灵性的圣湖。此湖海拔5300米，据说能显现观湖人的前生来世，所以西藏历代达赖喇嘛和班禅大师的转世灵童寻访，均要到此观湖。据说曾有人在拉姆拉错观湖台喧哗吵闹，结果本来万里无云的晴天，骤然间下起了冰雹。

Spiritual power is the decisive factor of the status of any place. A sanctuary of the divine heightens mountains, and a refuge for dragons deepens the water, so the saying goes. Likewise, Lake Lhamo Latso is a lake full of spirits. It is 5,300 meters above sea level, and said to be able to provide a look into one's past and afterlives. For this reason, the search for the reincarnation of the Dalai Lama and the Panchen Lama started from this lake. It's said that people once came to the lake and made a loud noise. Suddenly a hailstorm broke from a clear sky.

摄影：车刚

晒佛节

Sunning the Buddha

雪顿节又称晒佛节。作为节日的序幕，晒佛是最令人瞩目的仪式，五彩丝绸织成的巨幅释迦牟尼唐卡可以覆盖整面山坡。在日出前把巨幅唐卡展开，让第一缕阳光照映佛祖祥和的容颜，伴着凝重庄严的诵经声和法号声，数万信徒和游客双手合十、顶礼膜拜，那种神圣、壮美，令人震撼。

The Shoton Festival is also called 'Sunning the Buddha'. As the prelude to the festival, the sunning of the Buddha is a remarkable ceremony. The huge *thangka* of Sakyamuni, woven with silk threads of five colors, can cover the entire mountain slope. This *thangka* will be spread before sunrise to let the first rays of sunshine fall upon the Buddha's peaceful countenance. Tens of thousands of followers and visitors then prostrate themselves in worship, with their hands folded, chanting dignified sutras and solemn dharma names. It's a kind of sacredness and magnificence that could stun anyone.

风土·管窥
Sights and Sounds

珠峰观景台
Mount Qomolangma Observatory

珠峰观景台建在海拔 5300 米的珠峰脚下，是非专业登山人士允许到达的最高处。在那里，人们或在拉经幡，或在堆玛尼石，或只是静静地凝视珠峰。有对天津老两口曾在博客上发了张张开双臂大喊的照片，他们说，那种不可抑制的激动心情只有在最接近天空时才会生成与爆发。

Mount Qomolangma observatory is located at an altitude of 5,300 meters, the highest place non-professional climbers are allowed to reach. There, some people place prayer flags, some pile *mani* stones, and some just quietly stare at Mount Qomolangma. There was once an old couple from Tianjin that posted a photo of themselves on their blog yelling with open arms. They said that that kind of uncontrollable excitement could only emerge and break out when they were that close to the sky.

属相年转山
Circling the Mountains on Their Zodiac Years

有人说，西藏人小时候听得最多的是关于山的传说，唱得最多的是山歌，走得最长的是转山的路。西藏人相信，在神山的属相年转山，一圈相当于十三圈的功德。所以，在这些年份，会有一些行动不便的人，委托别人带上一块自己喜欢的石头替自己转山，这样就如同自己转了神山一样。

What Tibetan children hear most are tales of mountains; what they sing most are folk songs of mountains; and what they walk on longest is the road of mountain circumambulation. Tibetans believe that if you circumambulate a mountain in a year that matches the mountain's zodiac, then one round will yield the merits of thirteen rounds. As a result, in such years, some disabled people entrust a piece of favorite stone to other circumambulators. In this way it's like they themselves have gone circumambulating as well.

评论

微观西藏
TIBET: FAST & FURIOUS

祈愿大法会
The Great Prayer Festival

祈愿大法会是西藏最盛大的节日之一，是为了迎接未来佛早日降临。西藏经书记载：只有千佛全部降临，人类才能解脱。释迦牟尼佛是第四位，他之后五亿七千万年第五尊佛才降临。所以千佛全部降临是一个无限漫长的过程，但乐观的西藏人每年还是虔诚地在祈愿大会上呼唤着未来佛的早日诞生。

The Great Prayer Festival is one of the grandest festivals in Tibet. It is for welcoming the arrival of the next Buddha. According to Tibetan scriptures, only after one thousand Buddhas have come to this world will human beings be completely relieved. Sakyamuni (the founder of Buddhism) is the fourth Buddha, and it will take 570 million years before the arrival of the fifth Buddha. This is an endless wait, but optimistic Tibetans still pray devoutly every year at the Great Prayer Festival for an earlier descent of the next Buddha.

布谷鸟节
The Cuckoo Festival

西藏人相信万物有灵，因此有很多有趣的节日，比如布谷鸟节。他们认为布谷鸟是百鸟之王，是带来春天和雨水的神灵。有民俗学家说，过去在泽当地区每年都要举行欢迎布谷鸟的盛典；藏北的热振寺也有一个延续千年的"布谷鸟供佛节"，当天僧俗群众要涌到寺中转经朝佛，还要到柏树林中抛撒青稞，供养布谷鸟。

Tibetans believe that all things have souls. Consequently, they have quite a number of interesting festivals, such as the Cuckoo Festival. They believe that the cuckoo is the king of birds and the spirit that brings spring and rain. One folklorist says that in the Tsethang region, an annual festival used to be held by local residents to welcome the cuckoos. The Reting Monastery in northern Tibet also had a Cuckoo Buddha Worshipping Festival with a history of a thousand years. On this festival, people would pack into the temple to circumambulate and worship, then they would head out to the cypress forest to throw barley around to feed the cuckoos.

萨嘎达瓦
Saga Dawa

藏历四月是佛月,藏语称"萨嘎达瓦"。寺庙大都会在这个月的十五日(佛诞日)举行特别盛大的跳神活动。僧人们对此极为重视,往往提前数周就开始排练准备。根据传统的说法,这个月中做好事的功德加倍,做坏事的业障也加倍,所以这个月的拉萨往往比平时更能给游客以惊喜。

The fourth month in the Tibetan calendar is a Buddhist month, called Saga Dawa in Tibetan. Most temples hold an especially grand *cham* dance (a masked dance that is performed for emotional and spiritual purification) on the fifteenth of this month (Day of Vesak, a celebration of Buddha's birthday). Buddhist monks pay great attention to this day, and they start to prepare and rehearse several weeks earlier. According to folk sayings, people get double merits if they do good deeds in this particular month. Similarly, bad karma also doubles if one does something wrong. Hence, in this month Lhasa is capable of giving tourists more pleasant surprises than usual.

清洗心灵的圣湖
The Holy Lake that Purifies the Soul

阿里地区的玛旁雍错被称作"圣湖之王",因为湖水是由冈底斯山冰雪融化而来,湖面极为碧透清澈,可以看到五丈以下的鱼群,所以被教徒们称作佛祖赐给人们的甘露。当地人更相信,"圣水"不但能清除人肌体的污秽,更能洗掉人们心灵上的贪嗔痴疑慢"五毒"。

Mapham Yutso in Ngari Prefecture is called 'the King of Holy Lakes'. Its water comes from the melted ice of Gangdise Mountain. The water is blue and clear. Fish can be seen five *zhang* (about 16.7 meters) deep. Therefore, believers think it is *manna* granted by Buddha. Furthermore, natives believe the 'holy water' can not only clean the filthiness of the body, but also wash the five poisons (greed, anger, drowsiness, envy, and sloth) off people's minds.

微观西藏
TIBET: FAST & FURIOUS

第一座王宫
The First Palace

雍布拉康是西藏第一座王宫，传说松赞干布就是在这里迎娶文成公主的。这座建筑耸立在一个小山包上，规模不大，但熠熠生辉的金顶和赭红色的边玛草墙在蓝天白云的映衬下显得格外壮观。去雍布拉康参观最好是上午，因为据说上午 10 点左右太阳会从山尖照过来，这时的雍布拉康是最美的。

Yumbu Lagang is the first palace in Tibet, and it is said to be the venue where Songtsen Gampo married Princess Wencheng. It was built on top of a hillock. The construction is not huge, but its gleaming golden roof and crimson walls make an amazingly grand sight under the canopy of the blue sky and white clouds. The best time to visit Yumbu Lagang is in the morning, because it is said Yumbu Lagang is most beautiful around ten, when the sun peeks over the mountains and beautifully illuminates the structure.

摄影：李建安

风土・管窥
Sights and Sounds

古突
Gutu

古突，就是腊九粥。"古"是九的意思，"突"是粥。这种粥，就是把羊毛、辣椒、木炭、瓷片等包进面疙瘩里。吃到羊毛，表示心地善良；吃到辣椒，表示嘴不饶人；吃到木炭，表示心肠很黑；吃到瓷片，表示好吃懒做。现在生活好了，有的西藏人把瓷片换成水果糖，辣椒改为羊肉干，但吃古突的习俗没有变。

Gutu is lajiu congee. Gu means 'nine', and tu means 'congee'. Gutu is made by putting wool, chili, charcoal, ceramic chips, and other materials into chunks of dough. When eating it, if one gets the wool, it means he or she is good-natured; if one gets chili, it means he or she is sarcastic; if one gets the charcoal, it means he or she has a black heart and misbehaves. A Tibetan friend told me, now their lives have improved, they have replaced the ceramic chips with fruit drops, and chili with dried lamb jerky. Nevertheless, the tradition of eating gutu has not changed.

辩经
Sutra Debate

拉萨色拉寺每天下午的辩经堪称一绝。辩经是辩论佛教教义的学习课程，是攻读显宗经典的必经方式。辩经时，一身绛红的喇嘛们光着脚，先单辩后群辩，嘴里嚷得叽里呱啦，手掌拍得噼噼啪啪，不明就里的人以为是在吵架，但能听懂的人却往往沉醉其中。

The sutra debate at Sera Monastery every afternoon can be called a miracle. Sutra debate is both a study course of Buddhist doctrines and a necessary way of specializing in Exoteric Buddhism. During a sutra debate, the bare-footed lamas dress in saffron robes and ask each other about dharma. First are the singles debates, then the group debates. Shouts boom from their mouths, while their palms slap against the ground. Anyone who doesn't understand what they're saying might think they're fighting, but those who do understand are drunk with excitement.

评论

微观西藏
TIBET: FAST & FURIOUS

"三口一杯"
'Three Sips for One Cup'

藏族敬酒讲究"三口一杯"。客人接过酒盅，喝一口，斟满；再喝一口，再斟满；最后再喝一口，斟满，才能一饮而尽。藏族有句谚语"一杯成仇敌"，就是说喝酒不能只喝一盅了事，因为西藏人认为"三口一杯"的"三"代表吉祥如意、功德圆满。

When Tibetans propose a toast, the rule of drinking is 'three sips for one cup'. When a guest takes the wine cup, he should take a sip and then fill it up and repeat it a second and third time before finally emptying the cup. One Tibetan saying is, 'One cup makes an enemy', which means people shouldn't drink a cup of wine all at once. This is because Tibetans believe that the number three represents good fortune and perfection.

第二敦煌
The Second Dunhuang

神奇的萨迦寺"经书墙"高十米，长六七十米，有七百多年历史，经书八万四千册，堪称世界之最。据介绍，这些经书中的一部分是在元初八思巴时期由书法家用金、银、珊瑚、象牙、珍珠等各种珍贵宝石研成墨汁，在传统藏纸上书写而成的。萨迦寺也因此得名"第二敦煌"。

The miraculous 'Wall of Scrolls' in the Sakya Monastery is ten meters high and sixty to seventy meters long, and the temple contains more than 84,000 scriptures from over seven hundred years. It is probably the largest of its kind in the world and it is recorded that some of these scrolls originated from the Phagspa Period of the early Yuan Dynasty. The scriptures were written on traditional Tibetan paper by the calligraphers of that period, with ink made from ground gold, silver, coral, ivory, pearls, and other precious materials. Therefore, the Sakya Monastery has been known as 'the Second Dunhuang'.

评论

风土·管窥
Sights and Sounds

摄影：蒋越

西藏最美的春天
The Most Beautiful Spring in Tibet

每年三月，当西藏第一朵桃花盛开的时候，"林芝桃花节"就拉开了序幕。有人描写说，这时候，西藏的冬天还未退去银妆，林芝的桃花却已如藏族姑娘脸上美丽的高原红，如醉霞绯云般地争相斗艳，不仅能让人欣赏雪域江南那独特的旖旎风光，更能让人领略西藏最浪漫、最美丽的春天。

Every March, when the first peach buds begin to bloom, 'Nyingchi Peach Blossom Festival' starts. At that time, Tibet's silver make-up from the winter has not completely receded, but the peach blossoms in Nyingchi are just starting to flourish, just like the rosy (or so-called 'plateau red') cheeks of beautiful Tibetan girls, and their colors dazzlingly contend with each other. Visitors can not only appreciate the unique scenery of a snowy southern China in Tibet, but also have a taste of the most romantic and beautiful Tibetan spring.

微观西藏
TIBET: FAST & FURIOUS

自我供养的僧人
Self-Supported Monks

在西藏，寺院不供给日常所需，僧人们需要每两三个月回家取一次，所以，过去很多富裕家庭在寺院中都有自己的寮房甚至院落。家庭、社会和僧人、寺院有着千丝万缕的联系，这也是藏传佛教深入人心的原因之一。

In Tibet, the temples do not provide food or other daily necessities, so the monks go back home and pick up supplies every two or three months. In the past, many well-to-do families had their own rooms or even yards in the temple. In Tibet, families, society, the monks, and the temples have numerous close ties. This is one of the reasons why Buddhism is embedded in Tibetans' hearts.

"流动银行"
'Walking Banks'

阿里的普兰县县城附近有个科加村，是赴尼泊尔的必经之地，这里藏女的服饰因其别致尤其是贵重而声名远播。一套完整的科加服饰在 2005 年价值已在百万元以上，是真正的集全部身家于一身，科加妇女也被外来人称作"流动银行"。

In Burang of Ngari, there is a village named Korqag, an unavoidable place if you are going to Nepal. Tibetan women's costumes here are widely known for their elegance and preciousness. A complete set of Korqag costume cost over a million yuan in 2005, and this is truly 'wearing all your wealth'. Hence, non-native people also call Korqag women 'walking banks'.

摄影：觉果

风土·管窥
Sights and Sounds

藏族人的姓
Tibetan Family Names

有人说藏族人没有姓，这种说法对不对呢？西藏解放前，只有达官贵人和高僧活佛才有姓氏，大部分藏族民众只有名字没有姓氏。现在，这种彰显身份的贵族姓氏正在淡出历史。有学者认为，藏族姓氏的变化，折射出西藏社会的巨大变迁，是西藏人实现平等的标志。

Some people say Tibetans don't have family names. But is this true? Before Tibet was liberated, only prominent officials, renowned personages, eminent monks, or living Buddhas could have family names. Most Tibetans only have given names. Nowadays, this system of family names that denoted social rank is fading. Some scholars believe the change in Tibetan family names reflects the vast transition the Tibetan community has experienced, and they think of it as a symbol for real equality in Tibet.

情人般的木碗
The Wooden Bowl-Like Lover

民俗学家廖东凡讲过一个故事：一次，有位朋友去看望他，他用酥油茶招待，朋友从怀中掏出一个比脑袋还大的木碗，结果五磅酥油茶都没能倒满他的木碗。藏族人酷爱饮茶，也酷爱茶具——木碗。有首情歌这样唱："丢也丢不下，带也带不走；情人是木碗该多好，可以揣在怀里头。"

Tibetologist Liao Dongfan told this story: once a Tibetan friend came to see him and he treated him to butter tea. His friend took out a wooden bowl that was bigger than his head, thus the result was the five-pound pot of butter tea didn't fill up his wooden bowl. Tibetans are very fond of drinking tea, as well as using wooden bowls as tea sets. As a love song goes, 'Leave you aside — I can't, take you away — I can't either. How nice would it be if a lover were a wooden bowl, then I could just carry you in my bosom.'

评论

微观西藏
TIBET: FAST & FURIOUS

为三头牛编故事

Making a Story for Three Cattle

画家余友心在米拉山口塑了三头牛的雕像。为表感谢，当地人为这雕像编了一个故事：牛一家三口去那曲回来路过这里，一位神女对他们说："这里更美，留下来吧。"于是它们就留了下来。这个故事让余友心很欣慰，藏民总是用他们的朴实打动着每一个为他们付出过的人。

Painter Yu Youxin made a sculpture of three cattle in front of Milha Mountain Pass. To show their gratitude, the local people made up a story for this sculpture: a cattle family of three passed by after returning from Nagqu. A goddess appeared and told them, 'Here it is more beautiful; why not stay?' Thus, the cattle family settled there. This story delighted Yu greatly. In their sincerity, Tibetans are always grateful to every person who has helped them.

带上一把伞

Take an Umbrella with You

有人注意到，在西藏人们似乎总是举着伞，不是在遮雨，就是在遮阳。这是因为西藏的天气变幻莫测，也许晚上还狂风大雨，一早起来就晴空万里了；也许太阳正火辣辣的，一块乌云一来，立刻阴雨绵绵。这样的天气也教会了当地人什么是无常。西藏人对于金钱、情感甚至生命的豁达态度，或许与这天气不无关系。

Some have noticed that Tibetans always seem to be carrying umbrellas, either for protection from rain, or for escaping the sunlight. That is because the weather in Tibet is very unpredictable. There might be fierce wind and heavy rain in the evening, but when you get up the next day you will find a bright clear sky. There might be burning sunlight, but a moment later dark clouds will cover the sky followed by a shower. Nevertheless, such weather has also taught the locals the meaning of impermanence. Perhaps the open-minded attitude Tibetans have toward money, emotions, and even life, is associated with this weather.

评论

风土·管窥
Sights and Sounds

摄影：车刚

不同分工的丈夫

Husbands with Different Responsibilities

西藏摄影家协会副主席车刚曾花了整整10年跟踪拍摄西藏的一个一妻多夫家庭。他说，兄弟共妻不分家，财产不散失，"这个一妻多夫的家庭看上去很和谐，每个丈夫都有不同的分工"。有专家说，政府尊重民俗，未加禁止，但随着社会经济发展，这种现象越来越少。

Che Gang, the vice-chairman of the Tibet Photographers' Association, once spent a total of ten years following a polyandric family. He said that four brothers shared one wife so the family would not be split, resulting in a unified family fortune. Che said, 'The polyandric family I followed seemed very harmonious. Each husband had his own responsibilities.' Some experts say that the government respects folk customs and does not prohibit them. However, with the development of social economy, such phenomena are decreasing.

爱过节的民族

This Ethnic Group Loves to Have Festivals

藏族宗教与民俗节庆之多在中国各民族中名列前茅，比如：藏历新年、达玛节、雪顿节、亮宝节、望果节、沐浴节、转山会、牧民节、俄喜节、谢水节、上九节、赏花节、观花节、赛马会、林卡节、大佛瞻仰节、牛王节……

The number of Tibetan religious and folk festivals tops that of other ethnic groups in China. For example, they have Tibetan New Year, Damar Festival, Sho Dun Festival (Yogurt Festival), Liang Po Festival, Harvest Festival, Bathing Festival, Nomad Festival, Hanging of the *thangka*, Dajyur Festival, Buddha Prayer Festival, Lingka Festival, Pilgrims' Festival, etc.

微观西藏
TIBET: FAST & FURIOUS

旷野中的道场
Rites in the Wilderness

玛尼石又叫"石贡",其作用一是祈福消灾;二是坚定信仰,随时匡正自己的思想和行为。在地广人稀的西藏,无处不在的玛尼石发挥着经堂与道场的作用,同时也反映着藏民的性格:豪放、坚毅、隐忍、达观。

Mani stones (prayer stones) are also called *shigong* (stone tribute). They are used for praying for good fortune, and for strengthening one's beliefs and rectifying one's thoughts and behavior from time to time. Hence in sparsely populated Tibet, the omnipresent *mani* stones play the role of sutra halls and places for Buddhist rites. At the same time, they reflect Tibetans' vigorous, firm, enduring, and optimistic character.

摄影:车刚

评论

风土·管窥
Sights and Sounds

布达拉宫的镇宫之宝
The Most Precious Treasure in Potala Palace

说起布达拉宫的宝贝，导游们会告诉你诸如玉镶绿松石八思巴像、文成公主陪嫁的琵琶、黄金嵌宝石头骨酥油灯等，但是布达拉宫的镇宫之宝是一尊从公元7世纪流传至今的松赞干布本尊木质观音像。据说这尊佛像由檀香木自然形成，在兵荒马乱中曾不止一次被掠到别处，但每次又都奇迹般地重返布达拉宫。

When speaking of the treasures in the Potala Palace, tour guides often tell you about things like the jade figure of Phagspa inlaid with turquoise, the pipa from the dowry of Princess Wencheng, the butter lamp made from a skull decorated with gold and gems, and so on. However, the most precious treasure in the Potala Palace is a wooden Avalokitesvara statue of Songsten Gampo that dates back to the 7th century. It is said that this statue was formed naturally on a piece of sandalwood. Though it's been plundered to other places several times during the chaos of war, it's always miraculously found its way back to the Potala Palace.

哈达
Hadas

哈达无疑最能体现西藏人对白色的喜爱，因为那代表雪山白云般纯洁，是表达感情的最好载体。有句谚语说：朋友不求多，就求挚友一个；哈达不求多，就求洁白一条。献哈达时，只有给平辈、晚辈才可以直接挂在脖子上，给盘坐的僧人要放在膝盖上，而给高僧活佛献哈达，只能放在他面前的桌子上或脚下。

There is no doubt the *hada* shows Tibetans' love of the color white best, because it symbolizes the pureness of snowy mountains and white clouds and conveys people's feelings best. A proverb states: 'I don't want to make many friends, but one intimate companion; I don't ask for many *hadas*, but a spotlessly white one.' When presenting *hadas* to people of the same or younger generation, the presenter can hang them around their necks. If the *hadas* are going to be presented to monks sitting cross-legged, they should be put upon their knees. If presented to eminent monks or living Buddhas, they can only be put on the table in front of them or in front of their feet.

贵重的针线包
Treasured Sewing Kits

藏族人对于针线包非常珍视，藏语称"珍布柯水"，讲究的人家还用银制作，成为妇女们最喜爱的华贵饰品。尽管藏民族是一个高度自给自足的社会，但是在过去，即使别的日用品能自己生产，但是打磨针器却绝非易事，所以他们视针线包为贵重物品，随时随地都当宝贝一样。

Tibetans highly treasure sewing kits. Some wealthy families even decorate the boxes with silver, making them the women's favorite luxurious accessory. Tibetans are known for being a highly self-sufficient society. In the past, Tibetans could produce most daily necessities on their own, but grinding needles wasn't an easy task. Hence they treat sewing kits as valuables, treasuring them at all times and places.

人獒友谊
Friendships Between Humans and Mastiffs

藏族人相信，一个人在本命年内若被藏獒咬伤，是好事而非倒霉，因为被咬那一刻就是这人厄运终结之时。如果这个人用糌粑蘸伤口上的血喂咬他的藏獒，这只通人性的藏獒会深受感动，将之视作山盟海誓，人獒之间会建立终生友谊。

Tibetans believe if a person is bitten by a Tibetan mastiff in a year that matches his or her birth animal, then that is something lucky rather than bad, because when that occurs, the person's ill fortune will end. If that person takes some *tsampa*, lets it absorb the blood from his or her wound, and feeds it to the mastiff that bit him or her, this mastiff will be deeply moved and consider that action as a solemn pledge. The person will have this mastiff's friendship for life.

评论

风土·管窥
Sights and Sounds

无处不飞的歌声
Songs that Exist Everywhere

西藏自然环境虽然恶劣，藏族人却用歌声回报。敬酒时他们唱："喝着甜香的美酒，唱起动人的酒歌。"锄草时，他们唱："耘锄的耙子，为什么掉了？耘锄的耙子，锄草时掉了。"剪羊毛时，他们唱："绵羊，绵羊，你太忙了，夏天的毛没剪完，冬天又来了。"

Despite Tibet's harsh natural environment, Tibetans celebrate their home with songs. When toasting, they sing: 'When you are drinking sweet wine, start singing the touching liquor melody.' When weeding, they sing: 'The handle on the hoe, why did it come off? While weeding, the handle fell off the hoe.' When shearing their sheep, they sing: 'Sheep, sheep, you make us too busy. We haven't finished shearing you in summer and winter is coming...'

圣山中的圣山
Supreme Among Holy Mountains

西藏人相信一切山海湖林皆有灵，西藏圣山甚多，但人们大多是转山而不爬山。在众多圣山中，冈仁波齐被各大教派奉为圣山之尊，信众认为绕圣山一圈可除尽一生罪孽，绕十圈可在五百年轮回中免下地狱。

Tibetans believe that all mountains, seas, lakes, and forests have their own spirits. Tibet has many holy mountains, but Tibetans usually circumambulate them rather than climb them. Among these holy mountains, Gang Rinpoche (Mount Kailash) is considered supreme in several religious sects. Believers hold that circling Mount Kailash once can extirpate all sins in this life, and that by circling it ten times, you can avoid the hell of *samsara* for the next five hundred years.

摄影：车刚

微观西藏
TIBET: FAST & FURIOUS

摄影：聂晓阳

亡魂寓所
Resting Place for Souls

在念青唐古拉山下，草地上到处都是一个个的小石堆。当地朋友说，那是灵魂离开肉体后暂时的家，"西藏人每到一处，都会先堆一个石堆，因为谁也不知道自己什么时候死在哪里，这样就可以方便灵魂就近安家"。

Many small stone piles can be seen in the meadows of Mt. Nyainqentanglha. A local says they are temporary homes for souls leaving their human bodies. 'When Tibetans go to a place, they will put up a stone pile, because no one knows the time or place he or she will pass away, and in this way the soul can settle down conveniently.'

数字中的吉凶
Auspicious and Unlucky Numbers

西藏有很多吉祥数字，比如13，每月13号可以有两天，而没有14号。他们对8不感兴趣，因为他们喜欢的吉祥数字都是单数，所以单日子才是好日子。朋友喝酒碰杯，第一次碰三杯，第二次再碰三杯，连碰三次，各饮酒九杯，这才是铁哥们。

Tibet has a lot of lucky numbers such as thirteen. Every month can have two thirteenths, skipping the fourteenth day. Tibetans are not interested in eight, they prefer odd numbers as their auspicious numbers. Thus, all odd-numbered days are good days. When friends are toasting, they have three glasses for the first toast, three glasses for the second, and again three glasses for the third. Finishing nine glasses in total shows that they are homies.

天葬台意外
Accidents at a Celestial Burial Site

有作家曾听朋友讲，在某地天葬台发生过这样两件事：一位姑娘轻生服用了大量敌敌畏，天葬后毒杀了十多只秃鹫；另一位大醉而死，于是天葬台也醉倒了一大片秃鹫。所以这样的人死后要送到特别的地方，在念经后火葬。

A writer once heard his friend talk about two accidents that took place at a celestial burial site. A young girl had committed suicide by taking a large amount of DDVP (a poisonous pesticide), which resulted in the death of more than a dozen hawks after she was celestially buried. Another man died of alcohol intoxication, and a number of hawks got drunk on the celestial burial site as a result. Thus, when these kinds of deaths occur, it is customary to take the body to a special site and perform cremation after chanting scriptures.

喝酒别太实诚
Don't Be Too Honest When Drinking

很多人参加藏式宴席常会醉得"不省人事"，其实是因为不知道如何应对藏族主人的豪爽。作家毕淑敏总结的经验是：主人帮你斟满酒，炯炯地看着你，你要是一饮而尽，他就会迅雷不及掩耳地为你斟满第二杯，这样你就只能一杯接一杯地喝了。若你留一点在碗底，他便知道你已尽兴，也就随你意了。

Many people drink until they pass out when they attend a Tibetan banquet. This is because they don't know how to cope with a Tibetan host's hospitality. Writer Bi Shumin summed up a few points: when the host fills up your cup, he watches you eagerly; if you empty the cup, he will fill your cup again with the suddenness of a thunderbolt. You can do nothing but drink cup after cup. But if you leave a little liquor in the cup, the host will understand that you have already had enough, and he will let you be.

评论

微观西藏
TIBET: FAST & FURIOUS

神仙的爱恋
The Love of Two Deities

每年藏历四月十五日贡堂寺有一个很有趣的神仙相聚仪式。保护神赤宗赞要被送到贡堂，与分别了一年的情人贡堂拉姆女神相聚。当地人为此举办盛大的仪式，让这对神仙眷侣贴着脸，同住一个神殿，倾吐情话。临别时，两位神仙还要依依惜别，由僧人背负神像，送出一程又一程。

Every year on the fifteenth of the fourth month of the Tibetan calendar, the Gungtang Temple conducts a very interesting ceremony for the reunion of two deities. The patron saint Tritsongsen is sent to the temple and reunited with his lover, the goddess Gungtang Lahmo. The locals then hold a grand ceremony and let this couple pour out endearments in the temple face to face. Before their parting, monks carry the statues together for some distance, to show their difficulties in saying goodbye.

抢供品
Snatching Tributes

"顿钦"是过去在布达拉宫举行的一个新年大摆供仪式。东大厅的中央会摆上十几米高的油果子和各式干果等。仪式一结束，挤在门外的年轻人就会一拥而上抢供品，抢不上的人就把挤在前面的人的皮袄剪个洞——捡漏，但被剪的人也不会生气，因为充满喜庆的抢夺只是为了祈求来年的好运。

In the past, *donqen* was a big Tibetan New Year's ceremony in the Potala Palace. At the center of the east hall, fancy foods and various dried fruits would be piled as high as a dozen meters. As the ceremony came to an end, crowds of young people outside would rush in and snatch up the tributes. Those who failed to grab anything would cut the jackets of people in front, and this was called 'leaking collection'. No one would get angry because this joyous contest was simply a prayer for good luck in the coming year.

评论

风土·管窥
Sights and Sounds

圆与圆满
Circles Upon Circles

有人说：也许因为太阳是圆形的，于是藏族地区牧民的生活也与圆结下不解之缘。他们筑造的棚圈是圆的，跳的舞是圆圈舞，他们绕着山转，沿着湖走，等他们走到起点与终点相交时，也就完成了一生。

Some people say that probably because the sun is round, the shepherds of Tibet have also many circular things in their lives. Their buildings are round. They dance in circles, and loop around mountain peaks and around lakes. When they finish their journeys at the meeting point of start and finish, they have made a complete circle.

牛粪是个宝
A Treasure Called Cow Dung

我们常感叹"唉，一朵鲜花插在牛粪上"，然而在藏地，牛粪却是个宝。"一块黑牛粪，一朵金蘑菇"，倘若一位过路的老阿妈发现路边有一块干牛粪，她会跟捡到宝贝似的，把牛粪装进围裙带回家去。西藏人不仅用牛粪来生火做饭，而且在民间礼仪中，牛粪还是一种象征着美好的吉祥物。

We often sigh that 'a fresh flower is stuck in a heap of cow dung.' However, cow dung is thought to be precious in Tibet: 'A heap of cow dung equals a golden mushroom.' If an elderly woman spots a piece of dry cow dung, she is as happy as unearthing some type of treasure and will put the dung in her apron to take it back home. Cow dung is not only something that Tibetans use to light fires and cook with, but also a talisman that symbolizes happiness in local customs.

摄影：车刚

微观西藏
TIBET: FAST & FURIOUS

摄影：觉果

送往天堂的歌声
Songs and Paradise

在西藏，凡是欢聚必须饮酒唱歌。婚礼宴席、婴儿降生、孩子上学、新房落成都要饮酒庆贺。有趣的是，人死后一周年之际，邻居亲友也要欢聚一堂，喝酒唱歌，祝贺死者投胎转世。人们慢慢饮酒，悠悠唱歌，似醉非醉，如梦如痴……

In Tibet, gatherings are always accompanied by drinking and singing. Just like in the traditions of the Han ethnic group, Tibetan gatherings take place on a variety of occasions. When there is a wedding ceremony, when a child is born or goes to school, and when a new house is built, there is bound to be a celebration that includes alcohol. The interesting part is that on the first anniversary of someone's death, his or her neighbors and relatives also have a get-together. They congratulate the reincarnation of the deceased by singing and drinking. They drink and sing slowly, enjoying themselves in a dreamy and half-drunken state.

古老的婚礼习俗
Time-Treasured Marriage Customs

雅鲁藏布江边的一些地方，还保留着一些古老的婚礼习俗。比如新郎迎娶新娘时，新娘的头会被氆氇或藏袍紧紧包裹，据说这是防止魔鬼的侵犯，也有研究者认为这是古代抢婚习俗的再现。

There are some places along the banks of the Yarlung Tsangpo River that still practice old wedding customs. For instance, when the groom goes to the bride, her head is wrapped in *pulu* (a kind of handmade wool for clothes and blankets) or a Tibetan robe, which is meant to prevent demons from intruding, but some scholars believe it is a derivation of the ancient 'bride-kidnapping' customs.

风土·管窥
Sights and Sounds

洗澡盛会
Gathering for Bathing

每年的藏历7月中旬，很多西藏人要举家来到拉萨河畔洗澡聚会，洗刷一年的风尘。这个时候，不论男女老少，都会在"大庭广众"之下，赤身在河中净身、戏水。在那种情况下，谁也不会有丝毫的邪念。

In mid-July of the Tibetan calendar, many Tibetans go to the Lhasa River and attend a bathing gathering with all their family members. The purpose of the gathering is to wash away the weariness accumulated throughout the year. At this time, people take off their clothes in public, irrespective of sex and age, splashing or bathing in the river. There and then, no one has the slightest wicked thought in their mind.

挽救月亮
Rescuing the Moon

过去西藏人认为月食是月亮被怪物吞掉了，月食之夜，要敲打一切能发出声响的东西，以驱走怪物。作家马丽华说，在香堆考察时，她曾遗憾地错过仪式。那晚，香堆人倾镇而出，敲着锣鼓铜盆，敲着干牛皮，连狗都激动地跑出来狂吠着，几乎就是全镇盛典，而她只在梦中听到嘈杂纷纭的声音。

The people of Tibet used to believe that a lunar eclipse was the result of the moon being swallowed by a monster. On the nights of an eclipse they would tap on anything that could make a noise in order to drive the monster away. On a tour of Yendum, author Ma Lihua regretted missing the ceremony. That night, all the people of Yendum went out and banged on gongs and pans as well as dried cowhides. Even the dogs ran around barking loudly, and practically the entire village went nuts, while she only heard the noises in her dreams.

评论

"赞"的世界
The Ghost World

藏族人相信有些人死后会变成"赞"（厉鬼）。有民俗学家调查发现，似乎在西藏地区，整个"赞"的王国是由形形色色充满怨恨、愤怒、欲念的不幸的灵魂组成的。它们颇有一些威风，对它们只能奉承，不能批评；只能祭祀，不能怠慢。

Tibetans believe that after some people die, they become *zan* (ferocious ghosts). Folklorists have discovered that this ghost kingdom is said to be a world composed of unlucky souls engrossed in hatred, fury, and wanton desire. It is quite an imposing realm, and one can only accept, not criticize; worship, not neglect.

无处不在的六字真言
The Six-Syllable Mantra That Is Everywhere

"唵嘛呢叭咪吽"这六个音的祷词，被称为"六字真言"，也叫"玛尼"，被认为具有赐福消灾的神秘力量。在西藏，随时随地都能看到或听到六字真言，人们静坐养神时念，缓步行走时念，可以说除了吃饭、睡觉外，其余时间只要有空，最优先的选择都是颤动着嘴唇念诵这六字真言。

'Om mani padme hum' is a six-syllable prayer that has been called the 'Six-Syllable Mantra' or *mani*. It is believed to have the power to bless the reciters and protect them from misfortune. In Tibet, you can see and hear this mantra everywhere. People whisper it while sitting or walking, except during meals and bedtime. As long as someone has a little time, they will move their lips and recite the mantra.

评论

风土・管窥
Sights and Sounds

绿松石
Turquoise

过去历代拉萨贵族所戴的珠宝中，黄金和绿松石是最主要的部分。不少西藏人相信，戴绿松石戒指可保旅途平安，梦见绿松石则意味着吉祥和新生活的开始。在一些地方，女人头发上如果没有佩戴绿松石，就会被看作对人不敬。根据一个古老的传说，绿松石还是人们灵魂的寓所，抛弃绿松石等于丢掉自己的灵魂。

Among the jewels Lhasa nobles wore in the past, gold and turquoise were the most common. Many Tibetans believed that wearing turquoise rings could bless their trip, and dreaming of turquoise meant good luck and the start of a new life. In some places, if women didn't wear a turquoise in their hair, it was regarded as disrespectful to others. According to an old legend, turquoise was the place where people's souls took residence, and dumping a piece of turquoise equaled dumping one's soul.

摄影：觉果

微观西藏
TIBET: FAST & FURIOUS

石头情结
Attachment to Stones

西藏人对石头的情感是至深的，如果在右耳垂戴一小块绿松石，那就表示斯文高雅。结婚时，如果男方送给新娘一块绿松石，就表示把心交付。西藏人看石头，不会想到值不值钱，只问自己喜不喜欢。他们认为石头也有灵性，可以相伴终生。

Tibetans have a strong attachment to stones. Wearing turquoise in the right earlobe represents elegance and gracefulness. At weddings, if the groom gives the bride a piece of turquoise, that signifies him handing her his heart. Tibetans don't care about the price of a stone, they only care about their feelings toward it. They believe that stones have spirituality like other creatures and can be lifelong companions.

桑烟唤醒清晨
Awakening Ritual Fires

一般藏族人家早晨起来要做的第一件事就是煨桑，西藏的清晨常由桑烟唤醒。据说煨桑不仅能讨得神灵欢心，还能净化周围环境，消除不洁、秽气等，因此成为藏区最流行的祭拜方式之一。在高山上、寺庙里，在每家每户屋顶上，常能看见袅袅升起的桑烟。

The first thing Tibetans usually do in the morning is to light a ritual fire, and Tibet is often awakened by the smoke. It is said that this ritual not only pleases the gods, but can also purify the surroundings and get rid of unclean stuff. It has, therefore, become the most popular ritual in Tibet. In the mountains, in monasteries, and in each Tibetan household, it's very common to see ascending ritual smoke.

摄影：聂晓阳

风土·管窥
Sights and Sounds

神圣的酥油灯
Holy Butter Lamps

酥油灯是藏族人的精神依托，他们对燃灯的酥油和灯盏都非常讲究。点灯前，必须把手洗净，有些人还用毛巾之类的布把自己的嘴捂上，以免呼出的气玷污了神灵。供放酥油灯的经堂也是打扫得最为干净的，如果主人让客人在经堂中睡觉，那一定是把他当作了最高贵的客人。

The butter lamp is a spiritual prop for Tibetans. Therefore, they are very fastidious about the butter and the lamp. Before lighting the lamp, they must clean their hands first. Some people may even cover their mouth with a piece of cloth to prevent their breath from polluting the divinity of the lamp. The sutra hall where the butter lamps are placed is always the cleanest room in a house. If a guest is allowed to sleep in the hall, then the host must consider him or her a most honorable visitor.

藏式灶台
Tibetan Stoves

"龙特"是藏族传统中最常见的一种灶。别看就是一个土灶，它可是一个家庭的生活中心，所以必须请专门的砌灶师傅来搭建，还得提前预订。师傅会把成品灶分为两个部分运到家里，再拼装到一起，用土坯和泥浆固定下来，涂上黑色的颜料。这种灶对燃料要求苛刻，只能烧上等的牛粪和易燃的柴火。

A *lungta* is the most common stove in Tibetan tradition. Although it's just a stove made of mud, it functions as the center of family life. To set up a *lungta*, a professional builder needs to be invited and an appointment must be made. The builder will carry the stove to the home in two separate shipments and assemble them. Adobe and mud are used to fix the stove in the kitchen and then it is coated with black paint. The stove is finicky to fuel. Only cow dung or other flammable materials can be used.

评论

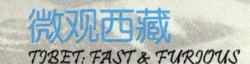
微观西藏
TIBET: FAST & FURIOUS

苦修洞
A Cave for Retreat

在藏域,很多修持佛法尤其是练习瑜伽和修习密宗的高僧,经常会选择一处洞窟苦修。在藏传佛教最早传道者莲花生大师建立第一座寺庙桑耶寺的青朴山,如今仍有40多个山洞供修行者苦修。历史上,一些大师在修行后,往往将自己用过或撰写的佛教典籍埋在洞中,留给后世有法缘人进行挖掘,这就是"伏藏"。

In Tibet, many eminent monks, especially those that practice yoga or study Esoteric Buddhism, often choose a cave and hold religious retreats. Master Padmasambhava, the earliest preacher of Tibetan Buddhism, built the first monastery, Samye Monastery, on Mount Qingpu. On Qingpu there still exist over forty caves for monks to do religious retreats. Historically, after some masters finished their retreats, they would often bury the Buddhist classics they had used or written in the caves for predestined people to find in the future. This is known as *terma*.

新生儿的洗礼
Purification of the Newborn

传统上藏民的新生儿在喂奶以前,要先喂一点酥油茶和糌粑糊糊。母亲还会把婴儿放在太阳下面晒一晒,认为这样孩子会长得更结实、漂亮。男孩在出生后的第三天、女孩在第四天要举行"邦色",也就是婴儿的洗礼。亲友们来到家中,用大拇指和食指捏一点糌粑,粘在初生儿的额头上,祝愿孩子吉祥健康。

Traditionally, Tibetans will give newborns some butter tea and *tsampa* paste before breast-feeding them. Some mothers will also put the babies under the sun since they believe the baby will grow stronger and prettier this way. On the third day of a boy's birth, and the fourth day for a girl, the family holds a purification ceremony for the baby. Relatives and friends come to the host's home and use their thumb and index finger to put some *tsampa* onto the baby's forehead, wishing good luck and health to the baby.

评论

风土·管窥
Sights and Sounds

终身享福的放生羊

The Happy Lives of Released Sheep

西藏一些地方有个习俗，如果家中有病人想要选择羊来放生祈福，就向羊群中扔一件衣服，衣服落在哪只羊身上，就把它挑出来，假装叫来一个屠夫，将要动刀时，主人过来阻拦，用钱把羊赎走。这只羊将成为终身受保护的羊，离开群羊，以糌粑为食，唯一的使命就是陪主人转经。

There is a convention in Tibet: if a family wants to choose a sheep to release for blessing a sick family member, they toss a piece of clothing to a flock of sheep. The one which the clothing falls on is picked. Then a butcher is invited to pretend he is slaughtering that sheep. However, just before the knife falls on the sheep, the owner comes and rescues it by paying the butcher. From then on, it becomes a released sheep that is protected for life. It will live away from the sheep flock and have *tsampa* as daily food. Its only duty is to go circumambulating with the host.

摄影：车刚

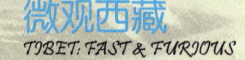

浑身上下有神灵
Gods All Over the Body

传统的藏族人相信，能伤害他们的神灵无处不在，甚至每个人的躯体里都有五群神灵，分别在头顶、一侧肩头、两个腋窝下以及心脏附近。这些神灵到处游走，如果碰巧触及某个神灵所在的位置，人就会不舒服或者毙命，所以在西藏最好不要随意碰触拍打对方。

Traditionally thinking Tibetans believe that gods who are able to harm them are everywhere. They believe there are five clusters of gods inside every person's body. They respectively reside on top of the head, on one side of the shoulders, under the two armpits, and somewhere near the heart. These gods can also wander around in people's bodies. Tibetans believe that if the part of the body the gods are in is touched accidentally, they will feel uncomfortable or even die. Therefore, you'd better not touch others casually in Tibet.

神灵也要"哄"
'Coaxing' the Deities

有人注意到这样的细节：西藏人相信万物有灵，并且这些神灵都像孩子一样需要爱护，有各种脾气，要十分小心。男人的生命神在右肩，女人的在左肩。把厨房弄脏了，灶神一生气全家就要生病。烧饭溢出来了，主妇们就会狡黠地"哄"神说：不是我，是邻居烧饭溢出来的啊。

A detail about deities: Tibetans believe everything in the world has spirituality, and these spirits have various checkered tempers, so they all need to be carefully treated like children. Males carry their god of life on their right shoulder, while females carry theirs on the left. If someone dirties the kitchen, the kitchen god will get angry and bring illness to the family. As a result, if a housewife spills food while cooking, she will slyly 'coax' the god by saying, 'It wasn't me; it was our neighbor who spilled the food.'

评论

风土 · 管窥
Sights and Sounds

"嘎乌"盒
Gawu Boxes

要说西藏人一生不离的,那就是"嘎乌"盒了,即挂在项上或背挎的佛盒,里面装着佛像或护身符。银制的嘎乌较普遍,也有金制的和铜制的,形状大小不一。男子用方的,女子用圆的。佩戴嘎乌,一方面有护身的意思,另一方面有装饰的意思。离了这个随身的经盒,很多西藏人出行做事都会觉得不踏实。

When talking about something that stays with Tibetans for their entire lives, you have to mention the *gawu* box, which contains a figure of Buddha or an amulet. Tibetans often hang it on their necks or carry it on their backs. *Gawu* boxes are made of gold, silver or copper, and the silver ones are the most common. They also have different shapes and sizes. Men use square ones, and women spherical ones. The *gawu* is not only an amulet for protecting yourself, but also an accessory. Without taking along this box, many Tibetans feel uncomfortable when going out.

死亡之后
After Death

西藏人家里有人去世时,要在大门上挂东西,告诉外人不要进门。西藏人相信,人刚死时是最关键的时期,因为死者的"本性"还在体内。这个时候如果受到打扰,就会迷失自己,影响往生。死亡三天后遗体通常会被送往天葬台,以便灵魂顺利进入"中阴",这是死亡和下辈子出生中间的状态,一般为49天。

When a person in a Tibetan family dies, the family will hang something on the front door to tell outsiders not to walk in for the time being. Tibetans believe that the period immediately following death is the most crucial, since people's souls are still in their bodies. If any disturbance happens in this period, the dead might lose themselves and their reincarnation could be adversely affected. Three days after people's death, their remains are normally sent to the celestial burial ground to facilitate their souls' entrance into *bardo*, which is the intermediate state between death and rebirth, usually forty-nine days long.

微观西藏
TIBET: FAST & FURIOUS

职业转山人
Professional Circumambulators

西藏有一个特别的职业：转山人。他们替身体状况差但又想实现愿望的人转山祈福。在冈仁波齐，替代转山的人每转一圈山，就会在山口拣一颗小石子作为标志。把这些石子卖给信徒，代表替转了多少圈。这笔买卖靠的是信任，没有人会监督替转人是否真的转了神山，石子也没有标价，全凭良心付钱。

Professional mountain circumambulators make up a special occupation in Tibet. They go circumambulating and praying for those who want to realize their wishes, but don't have the health to do so. Professional mountain circumambulators at Mt. Kangrinboqe pick up a stone at the mountain pass to signify that they have finished one circle of circumambulation. They later sell these stones to Buddhist disciples, as proof of how many circles of circumambulation they have done for them. These deals are based on trust. No one checks whether the circumambulators have really walked around the mountain, nor are the stones marked with a price — people just pay according to conscience.

开镰仪式
Ceremony for Starting Harvest

西藏农人播种要祭祀，收割的第一簇青稞也要进贡给各方神灵。有学者记录西藏农民开镰那天的仪式，一方面要给土地神献上青稞酒和糌粑，一方面还要念念有词地祈祷：今天我们开镰啦，请告诉青稞地里的神灵和生命，有头的藏起头，有脚的缩起脚，要不我手里的大家伙来了，弄出牦牛大的伤口我就不管啦……

Tibetan farmers need to offer a sacrifice to the gods when seeding, and must offer the first cluster of barley as a tribute during harvest too. One scholar recorded the ceremony at the start of harvest: Tibetans need to offer barley wine and *tsampa* to the god of earth and at the same time utter the following prayer: 'Today we start harvesting. Please tell the spirits and creatures on the barley land to hide their heads if they have heads, and curl their feet if they have feet. Otherwise, if my long sickle causes you a bad wound, I won't be responsible.'

风土·管窥
Sights and Sounds

加持
Blessings

在西藏人看来，佛像、佛经、佛塔、佛殿、木雕、塑像、唐卡等上师随身之物，就等同于上师的真身，要特别敬重，无论什么时候都要庄重以待，这样，就能获得上师的"加持"。如果一位普通人对你说"吉祥如意"，那只不过是一句问候；如果一位你虔诚信任的上师对你说"吉祥如意"，那就能带来极大的好运。

In Tibetans' perspective, Buddhist images, scriptures, pagodas, wood sculptures, statues, *thangkas*, and Buddha Halls all represent the incarnation of prominent Buddhist masters, so seeing them is equal to seeing the masters. People facing them should revere these objects at all times, so that they can receive the masters' blessing. Tibetans believe that if an ordinary person says 'good luck and happiness to you,' it is just a greeting; if a master you respect says the same thing, it will indeed bring you very good luck.

摄影：聂晓阳

微观西藏
TIBET: FAST & FURIOUS

善妒的神灵
Dealing with Envious Gods

西藏人办婚礼时，新娘家的人要特意请法师祷告各路神灵，不要因为新娘出嫁就生气，也不要对新娘纠缠不休。法师甚至还"威胁"神灵说：新郎家不会厚待它们，还是待在原地比较划算。如果有人要砍一棵树做房梁，人们也要念经请求树神的原谅，请它们不要发怒，不要在未来的房梁上"动手脚"。

When Tibetans hold a wedding, the bride's family often invite a master to pray to various gods, hoping that they don't become angry because the bride is getting married, and that they don't pester her in any way. The master even 'threatens' the gods, saying the groom's family will not tolerate their mischievous behavior, so it's better to stay where they are. If someone wants to hew down a tree to make a beam, people also need to recite scriptures to beg for forgiveness from the tree gods, hoping that they won't be angry or 'tamper' with their future beam.

祈福圣物
Holy Item for Blessing

在西藏，牧人们搭完帐篷的第一件事就是挂上经幡，祈求神灵的福佑；朝圣者走过一个新的山头，会在山石或树上挂上经幡，祈求旅途平顺；农民们开犁播种，也会在耕牛的头角上插挂经幡，祈求风调雨顺五谷丰登。经幡是人们表达崇拜与礼赞、祈求幸福与好运的圣物，是万不可乱动和不敬的。

In Tibet, the first thing herdsmen do after setting up a tent is to put up prayer flags and pray for the gods' blessings. When pilgrims climb to the top of a new hill, they will also put up prayer flags on the rocks or trees to pray for a smooth journey; when farmers start plowing and seeding, they put up prayer flags on cattle horns to pray for favorable weather and a good harvest. Prayer flags are a holy item for Tibetans to express their admiration and praise, and to pray for happiness and auspiciousness, so you should not move them casually or be disrespectful toward them.

风土·管窥
Sights and Sounds

石头妈妈
The Mother Rock

过去，拉萨农人春种秋收时，都要祭祀一块称为阿妈色多（金石头妈妈）的白石头。春天放在田间，请它保佑风调雨顺。秋收祭祀时，在它周围留下小片青稞麦穗，然后将它带回家中供奉。在老一代农人心中，这块石头非常神圣。

In the past, when the farmers of Lhasa planted in spring and harvested in autumn, they would perform a ritual with a white stone, known as the 'Mother Golden Rock'. In spring it would be placed in the field, and they would pray to it for favorable weather. In the autumn, they would leave a few ears of barley around it, and then take it home to be worshipped. In the hearts of previous generations, the rock was highly sacred.

超越亲疏
Treating Others Like Your Family Members

在西藏，人们把钱换成一毛一毛的，在大小佛像前都要捐功德。走在路上布施给乞丐的钱，多少不重要，但是要尽量不错过任何一个。西藏人不仅相信来世，也相信前世，"无史以来"每个人都可能是自己的亲人，所以他们更能超越亲疏平等视人。

In Tibet, people exchange their money into coins so that they can donate for merits in front of the Buddha statues of all sizes. When giving money to the beggars in the streets, what's important isn't the amount, but that you not miss any of them. Tibetans believe in both the afterlife and previous existences. From time unrecorded, everyone could have been their own relative, thus they treat others equally beyond their present affinity.

评论

微观西藏
TIBET: FAST & FURIOUS

摄影：聂晓阳

颜色的象征意义

The Symbolic Meaning of Colors

西藏人最常用的颜色是白、红、绿、黄和蓝，无处不在的五彩经幡就是由这五种颜色构成的。在西藏，每种颜色都有特定的象征：白色象征纯洁善良，红色象征兴旺刚猛，绿色象征阴柔平和，黄色象征仁慈博才，蓝色象征勇敢机智。

The most common colors Tibetans use are white, red, green, yellow, and blue. The prayer flags seen everywhere in Tibet are composed of exactly these five colors. Each color has a specific implication: white symbolizes purity and kindness; red stands for prosperity and vigorousness; green designates tenderness and peace; yellow signifies mercy and intelligence; and blue represents bravery and wisdom.

评论

风土·管窥
Sights and Sounds

小心翼翼
With Great Care

传统的藏族人认为神灵无所不在，人应该时刻小心翼翼。一个人来到从没到过的大山或峡谷，不能大声喧哗，因为这样会打扰神灵，引起不悦；人们不能在屋里吹口哨或大声哭叫，因为这样屋子内外的神灵会不高兴。

Traditional Tibetans believe that the gods are omnipresent, and people should be scrupulous at all times. People should not shout loudly when they come to a mountain or valley that they have never been to, because doing that might disturb the deities and displease them. People are also forbidden to whistle or cry loudly in a room because this will displease gods inside or outside the room.

楼梯阻鬼
Stairs to Block Ghosts

在西藏，人们认为如果死者不能得到很好的超度，就会迷失在阴间，变成"赞"（厉鬼），为害亲人和村民。在传统上西藏房屋的门很低，楼梯也很陡，据说就是为了防止被厉鬼追逐。在西藏还有一种神秘的"回阳人"，就是经历过死亡然后又复活过来的人，他们往往被看作世人和亡者之间的信差。

In Tibet, people believe that if a dead man's soul is not released smoothly, it will be lost in the underworld and turn into a ferocious ghost, hurting relatives and villagers. Traditional Tibetan houses have low doors and steep stairs because such arrangements are supposed to prevent the entry of ferocious ghosts. There are also some mysterious 'returned men', who have experienced death and become alive again. 'Returned men' are seen as messengers between the living and the dead.

先给狗过年
Dogs Celebrate the New Year First

西藏林芝地区有个民间传说，说是狗带来了青稞种子，才有了当地的农业。所以在林芝地区，过年的时候要先给狗过年，把各种好吃的东西放在一个大盘子里先喂狗。

In Nyingchi, a county in Tibet, there is a legend saying that dogs first brought barley seeds to this land, thus starting agriculture in this area. Hence the first celebration of the New Year in Nyingchi is to put lots of tasty food onto a big plate to feed the dogs.

微观西藏
TIBET: FAST & FURIOUS

门巴族的婚礼习俗
The Wedding Traditions of the Monpas

婚礼后，新娘家人突然拉着新娘往外走，男家急忙去追，双方乱成一团，最后还要媒人调解，女方家人才放手。这是西藏门巴族人的婚礼习俗。在西藏，以藏族为主体，还有汉、回、门巴、珞巴、纳西、怒、独龙等十几个民族世代居住。此外，还有夏尔巴人和僜人，不过人数很少，只有几千人。

After the wedding ceremony, the family members of the bride will lead her out suddenly, and the groom's family will run after them, creating a chaotic situation. In the end, the matchmaker comes in and does a mediation, and the bride's family will stop. This is a wedding custom of the Monba ethnic group in Tibet. Besides Tibetans, which are the dominant group, there are also a dozen other ethnic groups like the Han, Hui, Monba, Lhoba, Nakhi, Nu, and Derung, all living together for generations in Tibet. Moreover, there are also the Sherpas and the Deng, but only a fairly small number of them reside here, merely a few thousand people.

白色崇拜
Admiration of the Color White

清朝时有西藏官员去北京朝觐皇帝，看到有人办丧事穿白衣很惊奇，因为西藏人只有庆祝时才穿白衣服。对西藏人来说，白色是白云、雪山、乳汁的颜色，是纯洁、正义、力量、吉祥和喜庆的象征。对他们来说，对一个善良的人的最高评价，就是说他的心"很白"。

In the Qing Dynasty, Tibetan officials were surprised to see people wearing white clothes at funerals when they went to Beijing to present themselves before the emperor, because Tibetans only wore white clothes when they were celebrating. For them, white is the color of clouds, snow mountains, and milk. It is a symbol of purity, justice, power, luck, and joy. Their highest praise for a kind man is that his heart is 'so white'.

评论

滥杀才是罪
Slaughter Is a Sin

藏族学者平措次仁：在西藏，为了谋生的捕猎不算杀生，只有滥杀才是罪过，所以猎人捕猎不会超过自己的需要。西藏人认为，一头牛和一条鱼同样都是一条生命，但是宰杀一头牛可以供很多人吃，杀一条鱼却只够很少的人吃，所以西藏很多人是不吃鱼和其他小动物的。

Tibetan scholar Phuntsok Tsering says that in Tibet, hunting animals for a living doesn't count as destruction of life, only slaughter is considered a sin. So hunters will not hunt more animals than they need. Tibetans believe that both cows and fish are worthy of life, but killing a cow can offer food to many people, while a fish can only feed a few. Hence, many Tibetans don't eat fish or other small animals.

八大藏戏
The Eight Great Tibetan Operas

藏戏取材于佛经故事和民间传说，传统上有八大藏戏，其中有一部叫《文成公主》，讲述松赞干布使者依靠机智赢得文成公主以及她进藏以后的故事。藏戏中面具发挥着重要作用，在不同颜色的面具中，白色代表纯洁，红色代表威严，绿色代表柔顺，黄色代表吉祥，而半黑半白的面具则象征两面三刀的性格。

Tibetan operas are based on Buddhist stories and legends. Traditionally there are eight major Tibetan operas. One of them is called 'Princess Wencheng', and tells the story of Songtsen Gampo's envoy winning the hand of Princess Wencheng by his intelligence, as well as stories from after she entered Tibet. Masks play an important role in Tibetan operas, as do their colors: white represents purity, red represents majesty, green represents mildness, yellow means luck, and the half-black, half-white mask indicates a double-dealing personality.

摄影：聂晓阳

微观西藏
TIBET: FAST & FURIOUS

为神唱歌
Sing for Gods

在西藏，很多人到了山顶、河边或者祭祀的时候，都要放声高歌，因为他们相信，山上、河里和空中的所有的生命听到歌声都会很高兴，别人高兴了，自己也有好运。同时，通过歌声取悦神灵，神灵就不会降祸给自己。

In Tibet, many people sing aloud when they reach the top of a mountain, go to the riverside, or offer sacrifices to the gods, because they believe that all lives in the mountains, rivers, and sky feel happy when they hear their songs, thus bringing the singers good luck of their own. Furthermore, pleasing gods by singing can help prevent the gods from harming them in any way.

庆祝圆寂
Celebrating Death

西藏旧时传统不庆祝上师的生日，而是庆祝他的圆寂。藏传佛教相信，心获得自由的最好机会，就是死亡那一刻。一个人在死亡时反而最容易解脱，也就是说，只有人死亡时，凡夫之心和愚昧才会跟着死亡。只有死亡的瞬间才能解脱成佛，所以很多高僧大德是欢乐地迎接死亡的。

According to the old traditions, Tibetans did not celebrate the birthday of a guru (Buddhist master), but instead, they celebrated the day of his death. Tibetan Buddhism believes that the best chance for a man's heart to acquire freedom is when he dies. The easiest time for him to break away from *samsara* was upon his death. That is to say, when he dies, his mundane heart and ignorance vanish together. The moment of death is the only opportunity to free oneself completely and become a Buddha, therefore, many eminent monks are quite willing to welcome death.

评论

圣城·拉萨
Lhasa, a Mystical City

影：车刚

微观西藏
TIBET: FAST & FURIOUS

摄影：车刚

佛国圣地
The Holy Land of Buddhism

藏语中，"拉"是"神、佛"的意思，而"萨"的意思是"大地"，所以合在一起，"拉萨"的意思就是"圣地"。

In the Tibetan language, *Lha* means 'god' or 'Buddha', while *sa* means 'earth', so putting them together, 'Lhasa' means 'Holy Land'.

西藏的"犹太人"
Tibet's 'Real Businessmen'

拉萨第一街八廓街上，精明能干、善于交际的生意人，大多是康巴人。藏东的"康巴汉子"威名远播，而迁徙到拉萨的康巴人，尤其是康巴女人，却是以善做生意闻名的。他们被称作中国西藏的"犹太人"。

Most of the smart, capable and communicative merchants at Lhasa's famous Barkhor Street are from Kham. 'Khampa men' from eastern Tibet are well renowned. Those that migrated to Lhasa, especially Khampa women, are well known for their skills in doing business. Thus they are known as 'Tibet's real businessmen'.

日光与湿地
Sunlight and Wetlands

拉萨是座太阳辐射强、日照时间长的日光城。初到拉萨的人，即使每天喝很多水，也治愈不了干裂的嘴唇。就是这样一座燃烧的城堡，却有一片水草丰美的湿地，黑颈鹤、白唇鹿、赤麻鸭、斑头雁等常常出没。有人说，拉萨人同湿地与日光的关系，是世界屋脊上最微妙的一种关系。

Lhasa is a sunny city with long daylight and strong solar radiation. Newcomers to Lhasa have no cure for their chapped lips, even if they drink a lot of water every day. However, in this very town, you can find a rich wetland with lush aquatic plants. Moreover, you can often see black-necked cranes, white-lipped deer, ruddy shelducks, and bare-headed geese there. Some people say that the relationship which Lhasa people maintain with the wetlands and the sunlight is the most subtle tie on the roof of the world.

是回忆让我们变得不同
Memory Made us Different

女作家央珍说："拉萨城本身就是一种气息，一种意境，它是我灵魂依托的地方。我认为，任何文学作品的创作和阅读，都是回忆与缅怀，我的小说正是在往事力量的推动下完成的，是在老拉萨城安谧的陈年气息中展开的。"人每天之所以变得不同，是因为拥有了更多的回忆，而关于拉萨的回忆，总是悠远绵长。

Female Tibetan writer Yangdron says, 'Lhasa itself is a kind of sensation, and a kind of artistic concept. It is the place that supports my soul. I believe that any creation or reading of literary work is a recollection and appreciation. My novels were completed precisely because of the pressure of reminiscent power, and they were launched in the aged and tranquil breath of old Lhasa.' People are different from day to day because they have more memories, and those memories about Lhasa always bear a lingering aftertaste.

评论

微观西藏
TIBET: FAST & FURIOUS

格萨尔王庙的指示牌
The Signpost for the Temple of King Gesar

在异乡，也许你只是不停地奔向目的地，而错过了身边的风景。格萨尔王庙是不少游客旅程中的一站，却很少有人看过它的指示牌。一位作家说，在拉萨西郊的北京中路上，一块白漆小木牌钉在大树上方，箭头指向帕玛日山，牌子上用碳素笔写了一句不同寻常、却耐人寻味的指示语"那山上有格萨尔王的庙"。

When you get to a new place, you might keep running toward your destination, and miss the scenery around you. The Temple of King Gesar is a stop on many tourists' journeys, but few have seen its signpost. A writer says that on Beijing Middle Street in the western suburbs of Lhasa, a white wooden sign was nailed to a giant tree. The arrow of the sign pointed toward Parmari Mountain. On the sign an unusual yet intriguing instruction was written in carbon pen: 'That mountain contains the Temple of King Gesar.'

专心致志地发呆
Staying in the Moment

在拉萨，时间有时候似乎是静止的，人们经常以一种几乎感觉不到的速度行进，如天空中悠闲的白云一样，在拉萨的大街小巷悠然自得。在这里，不必做被强迫的事，不必烦恼悲欢离合的故事，在这里只需要专心致志地发呆、忘却、飘摇。时间老人似乎对这片土地过于厚爱，给了它太多的恩赐，让它用于"挥霍"。

In Lhasa, sometimes time seems to stand still. People often seem to be walking at a speed that can hardly be felt. Just like the carefree white clouds in the sky, they comfortably tour the streets and alleyways of Lhasa. Here, you don't need to force youself to do business, nor worry about stories of partings and reunions. Here, you just need to dedicatedly stay in the moment, forget, and drift about. Father Time seems to have treated this land too kindly. He blessed this plateau with much time to 'idle away'.

评论

圣城·拉萨
Lhasa, a Mystical City

包容度惊人
Amazing Levels of Tolerance

有 80 后女作家说，拉萨在某些时候让我想到纽约，它的包容度惊人：只要你在这里，无论是常驻还是暂留，只要你有一颗开放、平等、亲和的心，放下自以为是的姿态，你就能感觉到这城市回应的热情。

A young female author who was born in the 1980s says, 'Lhasa sometimes makes me think of New York. It has a high level of tolerance: Chinese, foreigners, travelers, locals — whether staying long-term or just for a quick stop, as long as you have an open, equal, kind and unaffected heart, you can feel the passion of the city.'

"偶遇"之城
A City of Romance

有人说，拉萨的"偶遇指数"已经超过了丽江、阳朔和大理，大有成为"偶遇圣地"之势。那些生活在都市的钢筋水泥楼林里、难以找到自我的人，来到离天最近的拉萨，心灵得到触动，于是拉萨制造了数不清的偶遇故事。

Some people say that the probability of having an affair in Lhasa is higher even than in Lijiang, Yangshuo, and Dali (all popular tourist attractions). Lhasa is on its way to becoming the most popular place of romance. When those who have lost themselves in the reinforced concrete and cement buildings of modern cities come to Lhasa, the place closest to paradise, they often find their hearts touched. As a result, this city has produced endless romantic stories.

摄影：车刚

微观西藏
TIBET: FAST & FURIOUS

摄影：聂晓阳

拉萨"小资"
Lhasa 'Xiaozi'

拉萨，旅客眼中古老、神秘的信仰之都，在新一代藏族人眼里它年轻、小资的一面正在被不断地塑造。70后作家凌仕江讲述了他眼中的一位藏族"小资"：闲暇时光坐在沙发上听听音乐，喝喝咖啡，翻翻茶几上的中英文时尚杂志；出门时要擦香水，抹啫喱水；呼朋唤友下馆子，先点一杯不加酥油的咖啡。

Lhasa is an old and mysterious city of faith in tourists' eyes, but in the eyes of the new generation of Tibetans, one perspective of its youthful and *xiaozi** character is being constantly shaped. Born in the 1970s, writer Ling Shijiang described a Tibetan *xiaozi* in these terms: 'During leisure time he would sit on the sofa, listen to music, enjoy a cup of coffee, and read a few pages of a fashion magazine in Chinese or English; when he went out, he would wear some perfume and use a hair spray; when inviting friends to eat out, he would first order a cup of coffee without butter.'

* A Chinese term describing fairly well-off people who seek modern tastes, and enjoy a comfortable life.

圣城·拉萨
Lhasa, a Mystical City

八廓街的喧闹与宁静
Exciting and Quiet Barkhor Street

作家央珍这样描述如今的八廓街：在这里，大昭寺庄严的包铜红门与街面上店铺的棕色小木门同时打开；六字真言与讨价还价声混合在一起，美元港币与人民币紧捏在一起，古老质朴的西藏民歌与疯狂的迪斯科混响在一起。在这里，虔诚与钱财、佛国与尘世、精神与现实、喧闹与宁静共存。

This is a description of the current Barkhor Street by writer Yangdron: 'The solemn red copper-clad doors of Jokhang Temple and the brown wooden doors of shops are opened at the same time. Scripture chanting is mixed with haggling. U.S. dollars, Hong Kong dollars and yuan are squeezed together. Plain traditional Tibetan folk songs and wild discos echo simultaneously. On Barkhor Street, devoutness and wealth, the Buddhist realm and the secular world, spirit and reality, excitement and quietness, all exist side by side.'

在拉萨晒太阳
Sunbathing in Lhasa

"驴友"李小平：冬季在拉萨晒太阳，是这座古城里最惬意的一件事。可以独享，也可以同乐，其中的滋味只有亲自到这阳光中晒一下才能体会得到。正是这冬季的阳光，给这儿的人们带来了无穷的力量，无论生活条件多么艰苦，他们脸上始终荡漾着阳光般灿烂的微笑。可以说，是阳光塑造了他们乐观、豪放的性格。

A traveler named Li Xiaoping says, 'Sunbathing in the ancient city of Lhasa during winter is a heavenly enjoyment. You can do it alone or with friends, but the pleasure of sunbathing can only be experienced when here. The winter sun gives the people here unlimited power. Regardless of how tough their lives are, sunny smiles can always be seen on their faces. Possibly, it is the sunlight that has shaped their optimistic and uninhibited characters.'

评论

微观西藏
TIBET: FAST & FURIOUS

可触摸的小城

A Tangible City

画家张萍曾写道：八廓街是相当复杂的一条街，它的像迷宫一样的巷子，巷子拐角的尿骚气息，古老房子的酥油味道，黑色的茶馆里传来的印度歌舞片，茶馆外是各种摊贩，街的拐角则坐着诵经的喇嘛……拉萨是个很宽容的城市，它接纳着人们对它的想象。拉萨也是个可触摸的小城，生活着很多正常和微小的人们。

Painter Zhang Ping once wrote, 'Barkhor Street is a rather complicated street, almost resembling a maze, with its alleyways smothered in foul smells, or the drifting butter smell of the old houses. Floating music comes from Indian movies played in the black teahouses. All kinds stand of stalls outside the teahouses, and lamas are chanting at every corner. Lhasa is a tolerant city, accepting all kinds of visions from people. It is also a small and tangible city, filled with numerous ordinary and humble people.'

别样之城

An Extraordinary City

"驴友"杨林楠形容拉萨是一座具有别样情感的城：走在老城的石板路上，脚下踏过的是多少古往今来的故事。杂乱中除了匆忙穿行的喃喃祷告，还夹杂着肆无忌惮的叫卖声，这种和声不那么完美，但也难以找到太多的瑕疵。在古老和现代的对话中，也许只有在拉萨才不会显得太过别扭。

Backpacker Yang Linnan regards Lhasa as a city filled with extraordinary emotions: 'Walking on the flagstone roads of the old city, the stories of the ages were just under your feet. In the buzz, besides the murmurs of prayers from those hurriedly passing by, there were also cries from unscrupulous peddlers. This harmony of sounds was not perfect, but you could not find many flaws either. Perhaps Lhasa doesn't appear too weird amid the dialogue between the ancient and the modern.'

摄影：聂晓阳

圣城·拉萨
Lhasa, a Mystical City

宜居之地
An Ideal Place for Living

法国人 Emilien 曾觉得拉萨是一座高高在上的圣城，一座精神属性强烈的城市，但后来他发现拉萨更是一个适合生活的地方。"拉萨是一座非常悠闲也极具生活气息的城市，这里有便利的生活资源，同时随便城市里的哪个角落，都可骑自行车直达，就像我的家乡安纳西一样。"

Frenchman Emilien used to regard Lhasa as a holy city standing high above the masses, a city of strong spiritual attributes. However, later he found that this city was also a liveable place. 'Lhasa is a relaxing city full of the vivid breath of life. There are convenient living resources, and you can go everywhere by bike, just like in my hometown Annecy.'

古城画卷
A Scroll Painting of the Ancient City

旅居拉萨的艺术家尹文涛：站在那一栋栋紧密地联结在一起的藏式小楼前，看绣着吉祥八宝图案的门帘，被风一吹，便露出正在给女儿编辫子的藏族阿妈的身影。小巷幽深，人们的生活节奏都是缓慢的。商贩的叫卖声、茶前饭后的交谈声，构成了古城一幅动态生活画卷。

Yin Wentao, an artist sojourning in Lhasa, says, 'I stood in front of the closely connected Tibetan houses and looked at a door curtain embroidered with the Eight Auspicious Symbols (a set of symbols that closely relate to Buddhism and are common on things Tibetans use). When the wind stirred the curtain, the figure of a Tibetan mother braiding her daughter's hair appeared. The alleys were narrow, and people's pace of life was slow. Vendors' shouts and the chatting around the table formed a dynamic scroll painting of life in this ancient city.'

评论

微观西藏
TIBET: FAST & FURIOUS

遥远的拉萨
The Faraway Lhasa

作家白玛娜珍：拉萨，你的舌尖一旦发出这个声音，似乎就有一种神秘的力量注入你的体内，使你的心里有所希冀，有所颤动，有所莫名其妙，有所不一样。这就是拉萨，拉萨给你的诱惑。这种诱惑来源于它的遥远，来源于你对它的不了解或知之甚少。遥远的拉萨，成了许多人心灵的庇护所、幻想的家园。

Writer Pema Nadron says, 'When you produce the sound "Lhasa" on the tip of your tongue, some mysterious strength seems to have been infused into you, making your heart hope, quiver, grow confused, and feel different. This is Lhasa and the temptation this city gives you. This temptation comes from the remoteness of Lhasa and from your unfamiliarity with this city. The faraway Lhasa has not only become a sanctuary for many people's souls, but also a fantasized homeland in many people's minds.'

拉萨的雨
The Rain in Lhasa

从小生活在西藏的白玛娜珍对拉萨的雨有着别样的感情，她写道："拉萨的雨最顽皮了，烈日当头时，它会突然冲下来，把炎炎的路面弄得湿淋淋，但一转眼又不见了。有时你朝前一步是万里晴空，朝后半步就要挨暴雨乌黑的小拳头。那景象奇怪极了。但拉萨的雨大多在夜里说话，所以一般感受不到雨天的压抑。"

Pema Nadron, who grew up in Tibet, has special feelings toward the rain in Lhasa. She writes, 'Rain in Lhasa is the naughtiest. It can rush down along with the rays of the baking sun, wetting the burning road, and disappear very soon afterward. Sometimes, when you take one step forward, it is clear sky above you; however, if you retrace half a step, you'll be hit by the small dark fists of heavy rain — it's really a weird phenomenon. Nevertheless, the rain in Lhasa usually falls at night, so people seldom feel depressed on a rainy day.'

评论

圣城·拉萨
Lhasa, a Mystical City

摄影：车刚　　　　　　　　　　　　　　　　　　摄影：赵关深

流浪狗
Stray Dogs

民俗学家廖东凡说，过去拉萨到处可见流浪狗，甚至有人把旧拉萨称为"乞丐与狗"的城市。狗之所以在拉萨大量生存和繁衍，与这座城市的宗教环境和居民习俗密切相关。拉萨居民大多是虔诚的佛教徒，打狗、杀狗是绝对不允许的，许多老人尽管自己不富裕，也要节省一些粮食，定时定点地去喂那些流浪狗。

Folklorist Liao Dongfan says that in the past, stray dogs could be seen everywhere in Lhasa. Some people even called old Lhasa 'the city of beggars and dogs'. The reason that dogs were able to live and propagate in Lhasa is closely related to the religious environment and habits of the locals. Most inhabitants in Lhasa are Buddhists, thus beating or killing dogs is definitely forbidden. Some elders, who are not rich themselves, still save food to feed stray dogs regularly at a fixed time and place.

世俗的一面
The Hybridity of Lhasa

作家安意如：从城市形态上客观地讲，拉萨亦是极世俗的城市。从某些角度看过去，它还保留了乡镇粗野杂乱的气息。另一方面，拉萨确实是魔幻神奇的，太多人将自己流放至此，空气里都散发着人在天涯的味道。缘分在这里显现，很容易落地生根，似乎什么意想不到的事情都会发生。

Author An Yiru: 'In terms of urban form, Lhasa is also a very secular city. From certain perspectives, it retains the tough and disorderly feeling of the countryside. At the same time, it's a fantastic and fascinating place, with many people voluntarily making their exile here, immersing themselves in the atmosphere of remoteness. Fate comes into play here as well, and it's easy to put down roots — you never know what might happen.'

微观西藏
TIBET: FAST & FURIOUS

拉萨爱情鸟
The Lovebirds of Lhasa

拉萨河上流传着一段凄婉的传说，那里有三只美丽的鸟相依相伴，要飞一起飞，要落一起落，叫声凄婉，仿佛在倾诉内心的苦痛。据说那鸟叫"索吉毕吉"，是当地头人的女儿色姆和出身低下的情人明珠及他们的孩子所变。相传，明珠被色姆的父亲害死之后，色姆带孩子跳河，一起化身成了爱情鸟。

A sad story circulates along the Lhasa River. There are three pretty birds that always stay together. They fly together, land together, and tweet sadly as if pouring out the pain in their hearts. The locals say that these birds are called 'Sojibiji', and they are the incarnations of a local chief's daughter, her low-born lover and their child. The story goes that after the chief killed his daughter's lover, the daughter jumped into the river with her child, and they all became lovebirds.

慢生活
Slow Life

有人说，拉萨是一座可以让人忘记时间的"慢生活"之城，而甜茶正是这种让人健忘的"催化剂"。三两个朋友围坐一桌侃大山，时而啜一口甜茶，两三个小时就这么优哉游哉地过去了，"你喝进的每一口甜茶里，都夹杂了上百年的情感和思绪，这种充斥着记忆的气味，让人有恍若隔世之感"。

Some people say that Lhasa is a city of 'slow life', which helps you forget about the passage of time, and the 'catalyst' for this forgetfulness is sweet tea. When a couple of friends chat at a table and have a sip of sweet tea from time to time, two or three hours slip away very quickly. 'Every sip of sweet tea contains emotions and thoughts that have brewed for hundreds of years. This kind of taste is full of memories, making you feel that you have gone into past generations.'

评论

行旅·品味
Travel and Taste

微观西藏
TIBET: FAST & FURIOUS

"陌生人路径"
'The Route for Strangers'

据说，进入拉萨老城最好的线路是西路，陆续经过哲蚌寺、罗布林卡，沿着林廓（围绕拉萨核心区的转经路）顺时针行进，看过城北的古寺、城东的集市和城南的觉波里山，最后再进城。

It is said that the best route into old Lhasa is the west route, which passes Drepung Monastery and the Norbulingka, then heads clockwise along Lingkhor (a circumambulation road that surrounds the core area of Lhasa). After seeing the old monasteries in the north, the markets in the east, and Joboli Mountain in the south, you finally enter the old city.

行囊
Luggage

外来旅行者在拉萨，不是背着大包小包的衣物药品，就是端着长枪短炮的摄影器材，生怕行囊不够满、眼睛不够用。拉萨当地人可不这样，出门转经顶多牵头羊。有位活佛曾经说："来大昭寺，身上东西越少越好，这样就单纯了，没杂念了。"

Most tourists in Lhasa, if they're not carrying bags stuffed with clothes and medicine, are lugging around lots of expensive camera equipment and fearing all the while that they've lost something. Local residents in the city are never like this; they at most bring a sheep with them when they go circumambulating. A living Buddha once said, 'When you come to Jokhang Temple, the less you take with you the better, so that your mind can be pure and simple, and more focused.'

摄影：聂晓阳

行旅·品味
Travel and Taste

冰湖裸泳
Skinny Dipping in Icy Lakes

旅者海琪和男友托马斯曾有过一段特别的经历：在雪域西藏，托马斯忽然两眼发光地表示要去湖中裸泳。海琪说，虽然她男友在德国也经常去冬泳，可这是海拔几千米之上的冰河，不知道河水会不会把他冻成标本。"几分钟后，一丝不挂的托马斯扑通一声就下去了，他在水中不知是太冷还是太兴奋，一直吼叫着。"

Traveler Hai Qi and her boyfriend Thomas had a very special experience: in snow-covered Tibet, Thomas' eyes lit up as he suddenly decided to go skinny dipping in the lake. Hai Qi says that although her boyfriend often went swimming in the winter in Germany, she didn't know whether he would freeze to death and become a specimen in the icy lake at such a high altitude of thousands of meters. 'Thomas jumped naked into the lake with a splash, and he kept screaming in the water, and no one knew whether it was because he was too cold or too excited.'

一如初见
Love at First Sight

摄影师吕玲珑在谈到对藏文化发源地山南的印象时说，山南人"至今保持着我第一次见到他们时的古朴、纯净和沧桑感"。他说，他每次来都怀着一颗朝圣的心，虔诚地聆听来自西藏的声音，"对于我来说没有什么是最爱的，因为我爱的是这里完整的生活链"。

When photographer Lü Linglong talks about his impression of Lhoka (Shannan), the birthplace of Tibetan culture, he says the people in Lhoka 'have retained the sense of simplicity, purity and spiritual richness as the first time I met them'. He also says that every time he goes to Tibet, he carries along a heart for pilgrimage, devoutly listening to the sounds of this plateau. 'For me, nothing here is my favorite, because what I love is the complete Tibetan way of life.'

评论

微观西藏
TIBET: FAST & FURIOUS

看淡自己
Hold Yourself Lightly

商人李厚霖回忆说：当我在阿里走了40公里山路还找不到一顶帐篷，只能顶着寒风睡在外面的时候；当我平时引以为自豪的身体，被高原反应折磨得昏天黑地的时候……我会问自己这么容易就被打败了吗？但很快我又释然了。这种释然就是"看淡了"——把一切，连同自己，统统看淡。

Businessman Li Houlin recalls, 'When I walked for forty kilometers in Ngari without seeing a tent and had to sleep in the cold wind, while my usually fit body was severely tortured by altitude sickness, I asked myself, "Are you so easily defeated?" I let go of this feeling after a while. I was relieved by "taking things lightly" — holding everything, including myself lightly.'

雾里景色
Scenery Veiled in Mist

西藏的天气变幻莫测，有人讲过这样一个故事：朋友走了趟滇藏线，出发前信誓旦旦地说要去看看南迦巴瓦山峰。回来后我向他要照片，他传过来的只有一片茫茫云雾。我问他：南迦巴瓦呢？他答就在云后，自行想象吧。我莞尔：这就是西藏，除非亲自去，否则你永远看不到那层迷雾里面的真实世界。

The weather in Tibet is unpredictable. One man tells this story: 'My friend traveled along the Yunnan-Tibet Road and pledged to visit the Namcha Barwa Peak. When he came back, I asked him to show me his photos, but there were only clouds and mist in the photos he sent me. I asked him, "Where is Namcha Barwa?" He said, "It's behind the clouds. Just imagine." I smiled, "This is Tibet; unless you go there yourself, you'll never see the true world veiled in mist".'

评论

行旅 · 品味
Travel and Taste

摄影：张培中

地球上最后的秘境
The Last Wonderland on Earth

雅鲁藏布大峡谷长 500 多千米，平均深度 2268 米，最深处达 6009 米，江水流速最快达 16 米每秒以上，有人称之为"主河床上的瀑布"。藏东南这条全世界最深、最长的大峡谷，也是世界上山地生物多样性最丰富的地区，可以看到许多濒危珍稀动植物，体验一天四季的变化，堪称"地球上最后的秘境"。

The Yarlung Tsangpo Grand Canyon is more than 500 kilometers long and 2,268 meters deep on average, with the deepest point reaching 6,009 meters and the river running at a top speed of sixteen meters per second. Hence, some people call it a 'waterfall on the riverbed'. This world's deepest and largest canyon in southeast Tibet also accommodates the richest mountainous biodiversity on the globe. Here you can see many rare animals and plants and experience the change of the four seasons within a single day. It could be called 'the last wonderland on Earth'.

不愿说"艰苦"
You Couldn't Call It 'Hard'

摄影家车刚：刚进藏时生活很差，但人很真。直到今天，"老西藏"们见面依然很亲。所以有人要我讲西藏生活，我不愿用"艰苦"二字，因为人的精神状态特别好。

Photographer Che Gang says, 'When I first went to Tibet, life there was extremely difficult, but the people were very genuine. Even today, when "the old friends who have worked in Tibet for a long time" meet, they are still very close. Hence, if someone asks me about the life in Tibet, I'm reluctant to use the word 'hard', since people's spirits are very hight.'

微观西藏
TIBET: FAST & FURIOUS

摄影：车刚

一个人的布达拉宫
Having Potala Palace All to Yourself

冬季的西藏长期以来被看作旅游的禁地。但是，CNN网站旅游版曾刊文介绍说，西藏是"亚洲最佳的冬季旅游目的地"，因为在冬天去西藏不仅有"史诗般的火车旅行"，而且"布达拉宫里没有了夏日的拥挤，阴冷的走廊和阳光下的小道只属于你一人"。

Tibet in the winter has been regarded as a forbidden place for traveling. However, the tourism section on the CNN website once introduced Tibet as 'the best winter tourist destination in Asia', reasoning that in winter Tibet provides you with 'an epic train journey', and that 'the Potala Palace is not as crowded as in summer, so both the gloomy corridors and sunny pathways belong exclusively to you.'

高原反应也值得
Worthy of Suffering Altitude Sickness

高原反应就像顽皮的孩子，东躲西藏，使很多人对雪域高原望而却步。但收藏家马未都却说："尽管每个人都有轻重不一的高原反应，但西藏就是西藏，世界最高峰珠穆朗玛在此，世界最高海拔的湖纳木错也在此，这奇妙的一山一水让你有点儿高原反应又怎么啦？"

Altitude sickness is like a naughty boy. He hides himself from place to place, making a lot of people step back at the sight of this snowy plateau. However, collector Ma Weidu says, 'Although everyone has altitude sickness to certain degrees, Tibet is attractive all the same. The world's highest peak, Mount Qomolangma, and highest lake, Lake Namtso, are both there. Before these natural wonders, what is the fuss about a little altitude sickness?'

行旅・品味
Travel and Taste

天葬师
Celestial Burial Masters

天葬是藏族比较普遍的殡葬习俗，但天葬师这个职业在藏族人眼里却十分"低下"。女导演书云因为拍摄的原因请天葬师平措到日喀则的家中小坐，却遭到摄影组里所有藏族人的疏远。平措喝着自己带来的青稞酒坦然地说："我家好几代都是天葬师，八年前我接过这门手艺，就知道这是佛祖帮我定下的命。"

Celestial burials are a common funeral custom for Tibetans, but celestial burial masters are regarded as one of the lowest walks of life. Female film director Shu Yun once invited the celestial burial master Phuntsok to her home in Xigaze for filming, and all the Tibetans in the film crew were aghast. Drinking the barley wine that he brought, Phuntsok said calmly, 'My family have been celestial burial masters for generations. When I took over this craft eight years ago, I knew this was the destiny Buddha had set for me.'

让灵魂跟上
Waiting for Your Soul

支教者李文韬描写道：西藏的冬天只能用一个"慢"字形容，一壶酥油茶，一盘炸土豆，一副骰子，一个阳光明媚的角落，这是享受西藏冬天最好的写照。在这里，你不用与自然抗争，只需慢慢等待春天的到来。在大昭寺前，晒着太阳的边巴说："人走得太快的时候应该停下来，让灵魂跟上。"

Volunteer teacher Li Wentao declared Tibet's winter can only be described with one word: 'slow'. A pot of butter tea, a plate of fried potatoes, a pair of dice, and a sunny corner — this is the best portrayal of how to enjoy Tibet's winter. Here, you don't need to battle with nature; you only need to wait slowly for the arrival of spring. Basking in the sunshine in front of Jokhang Temple, a Tibetan named Benba said, 'When people are walking too fast, they should stop and let their soul catch up with them.'

评论

微观西藏
TIBET: FAST & FURIOUS

只为那最稀薄的空气
Just for that Thinnest Air

来西藏前会想，要去林芝去布达拉宫去纳木错，但到了西藏，觉得在八廓街看看藏民转经磕长头，闻一闻满街散发着的混杂了酥油香的藏香味道就心满意足了。这世上，逃课、私奔都算是疯狂，但最疯狂的莫过于不远万里只为呼吸几口世界上最稀薄的空气。

Before you come to Tibet, you might think of going to Nyingchi, to the Potala Palace, and to Lake Namtso. However, when you reach Tibet, you may feel satisfied just smelling the mingling fragrances of yak butter and Tibetan incense, while watching Tibetans circumambulating or prostrating on Barkhor Street. In this world, even cutting classes and eloping count as craziness, but the craziest thing is traveling a long distance, just to breathe a few mouthfuls of the thinnest air in the world.

雪域圣心
Sacred Heart of the Snow Land

初次进藏时觉得西藏人是友善的，再进藏，觉得西藏人甚至是调皮的。你看她，她就对你笑。你对她笑，她会对你挤眉弄眼吐舌头。这就是圣地培育出的圣心，圣心便是童心。

The first time you come to Tibet, you'll likely think Tibetans are very friendly. When you come to Tibet again, you will think Tibetans are even playful. If you look at a woman, she will smile back. If you smile at her, she will wink or stick out her tongue at you. This is the sacred heart fostered in this holy land, and at the core of the sacred heart is childlike innocence.

摄影：车刚

一块木板的温暖
The Warmth of a Wooden Board

西藏美协主席韩书力先生讲了这样一个故事:"冬天我下乡去采风,坐在冰冷的石头上画画,当地的藏民就把小木板放在太阳下晒热了然后悄悄递给我,还生怕打扰我画画。"在两个语言不通、生长环境迥异的人之间,藏民无所求的、真诚的举动,就温暖了另一个人的心,即使过了很多年。

Han Shuli, president of the Tibet Artists' Association, tells this story: 'I once went to the country to collect inspiration during the winter. When a local Tibetan saw me sitting on the cold stones while painting, he placed a small piece of wooden board under the sun and quietly gave it to me after it was warmed, being careful not to disturb me.' Between these two people who spoke different languages and grew up in very dissimilar environments, that Tibetan's simple and sincere act easily warmed another person's heart, even after many years.

风马旗
Prayer Flags (Wind Horse Flags)

最早的经幡上都印着一匹宝马,驮着燃着火焰的佛法僧三宝,这就是为什么经幡也叫作"风马旗"。据说经幡每被风吹拂一次,就等于系幡人吟诵了一遍经文,吟诵的次数越多就越能给自己和周边的人带来福分。"驴友"朵儿说,看到经幡,就看到了青藏高原。

The earliest prayer flags ever printed depicted a horse carrying the flaming Buddhist Three Jewels (Buddha, Dharma and Sangha) on its back, so prayer flags were also called 'wind horse flags'. It is said that once the flags are stirred by the wind, it means that the person who tied them has recited the scripture once. The more times he recites, the more blessings it will bring to himself and the people around him. Backpacker Duo Er says, 'When you see the prayer flags, you also see the Qinghai-Tibet Plateau.'

嫁给高原
Marrying the Plateau

画家韩书力这样描述他看到和体悟到的西藏高原独特的美:金色的阳光,碧蓝的天空,有体积有重量的祥云,广袤而荒寒的牧场村寨,庄严神秘的寺院,纯然朴素的民风,无求但友善的眼神,山歌、酒歌、驮马铃声的交响,人文与自然景观的智慧与和谐。正是这些让他的心留了下来,心甘情愿"嫁"给了这片高原。

Painter Han Shuli describes the unique beauty he saw and felt on the Tibetan plateau: 'The golden sunlight, the cyan sky, the voluminous and auspicious clouds, the vast wild pastures and villages, the solemn and mysterious temples, the pure and simple folkways, the plain but friendly eyes, the symphony of folk songs, drinking songs, and sounds of bells, and the cultural and natural sceneries of wisdom and harmony.' Such beauty settled Han's heart here and made him willingly marry this plateau.

敬畏
Reverence

作曲家三宝曾讲过一件事:他有次开着吉普车走很远的路去看纳木错湖。一路起伏不定、变幻莫测,然后眼前突然就出现了纯净湛蓝的天湖。那种感觉,像"踏破铁鞋无觅处,得来全不费工夫"的执着与解脱,又像"蓦然回首,那人却在灯火阑珊处"的意外与释然,让他产生了一种"顿悟之后的敬畏之情"。

Composer Sanbao tells this story: once he drove a jeep very far to see Lake Namtso. The journey was full of unpredictable ups and downs, but in the end the heavenly clear and azure lake suddenly appeared in front of his eyes. At that moment he experienced the perseverance and extrication described in a poem: 'You might have worn out a pair of iron shoes in fruitless search, yet by chance it came to you effortlessly.' He also felt the surprise and relief of another poem: 'You turned around, and there she was, standing under the scattered waning lights.' These experiences gave him a 'feeling of reverence as after sudden enlightenment'.

摄影：车刚

讨水却得鸡蛋
Asking for Water and Receiving an Egg

画家韩书力说："一次去采风，口干舌燥时敲开了一户普通人家的门想讨杯水。但主人不仅端来了茶，还煮了鸡蛋给我。"这鸡蛋是藏民甚至不舍得给孩子吃的。在西藏，一个人对你好，往往不是因为他对你有所求，而是因为在他的价值观里，与人为善便是天经地义，反之则是亏欠。

Painter Han Shuli says, 'I once took a field trip to gather inspiration. I felt extremely thirsty under the heat, so I knocked on an ordinary family's door and asked for a cup of water. However, the host didn't just bring me a cup of tea, but also boiled an egg for me.' At that time, eggs were something that Tibetans could not even afford to let their children eat. In Tibet, if a person is nice to you, often it is not that he or she wants to ask you for a favor, but because according to Tibetan values, helping others is the norm. If you do the contrary, it becomes a debt you owe.

评论

微观西藏
TIBET: FAST & FURIOUS

父母的期望
Parents' Expectations

中国藏学研究中心的格勒博士曾在西藏昌都地区询问了多个家庭的家长，问他们期待孩子将来从事什么工作。本来，他估计父母最希望孩子当喇嘛，因为藏区喇嘛地位很高，但没想到，60% 的父母希望孩子当干部，其次是医生，希望孩子当喇嘛的父母只占 3%。

Dr. Gelek from the China Tibetology Research Center once surveyed Tibetan parents in Qamdo, in order to find out what they expected their children to do. He originally thought parents would most likely expect their children to become lamas, since they enjoy high status in Tibet. To his surprise, 60% of the parents wanted their children to become cadres. Their second choice was doctors; only 3% wanted their children to become lamas.

简单的早餐
Simple Breakfasts

在一家西藏旅馆，也许你自认为吃了一份简单的早餐，但随即你会看到一位藏族姑娘的早餐只有糌粑和红茶。清晨的西藏从六毛一杯的甜茶开始。西藏人的生活很简单，他们认为：剩下是浪费，多吃亦是浪费，而浪费就是罪孽。

You may think you had a simple breakfast in a Tibetan hotel, but you'll change your mind when you see that a Tibetan girl's breakfast is only a bowl of *tsampa* and a cup of black tea. The morning starts for Tibetans with a cup of black tea that costs six dimes. Tibetans' lives are very simple. They believe, 'Leaving leftovers is wasting, but eating a lot is also wasting, and wasting is a sin.'

评论

行旅・品味
Travel and Taste

心如洗
Heart is Cleansed

有人说:"到了西藏,心如洗。"什么是心如洗?就是你在路边看到一头牦牛,你都觉得它是个有故事的无差别的生命,你甚至会不自觉地对它微笑。画家余友心说:"西藏对人的心灵有一种最透彻的清洗,甚至消毒。"

Some people say, 'Arriving in Tibet, your heart seems to be cleansed.' What does that mean? It is like when you see a yak on the roadside and feel it lives a life filled with stories no different from yours; you might even unconsciously smile at it. When painter Yu Youxin spoke about the excellence of Tibet, he said, 'Tibet is able to perform the most thorough cleansing, if not disinfection, of a person's heart.'

甜茶馆的秘密
Secrets of Sweet Tea Houses

现在西藏也开设了不少酒吧和咖啡馆,但是更有特色的还是村落中的甜茶馆。藏学家陈默在曲水采风时发现,下午 2 点到 6 点的甜茶馆里坐满了中年男子,他们花几块钱就能悠闲地消磨一个下午。而晚上 8 点以后,年轻人就聚在一起看汉语电视,唱卡拉 OK,甚至毫无顾忌地聊聊私密话题。

Nowadays, many bars and cafes have opened in Tibet, but the most distinctive are still the sweet tea houses in villages. When Tibetologist Chen Mo went to Quxu to investigate the local folklore, he found that from two to six sweet tea houses were filled with middle-aged men, who could spend a few yuan and stay there for the whole afternoon. After eight in the evening, young people would gather there to watch Chinese TV shows and sing karaoke. Sometimes they would even start chatting about personal topics without any self-consciousness.

摄影:觉果

微观西藏
TIBET: FAST & FURIOUS

山高人为峰
Becoming the Peak of the Mountain

1996年美国《户外》杂志记者乔恩·克拉考尔登上珠峰，他当时的感受是："当我步履沉重地缓慢登上通往山顶的最后几级台阶时，我有一种沉入水中、生命正缓慢前行的错觉。然后我发现，自己带着空空的氧气瓶跟一根残损的铝制勘测杆，站在一层薄薄的楔形的积雪上，再无更高的地方可攀了。"

Journalist Jon Krakauer wrote about his experience climbing Mount Qomolangma in 1996 in the American magazine *Outside*: 'When I slowly took those final few heavy steps toward the peak, I felt as if I were immersed in water and my life was slowly moving forward. Then I discovered that when I stood on top of a thin wedge of snow with a busted aluminum surveying rod and an empty bottle of oxygen, there were really no higher places to go.'

无人区的女子
A Woman in a Desolate Land

高原阳光强烈，纯朴的藏族姑娘就用酥油拌上煤灰涂在脸上防紫外线。西藏画派创始人之一余友心讲了这样一个故事：一次他外出采风，看到一位正在放牧的康巴女人拿着一面小镜子正在涂脂抹粉，而那里，是人迹罕至的"无人区"。

The sunlight is very strong on the plateau, so simple-minded Tibetan girls will coat their faces with a mixture of yak butter and coal ash to protect themselves from ultraviolet radiation. Yu Youxin, one of the founders of the Tibet Painting Style, told such a story: once he took a trip to collect inspirations and saw a Khampa woman herding sheep. She was holding a small mirror and putting on makeup, yet where she stood was a desolate land with very few visitors.

评论

行旅・品味
Travel and Taste

布达拉宫山下一晚
A Night at the Foot of the Potala Mountain

歌手朱哲琴曾描述过这样一个场景："我曾经在布达拉宫山下坐了一晚上。我就是静静地坐在那里，然后听风铃的声音，看月亮，到早上的时候，看见布达拉宫下的民居……第一盏灯亮起的时候，屋里的人开始走动，然后狗叫，人们开始转经。后来在《拉萨谣》里我试图倾诉那个时刻的情感，但也只能表达十分之一。"

Singer Dadawa describes a scene she experienced like this: 'I once sat for an entire night at the foot of the mountain the Potala Palace stands on. I just sat there quietly, listening to the sounds of the wind chimes, and staring at the moon. When the next morning arrived, I saw the dwellings downhill... When the first lamp was lit, people began to move about in the houses. Then the dogs started to bark, and people began their circumambulation of the day. In my song, "A Ballad of Lhasa", I tried to express the feelings of that moment, but I only succeeded in conveying a tenth of what I felt.'

茶路
Tea Road

茶，对于高原上的藏族人民来说，同粮食、水、空气一样重要。西藏不产茶叶，过去每年所需，都是靠人背畜驮、翻山越岭从四川或云南运进西藏。著名的茶马古道，雪山摩天，江河汹涌，断崖峭壁，道路凶险。在漫长的岁月里，商人们用自己的双脚，踏出了一条崎岖绵延的商贸通道和文化走廊。

Tea is as important as food, water, and air to Tibetans living on the plateau. Tibet doesn't produce tea leaves. In the past, their annual needs were met through the stocks carried from Sichuan and Yunnan provinces to Tibet. These stocks were packed on people's and animals' backs, tramping over hills and dales. On the famous Ancient Tea Route, you see the skyscraping snow mountains, the raging rivers, and the rough cliff walls, telling of the danger on the road. Over a long period of time, the merchants paced out a rugged commercial channel and a winding cultural corridor on foot.

微观西藏
TIBET: FAST & FURIOUS

把生命用来等待
Using Life for Waiting

在西藏，排队半小时也不觉得烦躁，来了这里就觉得自己似乎也没什么急事，像是回到了家，看看山，看看湖，然后心想：与其把生命用来奔跑，不如用来等待，至少在西藏可以这样尝试几次。

In Tibet, even if you stand in line for half an hour, you still won't feel annoyed. After you have come here, you seem to have nothing urgent to do; you feel as if you are at home. Looking at the mountains and lakes, you might think that it's better to wait than spend your life running. You should try this at least a few times in Tibet.

"醉人"的地方
An 'Intoxicating' Place

西藏是个"醉人"的地方，入时沉醉出亦醉。进入西藏时，醉于圣地美景，醉于醇香美酒，醉于风土人情；离开西藏后，还会"醉氧"，也就是因含氧量突然增高而昏昏沉沉，如同醉酒一般。

Tibet is an 'intoxicating' place. Upon arrival, you drown in its charms, and when you depart, you are still drunk on its aftertaste. When you enter Tibet, you become intoxicated by the scenery of this holy land, the aromatic mellow wines, and the local customs and folklore. Even after you have left, you might still get 'intoxicated by oxygen'. This is caused by the suddenly elevated levels of oxygen in the air, making people feel drowsy after leaving the high altitude.

摄影：李俊秀

"回到"?还是"回不到"?
To Return or Not to Return

西藏,有多少人梦寐以求。有人在歌中唱着"回到拉萨"。有人说:"坐在云朵下,听到内心一个声音在喊'你——快——回——来!'"但作家马原却说:"曾经以为它是我的,或者我是它的,或者我们互相拥有。21年往矣,它与我仍然迢迢万里。"

Many people dream of Tibet. Some people sing songs of 'returning to Lhasa'. Some people say that when they sit and have a rest they can hear their heart yelling, 'Come... back... soon!' However, writer Ma Yuan feels, 'I once believed that it belonged to me, or I belonged to it, or that we belonged to each other, but after the passing of twenty-one years, we are still separated by a vast distance.'

西藏把我点燃
Tibet Lit Me Up

到拉萨后,作家马原开创了一个西藏文学的新时代。他说:"如果不去西藏,可能我的小说会完全不一样。西藏使我脱胎换骨。""这都是拜西藏所赐……西藏是一个奇特的地方,能给你想象力,给你独特的角度和意境,没有任何一个地方可以和西藏做比较……西藏把我点燃了。"

After his arrival in Lhasa, author Ma Yuan spearheaded a new era of Tibetan literature. He says, 'If I'd never been to Tibet, my novels might have been completely different.' 'Tibet forged a different me. Tibet is an amazing place that pours inspiration into your head and gives you a unique perspective. Tibet really lit me up.'

微观西藏
TIBET: FAST & FURIOUS

海子的西藏
Hai Zi's Tibet

诗人海子曾去过两次西藏,并且写下了《西藏》《远方》等与西藏有关的诗。据说,他的墓碑正面有两个小龛,里面嵌着海子从西藏千里迢迢带回来的两块玛尼石,每块约有 20 公斤。他诗中说:"没有任何泪水使我变成花朵,没有任何国王使我变成王座",除了西藏。

The poet Hai Zi visited Tibet twice, and wrote 'Tibet', 'Remote Place' and other poems related to Tibet. It is said that on his tombstone there are two small niches in which two *mani* stones were inserted. He brought them from far-off Tibet, each weighing more than twenty kilograms. In his poem, he wrote, 'No tears can turn me into a flower, and no king can turn me into a throne', but Tibet can.

水在看你的心
The Water Watches Your Heart

作家凌仕江写过这样一件事:他曾在纳木错圣湖枯坐多日,面对那与世隔绝的蓝,他说自己想坐到天荒地老。而当他起身准备离开时,一位每天路过的老牧人,对他说了多日来的第一句话:你来纳木错看水,水在看你的心。

Author Ling Shijiang tells this story: once he sat at holy Lake Namtso for several days, and as he faced the incredible blue, he said to himself that he wanted to sit there forever. When he was about to leave, an old shepherd, who passed by him every day, talked to him for the first time in days: 'When you sit at Lake Namtso and look at the water, the water looks at your heart.'

评论

行旅·品味
Travel and Taste

摄影：车刚

难忘那顶帐篷
An Unforgettable Tent

一位"驴友"这样描述他在风雨来临之前走进的一个帐篷人家：帐篷里没有什么家具，几乎所有的东西都散放在地上，只有一尊佛像端放在正中的桌子上，佛像前成排的酥油灯也格外干净。

A backpacker describes a nomad's tent he went into before an imminent storm: 'There was little furniture in the tent, and almost everything was scattered on the ground. Only a Buddha statue was properly placed on the table in the middle, and the rows of butter lamps in front of it were also exceptionally clean.'

心灵的回归
Return of the Soul

藏族歌星韩红曾在接受采访时说，所谓的西藏采风，其实就是心情的放松和心灵的回归。"如果为了创作才去西藏，这样的做法岂不是太刻意了吗？"她说："我在唱歌的时候，闭上眼就是布达拉宫的红色和白色，那是一个宝地。"

Han Hong, a famous Tibetan singer, said in an interview that the so-called song-collecting impulse in Tibet is actually a relaxation of the mood and a return of the soul. 'If you go to Tibet just to find ideas for creating something, isn't this approach too instrumental?' Han went on, 'When I'm singing, if I close my eyes, the red and white colors of the Potala Palace will appear in front of me. That is a land of treasure.'

微观西藏
TIBET: FAST & FURIOUS

藏包子
Tibetan *Baozi*

藏包子以牛肉馅为主，形状同内地的包子类似。在过去，吃肉包子是一件奢侈的事，直到现在，许多老人依然认为吃肉包子是一件大事，而且还是一件"非常幸福的事情"。

Tibetan *baozi** uses beef as its principal filling, and its shape is similar to the mainland *baozi*. In the past, eating *baozi* with meat filling was considered a very luxurious thing. Even now, many old Tibetans still consider eating *baozi* with meat filling a big and also an 'extremely happy event'.

* A type of steamed, filled bun in various Chinese cuisines. There is much variation as to the filling and the preparations.

酥油茶
Butter Tea

陈坤在《突然就走到了西藏》中说，他"留恋着脚步丈量山路的喘息声，略咸的酥油茶，满脸皱纹的清澈眼神，纱纱的桑烟"。你有没有喝过"略咸的酥油茶"？据说，喝酥油茶，第一口异味难耐，第二口醇香流芳，第三口永世不忘。

Chen Kun, a Chinese actor, says in *Suddenly in Tibet*, 'I missed my breath when pacing the mountain path, tasting the slightly salty butter tea, seeing the clear eyes in the wrinkled faces, and drifting smoke of incense.' Have you ever tasted 'slightly salty butter tea'? They say that when drinking butter tea, the first sip delivers a strange and unbearable taste; the second sip leaves a lasting mellow feeling; and the third sip will leave a taste you never forget.

摄影：觉果

行旅·品味
Travel and Taste

味道
Tastes

最讲究的藏菜，牛肉要选日土产的，因其肉质细嫩；吊汤则选白定藏鸡，因其汤浓味鲜；野菜必选第一声雷声响前的，因其鲜嫩；吃鱼要吃藏历二三月间上市的，因其膘肥润香。藏菜最好的烹饪也许就是风与火。生牛肉片直接晒干，吃的时候蘸点盐末，就是一道绝佳的特色美食。

In the most exquisite Tibetan food, the beef needs to be chosen from Rutok County for its tenderness; cooking soup should use Tibetan chicken from Palding for a fresh, strong soup flavor. Wild vegetables must be chosen before the first sound of thunder for their delicacy. Fish should come to market between the second and third month of the Tibetan calendar, since they are then plump and have a smooth taste. The best cook of Tibetan food is perhaps just wind and fire. Dry the raw beef slices directly in the sun, sprinkle on some salt when eating them, and they will become an excellent local delicacy.

马未都眼里的朝圣者
Pilgrims in Ma Weidu's Eyes

收藏家马未都讲起西藏行遇到的两位朝圣者时说："在晨霭湿润的空气中，远处两位宗教虔诚者，一前一后地悠悠磕着长头，迈步，合十，举手，匍匐，五体投地，周而复始。我急喊停车，每个人都不停地拍照摄像。以人类自觉的行为让同类如此热衷关注，磕长头算是一个。"

When collector Ma Weidu talked about two pilgrims he met on his trip to Tibet, he said, 'In the moist air from morning mist, two devout pilgrims from afar calmly prostrated. They took a step, put their palms together, raised their hands, crawled and threw themselves onto the ground, repeating it over and over again in succession. I hurriedly asked the driver to stop our car, and everybody began taking pictures of them. Speaking of conscientious actions that can draw such attention from other humans, prostration counts as one of them.'

评论

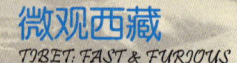

茶杯里的香格里拉
Shangri-La in a Teacup

做酥油,是把奶汁搅得水乳分离;做酥油茶,是把酥油和茶汁打到油茶交融。浓香扑鼻的酥油茶,是西藏人每天必不可少的饮料,它可以强筋泽气、和脾御寒。酥油茶里有西藏人对生存的体悟与智慧,有人说,酥油茶是茶杯里的香格里拉。

When making yak butter, one needs to churn the milk until the curds separate from the water. When making butter tea, one needs to stir the yak butter and tea until they blend well. Butter tea's aroma can easily fill one's nostrils, and it is an essential daily drink for Tibetans. Butter tea can strengthen the body, nourish the soul, coordinate dispositions, and keep out the cold. It contains Tibetans' comprehension and wisdom of survival. Some people say butter tea is 'Shangri-La in a teacup'.

生牛肉
Raw Beef

生牛肉是很多藏族人的最爱。有位旅游者这样描述第一次吃这种食物的经历:轮到我了,我用筷子搛了块生牛肉,在辣椒酱里边使劲地蘸,迟迟不敢放进嘴里。朋友说:"试试吧,非常爽口的。"我心一横,一口塞进嘴里。嚼了两口,绷紧的神经一下子松弛了,原来生牛肉并非想象中那样难吃,反而嫩嫩的,蛮可口。

Many Tibetans enjoy eating raw beef, and a traveler recounts his first experience of it: 'When it was my turn, I picked up a piece with chopsticks, dipped it in the chili sauce and hesitated before taking a bite. My friend encouraged me, "Try it. It's tasty." I knuckled down and put it in my mouth. After two bites, I felt it wasn't bad at all, but amazingly tender and delicious.'

评论

行旅·品味
Travel and Taste

藏面
Tibetan Noodles

西藏当地人最爱的面食就是藏面了。一碗捧出，精致发光的器皿，清亮的汤料，浑厚的面条，可人的牦牛肉丁，翠绿的葱花，配上一碟深红色的藏式酸萝卜和一小碗辣酱，令人垂涎欲滴。难怪有人在藏面馆里饱餐一顿后感慨说：这不但是最生活化的藏餐，还代表了西藏人的豪放与浓郁。

The favorite wheat-based food of Tibetans is the local noodles. When a bowl of Tibetan noodles is presented, the delicate gloss of the vessel, the clear soup, the thick noodles, the pleasant diced yak beef, and the chopped jade green scallions, along with a dish of crimson Tibetan pickled radish and a small bowl of hot sauce make people lick their lips. No wonder someone exclaimed, after having a big meal in a Tibetan noodle restaurant, 'This is not only the liveliest Tibetan meal, but it also represents the vigorousness and intensity of Tibetans.'

真正的石锅鸡
Real Stone-Pot Chicken

林芝八一镇的鲁朗石锅鸡也许是西藏最有特色的一道菜：锅用的是雅鲁藏布江两岸的天然岩石，挖空后，在江水中浸泡30天才可使用。放入藏香鸡和几十种药材炖上几个钟头才能做成欲罢不能的美味。有位旅游者说她恨不得带一口一千多块钱的锅回京，但因为新锅没有老锅的油润与气韵，只得作罢。

The Lulang stone-pot chicken in Bayi, the capital of Nyingchi County, is perhaps the most distinctive dish in Tibet. The pot is made of natural stones on the shores of Yarlung Tsangpo River. These stones are hollowed out and soaked in the water of Yarlung Tsangpo for thirty days before being used as pots. This especially delicious dish is made by putting Tibetan chicken and dozens of Chinese herbs into the pot and stewing it for several hours. A tourist once remarked how she was itching to take a pot home although it cost 1,000 yuan, but new pots didn't have the gloss or aroma of the old ones, so she had to give up.

微观西藏
TIBET: FAST & FURIOUS

茶与盐巴
Tea and Salt

每逢藏历新年，西藏人总在神龛上供上茶和晶盐用以敬神。婚礼时，在新娘经过的路上，乡亲们会在门口摆上茶叶和盐巴，迎亲者边收边走，收的不仅是礼物，更是大家的祝福。西藏人认为，来自内地的茶叶和当地的盐巴，在酥油筒内融合成芳香可口的酥油茶，是世界上最圆满的结合。

On New Year's Day of the Tibetan calendar, people put tea and salt in shrines as offerings to the gods. At wedding ceremonies, fellow villagers put tea leaves and salt at the doors along the road the bride passes. The groom's party, who escorts the bride, will collect it as they walk by. What they receive are not only gifts, but also blessings. Tibetans believe that the delicious buttered tea, made from mainland tea leaves and local salt in butter cylinders, is the best combination in the world.

甜茶是舶来品
Sweet Tea Is an Imported Idea

在过去，西藏人只喝酥油茶和青稞酒，甜茶是英国人和印度人爱喝的洋玩意儿。西藏人认为"甜茶是白糖加奶渣水，一没油性，二没酒性，没劲道"。但后来甜茶这种洋玩意儿渐渐成为西藏人茶桌上的新宠，在甜茶馆喝茶逐渐融入西藏人的生活里。

In the past, Tibetans only drank butter tea and barley wine. Sweet tea, in their minds, was a foreign product made for the British and the Indian people. Tibetans believed that 'sweet tea was only the mixture of milk dregs, water, and sugar, lacking oil, alcohol, and rich flavor.' But gradually this foreign product became a new favorite of Tibetans, and drinking tea in sweet tea houses eventually became a part of their daily lives.

评论

行旅・品味
Travel and Taste

藏家宴
The Particular Tibetan Dishes

拉萨的"藏家宴"是众多游客寻觅的宝地。有美食家带着儿子来享受酥油茶作为开场白的藏式大餐，主菜有血肠、风干牛肉、藏青菜、生牛肉酱、烤羊排、藏红花鸡汤，还有主食糌粑。不要问味道怎么样，看看11岁的小伙子摸着滚圆的肚皮走出来就知道了。

The 'Tibetan family feast' in Lhasa is a treasured experience many tourists seek. One food-lover took his son to enjoy this Tibetan feast which begins with butter tea. Its entrees included blood sausage, air-dried beef, Tibetan greens, raw beef paste, roasted lamb chops, saffron chicken soup, and the main course *tsampa*. Don't ask how it tasted, just watch that eleven-year-old boy and you will know everything — he walked away holding his round belly.

西藏的酸奶
Tibetan Yogurt

吃了西藏的酸奶，也许会颠覆你对酸奶的概念。西藏的酸奶黏稠、浓郁，但特别酸，即使加了白糖和蜂蜜，第一次喝的人仍会被酸得龇牙咧嘴。如果你爱上它的原始、厚重，每次吃酸奶的日子，都会像是过节。

After tasting Tibetan yogurt, your concept of yogurt might be completely changed. The yogurt in Tibet is thick and strong, but it's especially sour. Even with sugar and honey, people who taste it for the first time still wince at its sourness. However, if you begin to like this yogurt's originality and thickness, then every time you have this yogurt, it will seem like a festival treat.

摄影：车刚

微观西藏
TIBET: FAST & FURIOUS

生日也平常
Celebrating Birthdays Becoming Common

千百年来，尽管很多藏族人以"次吉"（初一）、"次昂"（初五）、"边巴"（星期六）等出生的日期作为名字，但大部分藏族人并不清楚自己出生的具体年月日，过生日更是很少有的事，一般只有高寿的老人才过一次。不过现在，越来越多的西藏人也开始以过生日为时尚了。

Though for centuries upon centuries many Tibetans have used *tseji* (the first day of every Tibetan month), *tseang* (the fifth day of every Tibetan month), *benba* (Saturday) and other dates of birth as their names, most Tibetans still don't know the specific year, month, and day they were born on, much less celebrate their own birthdays. Usually people celebrate their birthdays only once in their whole lives, and that's when they're very old. However, nowadays an increasing number of Tibetans are starting to celebrate their birthdays.

玛尼石上的圆圈
Circles on a *Mani* Stone

1994年，画家韩书力在藏东的一个玛尼石堆上发现了一块新刻的玛尼石，刻了很多嘴形的圆圈，不解其意。后来才知刻石头的是本村先富起来的人，目的是请众乡邻不要嫉妒，不要说东道西，这就是古老的观念在新时期的一种折变。

In 1994, painter Han Shuli found a newly carved *mani* stone on top of a *mani* stone pile in eastern Tibet. Many mouth-shaped circles were engraved on the stone, and Han was very confused about the meaning. Later he was informed that the creator of that *mani* stone was the first person who became rich in that village, so he used it to pray that the villagers would not envy nor dish dirt on him. This shows the change of old ideas in a new era.

评论

行旅·品味
Travel and Taste

摄影：聂晓阳

教育理念的改变
Changes in Educational Ideas

摄影家车刚谈到西藏人教育理念的改变时说：过去西藏老牧民家里最光荣的是出一个喇嘛，不是出个大学生。而现在更多的牧民不会要求孩子辍学回家放牧，而是更愿意他们继续学业，以便能够走出草原，到城镇寻求更好的发展。

When photographer Che Gang was asked to comment on the changes in Tibetans' educational ideas, he said, 'In the past, the most glorious thing for the family of a Tibetan herdsman was that someone in the family became a lama and not a college student. Nowadays, more and more herdsmen won't ask their children to drop out of school and do sheep herding at home. Many of them are willing to let their children continue studying so that they can get out of the grasslands and seek a better future in the towns and cities.'

在自家马厩里生孩子
Giving Birth in Stables

据纪录片导演书云记载：江孜县的卡麦乡政府为了鼓励当地妇女安全生育，规定：到卫生所生产奖励 200 元，否则罚款 200 元。可是一些女人忌惮鬼神，宁可交罚款也要在自家的马厩里生孩子，以图安心。现代医学在传统习俗面前只得暂时落败。

According to the records of documentary director Shu Yun, the government of Karmai Township in Gyangze County worked out a policy to encourage local women to give birth in health centers. The policy rewards those who go to health centers with 200 yuan and fine those who don't go with 200 yuan. Nevertheless, in their fear of ghosts, some women would rather pay the fine and give birth in their stables so that they can feel at ease. Hence, modern medical science has had to give way to traditional customs in these cases.

微观西藏
TIBET: FAST & FURIOUS

渺小的人类
Small Human Beings

有记者问西藏著名画师尼玛泽仁:"为什么你画中的人物在自然中都显得很小?"他答道:"人类在自然面前本来就是渺小的。藏族在那样一个物质贫瘠的环境中能生存下来,还能创造出灿烂的文化,靠的就是这种与自然和谐相处的精神。"

A reporter asked the famous Tibetan painter Nyima Tsering, 'Why are human beings so small in front of nature in your paintings?' He answered, 'Human beings are indeed small in front of nature. Tibetans depend on a harmonious spirit for surviving in this barren environment to create a brilliant culture.'

不可缺的酥油茶
Indispensible Butter Tea

传统藏族人每天起床要做的第一件事情就是烧茶打茶。要是早上没喝一杯酥油茶,一天都会觉得心里少点什么似的。传统藏族家庭的早餐就是酥油茶和糌粑。即使住在城里的年轻一代也没有几个人能抵挡得了酥油茶的香味,甚至很多人直接用它来喂养婴儿。

The first thing traditional Tibetans do when they get out of bed is brew tea. If they can't have a cup of butter tea in the morning, they will feel that something is missing all day long. The breakfast of a traditional Tibetan family is butter tea and *tsampa*. Even the young people who grow up in cities can't resist the aroma of butter tea. Many people even use it to feed their babies.

摄影:车刚

行旅·品味
Travel and Taste

随时随地"过林卡"
Spending a Day of *Lingka* Anywhere, Anytime

"林卡"在汉语里是"园林"的意思。挑一个好日子，男女老少"过林卡"是藏族的一种民族习惯。不过现在，过林卡不一定非得去一个正式的园林，只要有一片树林或一片草地，人们搭起帐篷就能过一个热热闹闹的林卡。即便连树林都没有，在一片开阔的空地上，搭起帐篷照样能开开心心地过一天。

Lingka means 'garden' in Tibetan. Picking a good day to 'do *lingka*' (or enjoy the outdoors) is a custom of Tibetans, regardless of age or sex. But nowadays, they don't necessarily have to go to a real garden or park. As long as there is an expanse of grass or a grove, they can set up a tent and have a lively *lingka*. Even if there aren't any trees in sight, they can still spend a joyous day setting up a tent in an open area.

现代祝酒歌
Modern Toast Songs

西藏人爱喝酒，而且是"无歌不欢"。在席间唱歌有不少讲究，歌词的内容一定要和所敬酒的人身份相符。比如敬家中长者时要唱"祝老鹰长寿，小鹰心情愉快"。而现在年轻人的肚子里装的都是流行歌曲，唱起来敬酒就会引来哄堂大笑，比如一个女儿敬爸爸时唱"我总是心太软，心太软"。

Tibetans love drinking, and they always have suitable songs to show their pleasure, believing in the sentiment 'no songs, no fun'. Banquet songs require that the content be pertinent to the person being toasted. For example, when you propose a toast to elders, the words should be: 'Here's to the elder eagles enjoying longevity, and the young eagles being happy all the time.' However, young people nowadays only remember popular songs. When they sing and toast someone, they often set the whole room in laughter. For example, picture a daughter singing, 'My heart is always too tender, too tender...' when toasting her dad.

评论

155

微观西藏
TIBET: FAST & FURIOUS

雅鲁藏布江上的活化石
Living Fossils on the Yarlung Tsangpo River

在雅鲁藏布江的航道上，仍然漂荡着着两千年前的金黄色身影——牛皮船，它似乎无视现代交通工具的挑战，运载货物、打鱼作业，优哉游哉，飘然来去。无怪乎廖东凡先生说：牛皮船，它是漫长岁月凝聚成的黄色化石。

On the Yarlung Tsangpo River float the golden shapes of cowhide boats that are 2,000 years old. Ignoring the challenges from modern transportation, they continue their work in shipping and fishing, drifting leisurely from here to there. No wonder folklorist Liao Dongfan said that the cowhide boats are 'yellow fossils formed over countless years'.

幸运与幸福
Luck and Happiness

到了西藏，除了寻幽探胜，更重要的是获得精神升华、心灵洗礼；但最重要的，是寻找属于这一方水土和人民的智慧，因为在这个纷繁的世界里，要有一双慧眼，才能看到真理。在西藏，一个"驴友"知道自己该看什么，是幸运的；而他知道该怎么看，那就是幸福的了。

When you arrive in Tibet, in addition to make unexpected discoveries, you'll have the chance to receive spiritual refinement and purification of the heart. Nevertheless, the most important thing is to search for the wisdom of the land and locals, since in this sophisticated world, you can only see the truth with a pair of inquisitive eyes. In Tibet, if a backpacker knows what to see, then he or she is lucky; if this backpacker also knows how to see, then that is happiness.

评论

行旅·品味
Travel and Taste

摄影：车刚

传统与现代共存
Coexistence of the Traditional and the Modern

小喇嘛扎西曾对采访他的记者说：柏油马路上可以开汽车，也可以跑马；收录机可以放在豪华房间里，也可以装在马背褡裢里；同样，一群乡下人可以一面接受医生的治疗，一面继续数捻佛珠、默诵经文，获得心理上的安慰，继续以信仰作为他们的精神支柱。

A lama named Tashi once told reporters in an interview that you can either drive a car or ride a horse on an asphalt road; likewise a tape player can be placed in a ritzy room or stuffed into duffel bags mounted on horseback. In the same manner, villagers can enjoy the benefits of modern medicine, and at the same time twist prayer beads, silently recite the scriptures, and maintain their spiritual pillar of faith.

劳动时要唱歌
You Should Sing When Laboring

藏族作家白玛娜珍注意到：一些现代化的工程队劳动时很严肃，从不唱歌嬉戏，三个月就能完成过去半年多的活；但传统的藏族工程队干活一般比较悠然，午休吃饭喝茶就要用两个小时，劳动时还要唱歌。

Tibetan writer Pema Nadron noticed that some modern engineering teams are very serious at work, and they would never sing or play with each other. Therefore, they could finish the work that used to take half a year in three months. However, the traditional Tibetan engineering teams usually seemed to be very relaxed at work. The noon break, during which they would go for lunch and tea, usually lasted nearly two hours. After coming back to work, they would sing as they labored.

微观西藏
TIBET: FAST & FURIOUS

"第一条"裙子
'The First Skirt'

旅居西藏多年的作家马丽华讲了一件有趣的往事：1985年夏天，马丽华穿着自己缝制的、据说是西藏"第一条裙子"上街，引起很多人围观。她说，现在，就算你穿着奇装异服，恐怕也不会有人多看你几眼。西藏这片土地同西藏人一样，海纳百川，包容万象，时尚与传统在这片土地上，共存而和谐。

Ma Lihua, a writer who sojourned in Tibet for many years, tells this interesting story: in the summer of 1985, Ma went into the street wearing a self-made skirt, allegedly the first skirt in Tibet, drawing many people's attention. She says that now, even if you wear some outlandish clothes, few Tibetans will stare at you. They are just like the land of Tibet, accepting everything and encompassing all behaviors. Both fashion and tradition live on this land, coexisting harmoniously.

别想多了
Don't Overthink

有人说，如果你给一位陌生的西藏人某种食物，他们可能只有两种想法：想吃就吃，不想吃就不吃。但对那些浸润在所谓现代文明中的人们来说，他们可能会有很多种想法，比如这食物干净吗？你为什么要给我吃？我吃了需要回报你什么吗？……既然到了西藏，请带着一颗纯净之心。

Some people say, if you give Tibetans some food, they may simply eat it if they want to, or not eat it if they don't want to. But people who are immersed in the so-called modern civilization could have many thoughts, such as, 'Is this food clean? Why do you give it to me? Do I need to give you anything in return?...' Since you have come to Tibet, please keep a pure heart.

评论

行旅・品味
Travel and Taste

摄影：聂晓阳

慈悲心
A Heart with Mercy

著名藏学家王尧先生在一次采访中提到，很多藏族人家围在一起喝茶吃饭，一定要开门看看外面是否有乞讨的人，如果有就一定要分一些食物给他们，因为他们觉得吃独食是可耻的。他说，他对藏族文化体会最深的是：慈悲心与同情心。

Famous Tibetologist Wang Yao once mentioned during an interview that the first thing many Tibetan families do when they gather around for some tea or a meal is to open the door and look to see if any beggars are around. If there are, they will certainly share some food with them, since they think eating alone is shameful. Wang remarked his deepest impression of Tibetan culture is hearts full of mercy and compassion.

生存之道
A Way of Surviving

为了避免恼人的高原反应，有人记录了这样一段东道主常会反复告诫来藏友人的话："吃饭不要太饱，走路不要快跑，说话不要太吵，喝酒更是要少。"几句叮嘱，其实说的是一些朴素的生存之道：知足、守常、宁静、清明。

In order to help avoid altitude sickness, someone has recorded a saying that the hosts often warn newcomers with 'Don't have too much when eating; don't go too fast when walking; don't speak too loud when talking; don't consume too much when drinking.' These words actually state the simple art of living: contentment, conservation, serenity, and sobriety.

微观西藏
TIBET: FAST & FURIOUS

西藏不是博物馆
Tibet Is Not a Museum

一位西藏学者说，到西藏旅行的人往往有两个极端，一种是带着无知狂妄的心态，来寻找落后的地方，甚至是找毛病、找污点；另一种则是带着顶礼膜拜的心态，来寻找所谓的香巴拉。但西藏不是博物馆，来西藏首先要有平常心。

A Tibetologist once said, 'There are two extremes among foreigners that travel to Tibet. One is coming with an ignorant and conceited mind in search of a backward place. Some even purposefully look for stains and faults in Tibet. The other is coming with a worshipping mind, seeing only the so-called 'Shambhala', or the Buddhist Pure Land. However, Tibet is not a museum. The first thing you should have when coming to Tibet is a balanced mind.'

高原反应的哲理
Philosophy of Altitude Sickness

高原反应真是让人琢磨不定，也许你身体很好，结果你反应最强烈，也许衣裳脱猛了，话说快了，路走急了，反应就来了。旅行是体会别人的生活，而西藏还给你一个体会"年迈"的机会，把自己想成耄耋老人，更低，更慢，更弱，只有这样，你才会是这雪域高原最终的强者。

Altitude sickness is truly unpredictable. Maybe you were fit as a fiddle, but your stress was fierce. Maybe you took off your clothes too quickly, talked too fast, or walked too hurriedly, then the altitude sickness struck right away. Traveling is to taste others' lives, and Tibet gives you an opportunity to experience an 'aged' self. Think of yourself as an elderly person; let yourself become quieter, slower, and softer. Only in this way can you become a strong person on this plateau in the end.

评论

行旅・品味
Travel and Taste

慢就是快
Slow Is Fast

对于高原反应，有人总结了三点：女人比男人容易适应，年长的比年轻的容易适应，体质较弱的比体质强的容易适应。但无论怎样，预防高原反应最重要的三点，第一是放慢，第二是放慢，第三还是放慢。在西藏，慢就是快。

If we must adjust to a high altitude, there are three points to remember: first, women adapt better than men; second, the old adapt better than the young; and third, people with weaker constitutions adapt more easily than those stronger ones. However, the most important precautions against altitude sickness are firstly, to take it slow; secondly, to take it slow; and thirdly, to take it slow once more. In Tibet, slow is fast.

西藏审美
The Tibetan Aesthetic

在八廓街拍照，你的镜头会不自觉地躲开那些帅哥美女，而转向那些饱经风霜的面孔，不是因为他们特别，而是因为在他们的脸上，你看到了岁月沉淀下的坚韧和智慧，这便是西藏审美。

When you are taking photos on Barkhor Street, your lens will unconciously stay away from 'hotties' and turn toward those weather-beaten Tibetan faces. Not that they are exotic, but because on their faces, you can find the tenacity and wisdom accumulated over time, and this is the Tibetan aesthetic.

摄影：车刚

微观西藏
TIBET: FAST & FURIOUS

摄影：聂晓阳

热烈与安静的碰撞
A Collision of Warmth and Quietness

西藏人是爱跳爱唱的，开心了唱歌，难过了也唱歌，休息时唱歌，劳动时也唱歌。西藏的建筑是活泼的，雪白乌黑喇嘛红，都是又浓烈又大胆的颜色。旅居西藏40年的画家韩书力却说："西藏是歌舞天堂，色彩海洋，但在人文环境中，西藏是安静的。"也许，西藏外在的热烈正是因为他们内心的平静。

Tibetans love dancing and singing. When happy, they sing; when upset, they also sing. They sing while resting; they also sing while working. The buildings in Tibet are vibrant. Snow-white, jet-black, and crimson (like the color of a lama robe) are all bright and contrasting colors. However, after residing in Tibet for forty years, painter Han Shuli said, 'Tibet is a heaven of songs and dances and an ocean of colors. Nevertheless, in terms of the cultural environment, Tibet is quiet.' Maybe the outside warmth is just a result of their minds' quietness.

不用擦掉的酥油茶渍
The Butter Tea Stains That Don't Need to Be Wiped off

喝酥油茶时，外来者会迅速擦掉沾到嘴唇上的茶渍，但当地人却不擦，因为西藏气候干燥，而酥油能很好地保护嘴唇。有人说，西藏人有最朴素而简单的生活方式，所以不要机械地用外来者的标准衡量他们。把心打开，才能发现一个更真实的西藏。

When drinking butter tea, tourists quickly wipe the remaining drops of tea from their lips, but the locals do not. This is because Tibet has a dry climate, and the yak butter from the tea is great for protecting lips. As some people say, Tibetans have their own plain and simple ways of living, so don't automatically use an outsider's criterion to judge them. Open your heart, then you can find the real Tibet.

楼梯哲学
The Staircase Philosophy

刚到西藏的人头上经常撞出很多包，因为藏式建筑楼梯非常陡，如果不习惯弯腰，就会经常撞到屋顶。把楼梯设计得陡一些本是为了防止"鬼"上楼，但低矮的屋顶却在不知不觉中提醒人们谦卑，而谦卑正是藏族人在高寒缺氧的世界屋脊上的生存之道。

People who come to Tibet for the first time often have many bruises on their heads, because the staircases of Tibetan buildings are very steep. If you are not used to bending over, your head will often hit the ceiling. Tibetans originally designed steep stairs to prevent ghosts from going upstairs, but the low ceiling has been unwittingly reminding people to be modest. This is how Tibetans have survived on this cold and oxygen-deficient roof of the world.

评论

微观西藏
TIBET: FAST & FURIOUS

缺氧到底是什么感觉
What Is Hypoxia Like?

作家毕淑敏刚进藏时曾问老兵："缺氧是不是像感冒时鼻子里堵满了鼻涕的感觉？"老兵笑了笑，给了个更确切的比喻："缺氧就像有人掐住你的脖子，然后用鞭子赶着你在玻璃罩里跑，喘不上气。"他还教了一个治缺氧头疼的土办法：用捆行李的带子在太阳穴上使劲多缠几圈。

When writer Bi Shumin first arrived in Tibet, she asked a veteran, 'Does hypoxia feel like having a stuffed up nose?' The veteran laughed and answered with a more precise simile: 'Hypoxia feels like being seized by the throat and whipped to run around in a glass container. You just can't catch your breath.' He also taught her an indigenous remedy for the headaches caused by hypoxia: wrap your luggage straps a few times around your temples tightly.

《西藏生死书》
The Tibetan Book of Living and Dying

演员陈坤可以说是一位藏缘很深的人，但他与西藏结缘还是因为另一个人——演员赵薇。一次，陈坤去帮赵薇搬行李，她的房间里有本书，封面上写着《西藏生死书》。赵薇随手递给陈坤说："给你看吧。"陈坤后来说，这本书带他走入西藏，改变了他的人生。

Actor Chen Kun has a deep and close attachment to Tibet. However, this connection was established by another person, i.e. Zhao Wei, a Chinese actress. Once, Chen helped Zhao move her luggage and found a book titled *The Tibetan Book of Living and Dying* in her room. Zhao casually handed him the book and said, 'Here, take it.' Chen later said that this book led him to Tibet and finally changed his whole life.

评论

仍是祖先的姿势
Sitting Like His Ancestors

有作家在藏北考察时,发现当地牧民认为自己生活中的一切都是天经地义、命中注定。她曾看到一位牧民盘坐在炉前,左手握着羊皮风袋,右手向炉内撒羊粪蛋。她的第一个念头是:他以他祖先的姿势坐在那里。

An author went to the north of Tibet and discovered that the local residents viewed everything in their lives as predestined and unalterable. She once saw a shepherd sitting cross-legged in front of an oven, his left hand holding a sheepskin bellows and his right hand feeding the fire with dried sheep manure. The first thing she thought was, 'He sat there in the same posture of his ancestors.'

高原上的牧女
Shepherdesses on the Plateau

年轻的牧女往往被形容为高原上盛开的鲜花。有人这样描写她们:她们的头发往往梳成很多小辫,装饰着各种金银首饰珊瑚松石,从前额分两边披在身后;腰间挂着奶钩、小刀、针线盒等心爱之物。她们在牧场上急行缓走,头上和腰间的配饰叮当作响,如同奏起一支支愉悦的曲子响彻苍茫牧野。

Young shepherdesses are often described as plateau flowers in blossom. Their hair is plaited into many braids and decorated with gold and silver ornaments, coral and turquoise stones. They part their hair in the middle on the forehead and let it hang down at the back. Milk hooks, knives, sewing boxes and other things they treasure hang from their waists. When they walk across the pasture, either hurriedly or slowly, their head and waist ornaments tinkle like joyous songs in the wilderness.

摄影:车刚

微观西藏
TIBET: FAST & FURIOUS

藏式民居
Tibetan Dwellings

"驴友"梁会平曾这样描写藏式民居：门庭的修饰是最为艳丽的色彩，底色多为纯净的蓝。门的顶端多半会放置一具牛头骨架。房子四周的最高处都会插上五彩经幡。在高高的山上，在横跨溪流的两岸，在这样通透的纤尘不染的天幕下，也只有这样的房子才相配。

Backpacker Liang Huiping describes Tibetan dwellings like this: 'They decorated the doors with the most brilliant colors, using pure blue as the background. A set of cow skulls was often placed on the top of the door. At the highest spots around the house would be placed colorful prayer flags. Often sitting on hillocks or beside streams, only these kinds of houses could match the transparent and perfectly unstained canopy of heaven.'

马未都的感慨
Ma Weidu's Sigh

文化名人马未都曾感慨说："西藏太神秘了，一个不宜于人类居住的高原环境，至少两千年前就有藏族祖先居住，他们不仅创造了生命的奇迹，还创造了举世震惊的文化。"他说："多数时候我们想不通历史，更想不通人生，那就去西藏吧，它能帮我们想通。"

Intellectual celebrity Ma Weidu once sighed with emotion, 'Tibet is too mysterious. More than 2,000 years ago, Tibetan ancestors began to live on this plateau that was not suitable for human beings. They have created not only a miracle of life, but also an astonishing culture that struck the world with amazement.' He went on, 'Often we cannot understand history, not to mention our own lives. Go to Tibet then. It will help us figure it out.'

评论

印象·讲述

Impressions and Expositions

微观西藏
TIBET: FAST & FURIOUS

去除魅惑
Disenchantment

说起西藏，无论是去过还是没去过，似乎所有人都能说上两句，有时这并非基于事实，而是基于想象。很多人希望那里是纯精神的、单纯的、浪漫的，但藏族作家阿来却说："西藏首先是一个族群的现实生活。我的写作不是为了渲染它的神秘，而是为了去除魅惑，告诉世界，这个族群的人也是人类大家庭中的一员。"

When talking about Tibet, everyone, no matter whether he or she has been there or not, seems to be able to say something about it. Sometimes their remarks are only based on fantasy rather than facts. Many people assume that Tibet is purely spiritual, simple, and romantic, but Tibetan writer Alai once said, 'Tibet is first related to the real life of an ethnic group. My work is not to render it mysterious, but to help remove the fantasies that shroud it, and to tell the world that this ethnic group is also a member of human society.'

信仰的力量
Strength of Faith

藏族作家次仁罗布说，最近几年中国国家级文学奖获奖作品中，少数民族作品比较突出，这是因为少数民族文学里有更多精神的东西，有一种信仰的力量。随着现代文明的侵入，传统与现代之间会有很激烈的争斗，有些东西将会消亡，但那些真正对人有内在吸引力的传统将最终赢得生存。

Tibetan author Tsering Norbu says that these past few years, among the works that have won China's national literary awards, those from minority ethnic groups stand out the most. This is because there is more spiritual content in minority literature and there is a power of belief. With the invasion of modern civilization, traditional and modern cultures have been in fierce conflict. Some things will die out, but those traditions that have a real inner attraction for people will generally survive.

评论

摄影：聂晓阳

乐天知命
Easily Contented

作家次仁罗布：在藏北，很多牧民仍然很穷，但是这并不意味着他们不快乐，而他们的快乐，就来自于他们有信仰。他们相信今生的现状是上辈子的言行造成的，所以乐天知命，对什么都能够接受。同时，他们也努力过好这辈子，希望下辈子可以得好报。有信仰，他们过得就更加认真专心。

Author Tsering Norbu says, 'In Tibet, many herdsmen are still poor, but this doesn't mean that they are unhappy. Their happiness stems from their beliefs. They believe that this life's circumstances are caused by the previous life's words and deeds, so they are easily contented and capable of accepting anything. Meanwhile, they also try to live a good life, hoping for a good reward in their next reincarnation. With this belief, they can live more earnestly.'

看友识人
Understand People by Seeing Their Friends

藏医丹增塔克：我看一个人值不值得信任，就要看他交朋友的时间长不长。一个人没有老朋友，那这个人是不可靠的。我认识的藏族邻居中，大部分人都有很多老朋友，他们交朋友不那么功利，不是为了互相利用，而真正是因为大家谈得来才交朋友。

Tibetan doctor Tenzin Take says, 'When I'm judging whether a person is trustworthy or not, it will depend on how many old friends he has. If a man has no old friends, he must be unreliable. Most Tibetan neighbors I know have lots of old friends. They make friends not for personal interest, nor for taking advantage of each other, but for the reason that they can talk freely with each other.'

微观西藏
TIBET: FAST & FURIOUS

摄影：车刚

原来你也在西藏
You Are Also in Tibet

有人说，西藏是离太阳最近的地方，是世界上最后一块净土。一碧如洗的晴空、雄伟超拔的雪山、随风飘扬的经幡、神秘虔诚的玛尼堆、一路风尘的朝圣者、永不停歇的转经筒……很多人向往西藏、痴迷西藏，若在这里遇见，记得说一句：哦，原来你也在西藏。

Some people say Tibet is the closest place to the sun. It is the last pure land in the world. A clear sky as if it has been washed, the magnificent and steep snow mountains, the prayer flags fluttering in the wind, the mysterious and devout *mani* stones (prayer stones), the windswept pilgrims, the permanently spinning prayer wheels... Many people yearn for or even become obsessed with Tibet. Tibet is like the spiritual home for modern people's souls. If you come across an acquaintance here, do remember to say, 'Oh, so you are also in Tibet.'

某种意义上的"天堂"
A Kind of Heaven

书云拍摄的纪录片《西藏一年》在英国首播，获得了西方主流媒体的高度评价。同名图书随后出版，也引起了轰动。书云说过一句话："旅行指南说，西藏接近天堂。我想说，西藏就是某种意义上的天堂。"

After the documentary produced by Shu Yun, *A Year in Tibet*, premiered in Britain, Western mainstream media highly recommended it. Following the documentary, she published a book of the same title, which also caused quite a stir. Shu Yun once made a remark, 'Travel guides say Tibet is close to heaven. I want to say, in a sense, Tibet is heaven.'

印象·讲述
Impressions and Expositions

看山只是山
Seeing the Mountains Just as Mountains

一位研究西藏的学者说，他起初是被这里秀美的风光与淳朴的民风所吸引，"看山是山，看水是水"。逐渐地当美景被信息闭塞、运输不便以及思乡情磨蚀后，他的眼中早已"看山不是山，看水不是水"。最后当他的精神得到沉淀、净化、洗礼与升华后，留在他眼中的则是"看山只是山，看水只是水"。

A Tibetologist says he was first attracted by the beautiful scenery and simple folkways in Tibet, 'seeing the mountains as mountains, the water as water.' Then, after he was gradually tormented by the dearth of information, transportation inconvenience, and homesickness, his eyes 'saw the mountains were no longer mountains and the water was no longer water.' Finally, after his spirit became purified, cleansed, and sublimated, his eyes began to 'see the mountains just as mountains, the water just as water' again.

美景背后的人心
Hearts Behind the Beautiful Scenery

扎根西藏40年的画家韩书力说："我对西藏经历了从俯视到平视再到仰视的过程——初到西藏，觉得这里蛮荒粗野；走走看看，就开始被这儿的风景折服，进入了寻幽探胜的平视期；等到发现美景背后是更加纯洁的人心时，就不得不仰视并感叹这里的精神高度。"

Having settled in Tibet for forty years, painter Han Shuli says, 'My knowledge of Tibet went from a downward view to a horizontal view, and eventually to an upward view: when I first arrived, I thought Tibet was wild and savage. When I started walking and looking around, I became impressed by the landscape here, moving into a period of exploration with a horizontal view. When I found what stood behind the pure scenery were the purer hearts of the people, I had to look up and marvel at the height of the spirit in Tibet.'

评论

微观西藏
TIBET: FAST & FURIOUS

快乐便是美
Happiness Is Beauty

有人说："世界上有不穿衣服的民族，但没有不爱美的民族，藏族是爱美也是会美的民族。"藏袍修身而不裸露，大气而不刻板。更重要的是，西藏人相信，如果没有一颗能够随时快乐起来的心，那么任何外在的美都是没有价值的。

Some people say, 'There are ethnic groups that don't wear clothes, but there aren't any that don't like to be beautiful, and Tibetan people not only are beauty-loving, but also know how to be beautiful.' Tibetan robes are long and cover the body completely. They are grand but not rigid. Nevertheless, more importantly, Tibetans believe that without a heart capable of enjoying life whenever possible, any outer beauty is of no value.

死亡这件"大事"
Death, the 'Big Event'

西藏人对待死亡的看法，应该是他们上千年形成的价值观的集中体现和升华。如果你有机会去参加西藏人的葬礼，你会觉得，死亡是件大事，但也仅仅是比其他事大一点而已。同理，你所认为的生活中所有大事，也仅仅是比其他事大一点而已，比如失恋。

The Tibetan view of death is perhaps a concentrated reflection and sublimation of values that formed over several millennia. If you have the chance to attend a Tibetan's funeral, you will feel death is a big event, but it is only a little bigger than everything else. Similarly, all those events you consider as big in life, such as breaking up with your lover, are also just a bit more siginificant than other things.

评论

印象·讲述
Impressions and Expositions

空，不空
Empty, Not Empty

在藏民家喝茶，哪怕喝了一小口，主人也会立刻帮你添满。西藏人忌讳空不是为了显摆或祈求富有，而是因为在他们的观念里，拥有就是用来分享的。这也是这片物质匮乏的土地上人们内心的富有和质朴。

When you are drinking a cup of tea with a Tibetan family, even if you have only taken a little sip, the host will still fill it up immediately. Tibetans avoid emptiness not for showing off or praying for wealth, but because in their view, possessions are there to be shared. This is also shown in the richness and plainness of Tibetan hearts, in a land that has scarce resources.

进藏心态
Mentality for Visiting Tibet

扎根西藏 40 年的画家韩书力对人们的进藏心态给了三点建议：第一，用平视的眼光进藏，平视就是不怀偏见的注视。第二，用平常心进藏，不要一惊一乍。第三，用包容的心态进藏，不要以牧师的心态试图去改变，那样只是单相思，适得其反。

Having settled in Tibet for forty years, painter Han Shuli gives three pieces of advice to people visiting Tibet. First, enjoy Tibet with a 'horizontal' or unbiased perspective. Second, come to Tibet with a balanced mind; don't overreact to things that surprise you. Third, visit Tibet with a tolerant heart. Don't try to change it as a priest might do. That is just an unrequited love and might lead to results contrary to your wish.

摄影：车鸣

微观西藏
TIBET: FAST & FURIOUS

用画笔朝圣
Use the Painting Brush for Pilgrimage

有朋友曾建议旅藏画家韩书力留在巴黎,但他最后还是回到拉萨。他说:"我就像一根草,西藏是我的家园,把我挪到别的土去,不是不能活,但终究长不好。"也许这世上有很多地方能够作画,但只有西藏能让这样一位画家用画笔朝圣。

A friend once advised traveling painter Han Shuli to stay in Paris, but he still went back to Lhasa eventually, saying, 'I am like a blade of grass; Tibet is my home. If you move me to another soil, it's not like I couldn't live anymore, but I wouldn't grow as well for sure.' Perhaps there are many places in the world for painters, but only in Tibet can a painter use his or her brush for a pilgrimage.

爱情圣地
A Holy Land for Love

在西藏,不用接吻,也不用牵手,你们就肩并肩地走,心里便什么都有。如果你恋爱了,和 TA 到西藏去吧,不是要雪山圣湖见证你们的爱情,而是要你们自己知道,爱情不是山盟海誓,也不是生死相依,爱情,仅仅是两颗心的共鸣。

In Tibet, you don't need to kiss, neither do you need to hold hands. Just walk side by side, and then you have all your heart wants. If you have fallen in love, go to Tibet with him or her, not to let the snow mountains and sacred lakes witness your love, but to let yourself understand that love is not pledges or promises nor leaning upon each other. Love is merely the resonance of two hearts.

评论

印象·讲述
Impressions and Expositions

摄影：陈永平

处处是彩虹
Rainbows Everywhere

在西藏，彩虹不仅在口口相传的美丽故事里，还被广泛地装点在生活中。在作家叶玉林眼中："年轻姑娘们腰间的彩裙是飞舞的彩虹；墙壁和栋梁上的线条图案是储存在房里的彩虹。在项链、首饰、牧羊鞭、牦牛角、靴子上，也往往能发现变换着的小彩虹。甚至在高原人的眼光里，也仿佛能见到闪闪的彩虹。"

In Tibet, rainbows not only exist in beautiful stories passed orally from generation to generation, but also as a decoration in daily life. In the eyes of author Ye Yulin: 'The multicolored skirts of young girls are moving rainbows; colored lines painted on walls and rafters are rainbows stored within a house. Moreover, necklaces, jewelry, sheep whips, yak horns, and boots exhibit shifting mini-rainbows. You can even catch shining rainbows in the eyes of the local people.'

微观西藏
TIBET: FAST & FURIOUS

回到本原
Returning to Origins

歌手朱哲琴：西藏具有这样的一个环境，使你得以回到本原的状态，在其中你可以回忆起最久远的过去，思考最遥远的将来。

Singer Dadawa (Zhu Zheqin) once said: 'Tibet is a place that makes you return to a primitive state, in which you can recall the remote past and visualize a distant future.'

干杯西藏
Cheers, Tibet

马原、扎西达娃、马丽华、皮皮、韩书力、车刚、牟森……这些总和西藏联系在一起的文化名人被画家于小冬画进了一个虚构的聚会里，画中 23 人各执一杯红酒，圣徒般立在一张大桌前，充满了宗教般的仪式感。这幅著名的画，就是《干杯西藏》。拉萨，像一席流动的盛宴；干杯，有青春的激情，也有未来的彷徨。

Ma Yuan, Tashi Dawa, Ma Lihua, Pipi, Han Shuli, Che Gang, Mu Sen — these renowned writers and artists with close ties to Tibet have been painted together in a scene by artist Yu Xiaodong, each of them holding a glass of wine before a large table in a scene like a religious ritual. The title of the painting is 'Cheers, Tibet'. Lhasa is a lasting banquet, and the act of a toast is filled with the fervor of youth and wonder as to what the future may bring.

绘画：于小冬

印象·讲述
Impressions and Expositions

神秘难绘
A Mystery Difficult to Paint

在北京三里屯的一个餐馆,有记者曾问画家陈丹青:"你画了十几年的西藏,是否还愿意为那些金色的城市发呆?"陈丹青回答说:"我的画布根本无法承载那来自空气中的极纯极辽阔的神秘。"无独有偶,当记者问另外一位西藏画师时,画师回答说:"我笔下是我心中的神。"

A reporter once asked painter Chen Danqing in a restaurant in Beijing's Sanlitun area, 'You've painted Tibet for so many years, are you still willing to spend your time thinking about those golden cities?' Chen replied, 'My paintings can never capture the extremely purified vast mystery in Tibet.' Similarly, when the reporter asked another Tibetan painter, the painter replied, 'I am visualizing my conceived god.'

以西藏为知音
Take Tibet as Your Bosom Friend

画家艾轩进藏30余次,谈起西藏最吸引他的地方,他说:"开始,西藏吸引我的是外在的东西,湛蓝的天空,人们黝黑的皮肤,鲜艳的配饰,草地上盛开的鲜花……我感觉那是完全不同的天地。后来我才感到,在那里能寻找到很符合我追求的一种精神。大自然激活了我深层的心理诉求,我找到了诉说的空间。"

Painter Ai Xuan has visited Tibet over thirty times. When talking about what attracted him most there, he said, 'At first, what attracted me were the external things: the blue sky, people's dark skin, the bright accessories, the blooming flowers on the grassland... I felt that Tibet was a totally different world from where I lived. Later, I found a spirit in Tibet that accorded with what I pursued. It was nature that aroused my inner appeal, and I found the place to articulate myself.'

评论

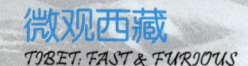

微观西藏
TIBET: FAST & FURIOUS

彻底的蓝
Thoroughly Blue

一位"驴友"这样描写西藏：久居都市的人们或许已经忘记天空其实是蔚蓝的，以至于面对西藏湛蓝的天空，竟一时失语。那是怎样的一种蓝色啊，举目是蓝，低头亦是蓝，蓝得那么彻底，你甚至无法回想起在哪里见过类似的色彩，亦无法确切地从调色板中找出它的色号。

A backpacker describes Tibet like this: 'Perhaps people living in cities have so long forgotten that the sky is actually blue that they would become speechless when facing the azure sky in Tibet. What kind of blue is it? When you raise your head, your eyes are full of blue. When you lower your head, that blueness still holds your eyes. The sky-blue is so abundant that you could hardly recall seeing any similar color elsewhere, nor could you find such color on the palette.'

一条短信
A Text Message

一位"驴友"说，午后，他站在八廓街，发了条短信给所有朋友：不到西藏，不知道天空有多蓝；不到拉萨，不知道空气有多新鲜；不到大昭寺，不知道信仰有多虔诚；不到八廓街，不知道逛街多有趣。他说，八廓街并不大，却让所有在这条街走过的人终生魂牵梦萦。

A backpacker recounted this story: he stood on Barkhor Street one afternoon and sent a text message to all his friends. The text read, 'If you haven't come to Tibet, you won't know how blue the sky is; if you haven't come to Lhasa, you won't know how fresh the air is; if you haven't come to the Jokhang Temple, you won't know how devout faith is; if you haven't come to the Barkhor Street, you won't know how interesting shopping is.' He said that though Barkhor was not big, every person who had walked it would find it in their dreams throughout the rest of their lives.

评论

印象·讲述

Impressions and Expositions

世界屋脊的屋脊
The Roof of the World Roof

羌塘在藏语中的意思是"北方高地",海拔4500米左右,是"世界屋脊的屋脊"。对这里,野生动物保护专家乔治·夏勒曾描写道:这里没有路,也不曾有过路,不见任何人的踪迹,除了野牦牛、藏羚羊或野驴的蹄印。江、湖、山脉都没有名字,岸和雪地都没有被任何旅行者的眼睛看到过,除了我。

Changtang in Tibetan means 'northern highlands', and with an average altitude of over 4,500 meters above sea level, it's the 'roof of the roof of the world'. Wildlife conservation expert George Schaller once described it as follows: 'There are no roads here, and never have there roads been here before. There are no traces of any human being, only the footprints of yaks, Tibetan antelopes, and wild donkeys. The rivers, lakes, and mountain ranges were never named. The river banks and snow have never been set sight on by any traveler but myself.'

忘了喧嚣
Forgetting the Bustling

演员陈坤在拍完以西藏为背景的电影《云水谣》后说:"西藏的一山一水都是那样富有灵性,藏族同胞是那样的友善和淳朴,置身在西藏的寒冷雪山前,才明白并体会到一个善意的微笑能带给人多么珍贵的温暖。"他还说:"在这样纯净的地方,心很静,人很纯粹,忘掉了尘世的喧嚣复杂。那一刻,只有自己。"

After finishing the movie *The Knot*, which uses Tibet as its background, actor Chen Kun said, 'The mountains and water in Tibet are full of spirituality, and Tibetans are simple and friendly. Only after you have gone to the snow mountains in Tibet will you understand how precious the warmth of a friendly smile is.' Chen also remarked, 'At such a pure place, the heart becomes peaceful, and thought becomes simple. People can forget about the buzz and complexity of daily life. At that moment, your self is everything.'

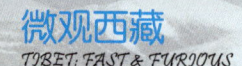

微观西藏
TIBET: FAST & FURIOUS

我把西藏比壁画
Comparing Tibet to Murals

摄影师平老虎：我去过东西南北很多风景地，如果把内地的很多风景地，比作尺把高的朦胧柔美水粉画，或者是一米来高光影动人的油画。那么，西藏就好比一幅画在高大教堂里的几十米长的壁画，驻足远观，壮美雄浑，疾行许久，仍在画中。而趋近揣摩，每个细节都那样的瑰丽精致，动人心魄。

Photographer 'Tiger Ping' says, 'I have been to many sights around China. If I compare the mainland spots to a soft and hazy gouache about one foot high or a shadowy oil painting as high as a person, then the sights in Tibet are like a mural in a lofty church, dozens of meters long. If you stand afar to view it, you'll see its magnificence and vigorousness; if you walk for a while, you can still find yourself in the painting; if you approach the painting and appreciate it carefully, you find every detail is so delicate and heart-lifting.'

忘了恩怨情仇
Forgetting about Love and Hatred

有人形容说，西藏海拔高度上的寒冷，把那些鸡毛蒜皮的恩怨情仇好像都冻掉了，只剩下自我与生命的对视，默默无言。大概也是因为生命感受到了大自然的震撼，有无法承受之重，让自己融入自然的空灵中，有种滴水汇入汪洋的归属感，心都融化了。

A description of the coldness at a high altitude in Tibet: 'It seemed to have frozen off all trifling grudges, silently leaving you and life eye-to-eye. Perhaps life itself also felt the shock brought by nature was unbearably heavy. When you blend yourself with the intangibility of nature, you feel like a drop of water returning to the vast ocean, and your heart melts.'

评论

印象·讲述
Impressions and Expositions

距离感
A Sense of Distance

作家海岩评论说，西藏题材的文学作品备受瞩目的一个原因，在于西藏的神奇与读者现实生活的距离。当一个场景的出现让人觉得有距离感时，人们才会感到新鲜，才会觉得有值得探求的东西。

Writer Hai Yan comments, 'The reason that literary works of Tibetan themes attract much attention lies in the distance between readers' real lives and their idealistic ideas of Tibet. Only when a scene in a book gives people a feeling of distance will it capture people and make them feel that there is actually something worthy of further exploration.'

余味悠长
A Lingering Aftertaste

有人说，西藏，只能在高原反应的眩晕中去体会，"在西藏时也并未感觉特别的瑰丽，西藏的美丽在其余味。一点点的回甘，蚕抽丝一般抽取着美好的回忆，那些风景就一缕一缕地慢慢飘过"。

Someone once said that Tibet could only be felt from the dizziness caused by altitude sickness: 'You might not feel the magnificence of Tibet when you are there, because its beauty lies in the aftertaste. The bits and pieces of sweetness will come back to you, extracting your pleasant memories like reeling off raw silk from cocoons. The scenery you have enjoyed will drift past your eyes bit by bit.'

摄影：程华德

微观西藏
TIBET: FAST & FURIOUS

摄影：车刚

赴藏如归
Coming to Tibet, Feeling at Home

很多人对洁净的蓝天白云有着特别的钟爱，因为那是小时候的记忆。每次看到没有污染的天空和白云，人们都会想起童年美好的往事，在记忆里，童年就是在这样的天空和白云下度过的。所以很多人到了西藏，恍惚间会忽然觉得像在故乡一样。

Many people have a special affection for blue skies and white clouds because they remind them of their childhood memories. Whenever they see the unpolluted sky and clouds, they think of the beautiful years of their past, when they lived under that kind of clear sky and white clouds. As a result, when people come to Tibet, they feel as if they have gone back to their hometown.

评论

印象·讲述
Impressions and Expositions

仪态万千的牦牛
Elegant Yaks

牦牛一般高一米二左右，长一米六左右，重可达千斤，十分魁梧。作家叶玉林曾风趣地写道："初看到牦牛，可能会想起《西游记》里和孙悟空斗法的牛魔王，以为它不过是粗鲁蠢笨的庞然大物。可在牧场上看久看惯了，觉得它倒仪态万千呢。"

Yaks are usually about 1.2 meters tall and 1.6 meters long. Weighing as much as 500 kilograms, they are quite burly. Author Ye Yulin once wrote humorously, 'The first sight of a yak might remind us of the monstrous Bull Demon King who battled with the Monkey King in *Journey to the West*. After getting used to seeing it on the farm, people see it as a noble animal rather than a dumb beast.'

骑行者
Cyclists

在西藏，常常能看到骑车的旅行者。他们悠悠而过，随行随止，全凭心情与风景。他们也曾经历孤独绝望、道路艰险、风雨兼程，忍受肉体和意志的双重考验，却始终在路上。一位骑行者说出了这样的感受："身体在地狱，眼睛在天堂。"

In Tibet, one often sees people traveling by bicycle. They go along at a leisurely speed, riding and stopping depending on the scenery and their mood. They might also have experienced loneliness, desperation, dangerous road conditions, unpredictable weather, and physical and spiritual challenges, but they stay always on the road. One cyclist summed up his experiences by saying, 'My body was in hell, but my eyes were in paradise.'

北京人在拉萨
A Beijinger in Lhasa

摄影家车刚说自己一个有趣的心态："每年冬天我回北京陪家人，很少出去应酬，就待在家里好好表现，做饭刷碗接孩子，目的是为了假期一结束赶快回西藏。"

Photographer Che Gang describes a very interesting attitude: 'When I go back to visit my family in Beijing every winter, I seldom go out and network. I just stay at home and try to be useful, which includes cooking, dish washing and picking up the kids. My purpose is to get released as soon as the vacation ends so that I can return to Tibet.'

微观西藏
TIBET: FAST & FURIOUS

西藏眼神
Tibetan Eyes

在西藏，无论美景或美食，都没有藏族人的眼神给人留下的印象更深。正如著名作家阿来所说，藏族人的眼神是清澈的和勇敢的，这是大自然赋予的。藏族人的眼神更是平和的，是超越了命运局限的平和，无论命运如何悲凉，他们从来不曾脱离自己的土地，脱离脚下的草原。

In Tibet, neither beautiful scenery nor delicious food impresses people more than Tibetans' eyes. As the famous writer Alai put it, 'Tibetans' eyes are clear and courageous; they are nature's blessing. Moreover, their eyes are placid, and so placid as to surpass the limit of destiny. No matter what desolate fate befalls them, they will never break away from their own soil or separate themselves from the grassland under their feet.'

行走在西藏
Walking in Tibet

有人把西藏比作天堂，演员陈坤这样描述在天路行走的感觉："站在海拔4300米的山峰上，俯瞰四周。远方的拉萨像一幅精心描绘的坛城，近处色彩鲜艳的经幡铺天盖地悬挂在我们曾走过的山脉间。那一刻，我的心充满了正面的能量。"

Some people compare Tibet to heaven. Actor Chen Kun describes his feelings when walking on 'heaven road': 'Standing on a mountain at an altitude of 4,300 meters and looking around, faraway Lhasa looked like a delicately portrayed *mandala* (a peaceful place which enshrines figures of bodhisattvas). Nearby, the mountains we passed were snowed under by brightly colored prayer flags. At that moment, my heart became filled with positive energy.'

评论

印象·讲述
Impressions and Expositions

摄影：车刚

好好吃饭
Eating Well

有人说在西藏吃饭格外香。为什么在水都烧不到100度的高原吃饭会格外香呢？也许是因为你的心变得格外宁静了。心静时，你看到的景色是美丽的，听到的音乐是优美的，口中的食物也是美味的。难怪雪域修行大师米拉日巴的格言是：好好吃饭。

Some people say that Tibetan food is particularly tasty. How can this be in a place where water boils at much less than 100 degrees? It may be because one's heart has become exceptionally quiet. When your heart is quiet, the scene you see becomes beautiful, and the music you hear becomes graceful, so, of course, the food you eat will also become tasty. It's no wonder that the meditation Master Milarepa's motto was 'eat well'.

平淡与极致
Dullness and Perfection

一位在西藏工作多年的外地人说："西藏的生活平淡但又极致。平淡是因为在高寒缺氧的世界屋脊，除了工作，真是无心更无力于其他。极致是因为，在这里，心灵得到了前所未有的洗涤。"

A non-local, who had worked in Tibet for many years, remarked, 'Life in Tibet is insipid yet perfect. It is dull since on this oxygen-deficient roof of the world you don't have the mood or even the energy to do anything besides work. It is perfect because your spirit is purified in an unprecedented way.'

微观西藏
TIBET: FAST & FURIOUS

神秘与灿烂

Mystery and Splendor

有人形容第一次从西藏回来以后的感觉,如同奥地利著名画家克里姆特的作品《吻》那样,金碧辉煌的基调、象征主义中潜在的神秘主义色彩、强烈的平面感和富丽璀璨的装饰效果,让人生出绚烂夺目的种种联想。

One person's feeling after visiting Tibet for the first time: 'It is like *Kiss*, the work of the famous Austrian painter Gustav Klimt. The fundamental atmosphere of splendor and magnificence, the potential mystic color in symbolism, the strong sense of plane surface, and the richly resplendent effects of decoration — all of these provide people with dazzling insights.'

永不过时的袈裟

The *Kasaya* That Never Becomes Outdated

大昭寺喇嘛尼玛次仁曾说:"我觉得袈裟很有趣,只要不烂,今年穿了明年再穿还是新的,样式永远不过时。"圣城拉萨,经轮转动,香烟缭绕,法号声声,就像永不过时的袈裟一样,总能轻轻地拨动人们的心弦。

Lama Nyima Tsering of Jokhang Temple once said: 'I think *kasaya* is very interesting, as long as it is not worn out; it will still be like new next year, even if you have worn it all this year. The style of this costume will never become outdated.' In the holy city of Lhasa, the turning of prayer wheels, the surrounding smell of incense, and the sound of chanting dharma names are exactly like a never-out-of-fashion *kasaya,* constantly plucking at people's heartstrings.

摄影:聂晓阳

印象·讲述
Impressions and Expositions

拉萨幻觉
Lhasa Illusions

一天下午,美国人龙安志和朋友坐在大昭寺附近宾馆的屋顶上,喝着酥油茶。远处可以看到布达拉宫,蓝天清澈透明,带来了一种幻觉,使人感到伸出手去能够摸到布达拉宫。龙安志试着去摸,只是想证实这仅仅是个幻觉。或许西藏改变了人对距离、空间、时间和音乐的感知能力。

One afternoon, an American named Laurence Brahm sat with his friends on the roof of a restaurant near Jokhang Temple, drinking butter tea. The Potala Palace in the distance and the clear blue sky gave them the illusion of touching the Potala Palace if they stretched out their arms. Brahm tried to touch the palace with his hands only to prove that it was an illusion. Perhaps Tibet changed their ability of sensing distance, space, time, and music.

西藏的星空
Starry Skies in Tibet

陈坤讲述他在西藏的一个普通夜晚:我和同学们在羊卓雍湖围坐一圈,分别讲述自己在行走中的感悟。大家讲完后,设计师提议把照明灯关掉。有人问:"为什么?"他说:"关上灯,抬头看。"大家抬头看,西藏的夜空繁星点点,他们从未见过这么闪亮和密集的星星。

Actor Chen Kun describes an ordinary night he had in Tibet: 'I sat with my classmates around Lake Yamdrok and we talked about our inspirations for walking. When we finished, a designer proposed to turn off the lights, and someone asked, "Why?" The designer answered, "Turn off the lights and look up." All of us raised our heads. The night sky was full of stars, and we had never experienced a night with such dense sparkling stars.'

评论

微观西藏
TIBET: FAST & FURIOUS

摄影：车刚

冬天的高原
Winter on the Plateau

画家张鹰：对于生活在高原上的藏族人来说，冬季正是他们出游朝佛的季节，因为一年中只有这时才是他们闲暇之时。旅游者都说，不到八廓街就等于没到西藏。如果说夏天的八廓街是招揽八方游客的胜地，那么冬天的八廓街才是朝佛人的圣地。冬天的西藏回归到高原的本来面目，就像强壮的汉子褪去了外衣。

Painter Zhang Ying says, 'For people who live on the plateau, winter is the time to start pilgrimages, because this is the only time of the year when they have free time. Travelers all say that Barkhor Street is a place you must visit if you go to Tibet. If Barkhor Street is the tourist destination for travelers from all over the world in the summer, then in winter time it is a pilgrimage destination. Tibet in winter has returned to its original color, as a muscular man finally undressed.'

"藏漂"
Tibetan Migrants

与"北漂"不同的是，"藏漂"来到西藏不是为了物质上的追求，更多人希望在精神层面上获取滋养。时间或长或短，一些人永久地停留在这片土地，而更多的人则带着"精神补给"重新从西藏出发。

In contrast to 'northern migrants' (people that come to Beijing in search of work), 'Tibetan migrants' come to Tibet not just for the pursuit of fortune; many people hope to obtain nourishment on the spiritual level. After varied lengths of time, some decide to permanently stay on the plateau, but more people leave Tibet stocked with their new 'spiritual supplies'.

印象·讲述
Impressions and Expositions

高天厚土的滋养
Nourished by High Sky and Thick Earth

旅居西藏 30 余年的画家余友心先生说：在雪域高原的圣山神湖之间行了几万里路，备尝这片高天厚土的滋养，你的形象外观不知不觉变为结实粗犷，你的心胸不知不觉变得坦荡博爱，你的作品更是不知不觉地从材质到风格一变再变，终成今天的面貌。

Yu Youxin, a painter who has sojourned in Tibet for over thirty years, said, 'I have walked tens of thousands of miles among the holy mountains and lakes on this snow-covered plateau and have enjoyed the nourishment of the high sky and thick earth. As a result, my appearance has become sturdy unconsciously, my mind has become broad and philanthropic, and my work has been changed again and again in both material and style and has finally arrived at what it is like today.'

天籁之音
The Sounds of Nature

有人曾写道：藏族人天生就有一副好嗓子，外人常说西藏人的歌声是天籁之音。但在我心里，那经幡飘动、经轮转动的声音才是最美最动听的。每当站在五彩经幡下，闭上眼睛倾听它随风飘舞的声音，我的心仿佛被震住了。多么奇妙的声音啊，这声音竟能让我的心平静如水，似梦似醒，如诗如梦……

Someone once wrote, 'All Tibetans have great voices. When others visit they're always amazed by how well Tibetans can sing. However, in my view, the fluttering sound of prayer flags and rubbing sound of prayer wheels are the true heavenly sounds. Every time I stand under those five-colored banners, close my eyes and hear them dancing in the wind, my heart seems stunned by this amazing sound, which brings peace to me, and puts me into a state of half-dream and half-awakening...'

评论

微观西藏
TIBET: FAST & FURIOUS

谦卑使人强大
Modesty Makes People Powerful

画家艾轩说:"在西藏我更多感受到的不是壮丽和辽阔,而是作为人的孤独和渺小。人在自然面前显得太单薄、脆弱和无奈,地平线那么辽阔,人那么渺小,被远方严峻的地平线回收和释放。"难怪有人说,在恶劣的自然环境下,西藏人得以生存,靠的绝不是对雪山圣湖的占有和征服,而是谦卑。

Painter Ai Xuan once said, 'In Tibet, what I felt the most was not its magnificence or vastness, but the loneliness and smallness of human beings. People seemed so weak, fragile, and helpless in front of nature. The stern horizon was so extensive, recycling and liberating our souls.' No wonder some people remark that in such a harsh natural environment, Tibetans' survival is in no way related to their occupation or conquest of snowy mountains and sacred lakes. They have survived just by virtue of their simple modesty.

"傻"人"傻"福
Fortune Favors Fools

画家韩书力说:"缺三分之一氧气的高原,刚好够我用有限的体力去做最想做的事,刚好够我用缺氧的大脑记住别人对我的友善关爱,而忘记了别人对我的恶意与伤害。"有人也说:"西藏为什么能给人心灵的洗礼?因为这里缺氧,人变'傻'了,人一'傻',想的事就少,就变得更单纯。"

Painter Han Shuli says, 'Lacking one-third of oxygen in normal air, the plateau offered me just enough energy to do what I wanted to do most: make me use my oxygen-deficient brain to remember the friendliness and love others gave me, and in the meantime forget the malice or harm I have received.' Some people also say, 'Why can Tibet cleanse people's spirits? Because it is oxygen-deficient, people become "silly", and when that happens, people start to think less, thus becoming simpler and purer.'

西藏的母亲
Tibetan Mothers

画家昂桑喜欢画西藏的妇女，尤其是藏北草原上那些在艰苦条件下把孩子抚养成人的母亲。她们站着，孩子们就在草地上奔跑，这些草原之子虽然衣着单薄，但实际上生活得无忧无虑。昂桑说："这些妇女心中有佛，又生活在圣地，所以她们的眼睛像佛的眼睛，很美。"

Painter Ang Sang likes to draw Tibetan women, especially the mothers who have brought up their children under poor conditions on the grasslands of northern Tibet. Mothers stand there, while their children run across the grasslands. Although these children only wear thin clothes, they enjoy a free life with few worries. Ang Sang says, 'These women keep Buddha in their hearts and they live in this sacred place, so their eyes are similar to Buddha's eyes, very beautiful.'

摄影：觉果

评论

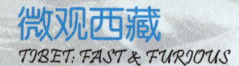

孤独与力量
Loneliness and Power

很多人将去西藏当作一次修行。曾在阿里待过 11 年的作家毕淑敏说：人在年轻的时候，远离城市，孤独地走进大自然的怀抱，会在一个大的恐怖之后，感到大的欣慰；会感到一种力量，从脚下的大地和头上的天空，从身边的每一棵草和每一滴水，涌进你的头发、睫毛、关节和口唇……你就强壮和智慧起来。

Many people consider going to Tibet a form of spiritual cultivation. Writer Bi Shumin, who stayed in Ngari for eleven years, says, 'When young people stay away from the city and walk alone into the arms of nature, they feel great horror and then great gratification; they feel a kind of strength, from the earth beneath and the sky above, from every blade of grass and drop of water around, flowing into their hair, eyelashes, joints, lips... then they become strong and wise.'

被阳光宠坏的民族
Ethnic Group Spoiled by Sunlight

作家扎西达娃讲，冬天的上午，西藏万里无云，一群群人在屋外晒太阳，这个离太阳最近所以被阳光宠坏了的民族并不在乎你如何形容他们，昏沉也罢，呆若木鸡也罢，重要的是，你别挡住他们的阳光。但在西藏人创造出的众多神灵中，却没有创造出一个辉煌的太阳神，这使他们的后代迷惑不解。

Writer Tashi Dawa describes the winter mornings of Tibet: 'There isn't one wisp of cloud in sight. Groups of Tibetans stay outdoors to bathe in the sunlight. This ethnic group, being the closest to the sun and thus spoiled by it, does not care how they are described. You can say they are drowsy or dazed, so long as you don't block their sunlight. But one thing has puzzled Tibetan descendants: out of all the gods Tibetans have created, there is no glorious god of the sun.'

评论

印象·讲述
Impressions and Expositions

摄影：车刚

摄影：聂晓阳

蓝天
Blue Sky

几乎每一个到西藏的人，都会被西藏的蓝天震撼、打动。有人说：在你抵达之前，西藏的天就这么的蓝，在你离开之后，它还将依然的蓝……天天天蓝，与谁都无关，天天天蓝，与谁都有关……天和蓝包容了万千纷纭的愁和欢。

Almost every person that has been to Tibet is shaken and moved by the Tibetan sky. An author once stated, 'Before you ever came, the skies of Tibet were blue; after you leave, it will still be blue as always... The sky is blue whether people are there or not... The sky and blueness are embracing a myriad of diverse joys and sorrows.'

多活了一辈子
Living One More Life

一位援藏干部说："我在西藏的生活就是一个不断挑战自己的过程，对于高山险峻，我敬畏但不恐惧，不断地去尝试去挑战，拓展了人生经历，也升华了人生体验，到西藏真觉得自己多活了一辈子。"也许西藏的魅力正在于它不但能给人激情，还能让人把心安住在此。

An official sent to work in Tibet says, 'My life in Tibet is a course of constant challenges for myself — steep mountains that I revere, but do not fear. I continuously accept challenges, which have expanded and enriched my life experience. I really feel I have lived a second life since coming to Tibet.' Perhaps the charm of Tibet lies exactly in that it can not only give a person passion, but also settle his or her heart on this plateau.

微观西藏
TIBET: FAST & FURIOUS

摄影：吕宇理

简单是一种智慧
The Wisdom of Simplicity

中国登山队队长王勇峰是中国登山界最负盛名的人物，他是中国最先登临世界七大峰的人之一，曾因严重冻伤，把三个脚趾奉献给了珠峰。面对用生命换来的荣誉，他很淡定：登山就像出趟差。他说他这个人很简单，因为"脑细胞在高山上死的太多了"。

Wang Yongfeng, the captain of the Chinese mountaineering team, is the most famous person in China's mountaineering community. He is one of the first Chinese to conquer the 'seven summits' (the seven highest mountains around the world). He has sacrificed three toes to Mt. Qomolangma because of frostbite. Facing the honors he has won at the risk of his life, he is composed: 'Mountain-climbing is like going on a business trip.' He says that he is a simple person, because 'too many of my brain cells died on high mountains.'

评论

印象·讲述
Impressions and Expositions

"遗忘"珠峰
'Forgetting' Mount Qomolangma

如果你问身在拉萨的藏族人，可能很少有人近距离接触过珠峰，甚至并不愿把这一自然奇景当作一种谈资。难道是因为冷漠？当然不是。17岁就在雪域高原上开始当兵的凌仕江说，"想要了解珠峰，就请不要去丈量她、征服她、念想她。我们都应该向拉萨人学习——在遗忘里，让她慢慢长高"。

If you ask a Tibetan living in Lhasa about Mount Qomolangma, he may not say much. Probably very few people have had close contact with Mount Qomolangma. They are reluctant even to use this natural wonder as a daily topic. Could it be that they are cold and indifferent? Of course not! Ling Shijiang, who once served as a soldier on the snowy plateau when he was seventeen, remarked, 'If you want to understand Mount Qomolangma, then please do not survey her, conquer her, or even think of her. We should all learn from Lhasa people — in oblivion, let her slowly grow taller.'

心中的度母
Tara in Her Heart

藏族女作家格央说：小时候走夜路心里害怕，就不停地念度母心咒，它带给我力量和安全感。在我心灵深处，对度母有着太多的依赖、感激和盼望。我的家乡也有被认为是度母化身的山，我还清楚地记得：山是美的，果子是甜的，空气是洁净的，那林中忽隐忽现的是最动人的歌声，而那歌者就是漂亮慈悲的度母。

Female Tibetan writer Goyon says, 'In my childhood, I was afraid of walking the road at night, so I kept reciting the Tara Mantra, which would give me power and a sense of security. Deep in my heart, I feel much dependence, gratitude and also expectation from Tara (a female bodhisattva representing the virtues of success in work and achievements). Even a mountain in my hometown is regarded as an incarnation of Tara. I can still clearly remember that the mountain was majestic, the fruit was sweet, and the air was clean. The sounds drifting out of the forest at times were the most touching, and the singer was not anybody else but the beautiful and merciful Tara.'

微观西藏
TIBET: FAST & FURIOUS

有限的面积，无限的空间
Limited Area, Infinite Space

面对布达拉宫，看一眼，拍一张，很多人都有这样的经历。但，想的是什么，却因人而异。作家马丽华说："西藏本身并不具备更多，除了石头和冰雪，但通过对它的凝视，一瞥亦可成为无限。"所以，西藏拥有有限的面积，却有无限的空间。

Facing the Potala Palace, many people first take a glance, and then take a photo. Nevertheless, what people think varies from person to person. Writer Ma Lihua said, 'Tibet itself doesn't possess anything greater than stones or snow, but just through gazing at them, a glance can become infinity.' Hence, Tibet has a limited area, but holds an infinite space.

西藏与灵魂有关
Tibet Is All About Souls

学者李敬泽说："1985 年，扎西达娃发表短篇小说《系在皮绳扣上的魂》，西藏第一次以神奇的形象进入汉语文学。西藏不再被置于进步—落后的客观历史判断之下，西藏与灵魂有关，它不再是等待改造的对象……寻觅不是为了印证我们的'有'，而是为了印证我们的'无'。"

Scholar Li Jingze says, 'In 1985, Tashi Dawa published a collection of short stories titled *A Soul In Bondage*. This was the first time that Tibet was presented in Chinese literature with a mystical image. Tibet was no longer viewed in terms of a "forward vs. backward" dichotomy, but in the spiritual perspective. It was not a place waiting for reforms anymore... We were seeking not to prove what we "have", but rather what we "do not have".'

评论

印象·讲述
Impressions and Expositions

淡定
Calmness and Tenacity

走在拉萨的大街上，会发现西藏人很少勾肩搭背、蹦蹦跳跳，他们的表情常常是那么沉着冷静，不过分兴奋，也不过分忧伤。也许藏族人之所以能在最恶劣的环境下创造了毫不亚于其他地方的快乐社会，正是因为他们的淡定和坚韧。

If you walk the streets of Lhasa, you seldom find Tibetans back-slapping or hopping around. Their facial expressions are often composed, without much excitement or sadness. Maybe it is exactly because of Tibetans' calmness and tenacity that they have been able to create a happy society comparable to those in other places in such a severe environment.

摄影：聂晓阳

微观西藏
TIBET: FAST & FURIOUS

摄影：车刚

在西藏没法作画
Painting Is Impossible in Tibet

画家薛继业说自己一直靠想象作画，而一趟西藏之旅几乎破坏了他的画画欲望。他说："西藏是不太能以我的方式绘画的。"一日，他独身坐在纳木错湖畔，心顿时被西藏这"不俗的真实"打乱：不愿想象作画，怕坏了真实；更不愿在画画时追求完美，怕失去一份原始而略有缺失的美。

Painter Xue Jiye has always said that he painted with his imagination. However, his trip to Tibet almost ruined his desire to draw. He says, 'Tibet isn't something that I could draw in my way.' One day, as he sat alone by Lake Namtso, his heart became disturbed by the 'unusual truth' of Tibet. He didn't want to imagine his drawings for fear that he would ruin the reality. Moreover, he didn't want to pursue perfection when painting, as this would ruin the slightly flawed but primitive beauty.

无人区的生灵们
Creatures in No Man's Land

关于藏北无人区，有段文字写道：那里只是无人而已，并不荒凉，大自然对它并不吝啬。这里，仍然是有花有草，流水潺潺；汽车在无人区奔驰，大地任你驰骋，常有一群群野驴、野马和黄羊，跟汽车赛跑；野鹿和野牦牛，也会毫不在乎地挡住你的去路。

One description of the no man's land in northern Tibet: 'It is uninhabited, but not desolate. Nature wasn't stingy toward it. Grass and flowers flourish, and streams quietly flow past. You can drive a car freely in this area, and herds of wild donkeys, horses, and flocks of Mongolian gazelle often race with your car. Wild deer and yaks will also block your way quite casually.'

印象·讲述
Impressions and Expositions

取悦自己
Please Yourself

西藏人喜欢唱歌与他们的生活环境不无关系。作曲家三宝说："在广袤的草地上，一望无际，能见到的人很少。地方太大，根本看不到人，这时唯一特想做的事就是大喊。"西藏人的歌声之所以格外美妙，也许是因为他们的歌声不为取悦别人，只为快乐自己。

Tibetans' habit of singing is strongly related to their living environment. Composer Sanbao says, 'On the vast grassland that stretches to the horizon, you can hardly see anyone. The land is simply too large, you can see no one at all. At this moment, all you want to do is to shout loudly.' Tibetans' singing is exceptionally beautiful, perhaps because they sing not to please others, but to enjoy themselves.

藏獒的今生
Tibetan Mastiffs Today

近些年来，藏獒突然成为受到狂热追捧的都市宠物。而藏獒的粗犷、剽悍、刚毅、威猛等特征，却处在不断的退化中。据不完全统计，"目前世界各地约有 30 万头藏獒，但纯种藏獒已不足 100 头"。"传说，离开草原的喜马拉雅纯种獒死的时候会流血，那是灵魂消失的征兆，因为它们拒绝来世。"

In recent years, the Tibetan mastiff has become widely sought after as a pet in large cities. However, the animal's natural fierceness, courage, fortitude, and mightiness has been steadily degrading. Statistics show that while there are more than 300,000 Tibetan mastiffs in the world, less than a hundred purebreds remain. According to legend, when a Himalayan purebred mastiff leaves the grasslands and dies, it will bleed, signifying the disappearance of its soul and its refusal to be reincarnated.

评论

微观西藏
TIBET: FAST & FURIOUS

摄影：车刚

外国游客的拉萨感受
Foreign Visitors' Feelings About Lhasa

美国人龙安志说，很多外国游客一到拉萨就感到迅速宁静下来，很舒服，很自在，就像把自己已经失去的一种东西找回来了。但是，一旦回到了家，他们又会忙碌起来，时间上的紧迫感又会污染他们的灵魂和心境。

An American named Laurence Brahm says, 'Many foreign visitors feel calm, comfortable, and at ease soon after they arrive in Tibet, as if they have recovered something lost a long time ago. However, when they get home, they return to their bustling lives. A sense of stress will again pollute their souls and moods.'

印象・讲述
Impressions and Expositions

无理由爱上西藏
No Reason for Falling in Love with Tibet

为什么爱西藏？也许有人第一秒会说：我爱阳光浓烈的布达拉宫、积雪的冰山、如明珠般璀璨的圣湖、雄浑巍峨的寺庙、有虔诚信仰的芸芸众生……然而，爱上西藏，何需理由？正如有人说：有些地方，只是听到名字，你就会知道，你与那地方定是有着千丝万缕的联系，在一瞬间洞穿你的灵魂。

Why do you love Tibet? Some may answer instantly: 'I love the sunshine-coated Potala Palace, the snow-covered mountains, the sparkling holy lakes, the spectacular temples, and the pious believers.' However, do you really need a reason to love Tibet? As some people put it, some places leap into your soul the moment you hear their names, and you notice that you have countless connections with them in thousands of ways.

去经历吧
Experience It Yourself

"驴友"小可：西藏是一个只有经历过、震撼过、感动过、哭过、笑过、惊过，你才能真正理解的地方。如果没有经过路途中的颠簸，没体验过初入西藏高原反应的不适，你就无法体会路之艰辛，也无法去感受那曲折险恶中行车的惊心动魄，还有沿途中哪怕只是一闪而过的美景。

From backpacker Xiao Ke: 'Tibet is a place that you can only truly understand after you have cried and laughed, been shocked, moved, and surprised. If you have never experienced the jolting on the way, and the uneasiness of altitude stress upon your first arrival, you cannot sense the difficulties of traveling, the breath-taking driving on the twisty roads, and the beautiful scenery, sometimes just a blur as you speed past on your journey.'

评论

微观西藏
TIBET: FAST & FURIOUS

身子苦，心里乐
Tired But Happy

演员陈坤：以前在城市里面，可能我每天都洗澡，弄得干干净净、漂漂亮亮的，但是心里经常因为各种各样的负面情绪而不专注、不畅快。这段时间，我们在西藏徒步，条件特别艰苦，行走也很累，住在野外，喝山泉水，帐篷就扎在牛粪旁边，但是心情特别愉快，身上臭烘烘，心里特别敞亮。

Actor Chen Kun says, 'When I lived in the city, I took a shower every day to look nice and clean. However, I could seldom concentrate or feel delighted due to various negative moods. When we hiked in Tibet, the living conditions were poor and the walking was tiring. We lived in the wild and drank spring water, and our tent was pitched next to cow dung. However, we were very delighted. We might be smelly, but our hearts were clear and open.'

越走越深
The More I Walk, the Deeper I Get

艺术家巴荒说：每走一遍西藏，都是一次朝圣的旅途；每一次朝圣，都是在自身未知的领域里再度旅行；每写一遍西藏，都是重新在高原上走一遍。我越走越深，从阳光灿烂的"风景"走到了历史深处扑朔迷离的"风景"，走到了人的情感和理性深处的"风景"。

Artist Ba Huang says that every trip she took to Tibet was like a pilgrimage. Every pilgrimage was like exploring the unknown areas of her self again, and every time she wrote about Tibet was like revisiting that plateau one more time. The more she walked, the deeper she got. She went from the brightly sunny 'scenery' to the whirling 'scenery' deep in history, and eventually came to the 'scenery' deep in people's emotions and rationality.

评论

精神・信仰
Spirituality and Faith

微观西藏
TIBET: FAST & FURIOUS

是艺术，更是信仰

It's Art, But It's All About Faith

西藏最后一名乌钦（旧西藏首席画师）扎西次仁这样描述唐卡：壁画和唐卡是信徒们顶礼膜拜的对象，所以不该把他们看作待价而沽的商品，绘画是我们对佛的敬畏和奉献，不是为了表达某种世俗情趣，所以一名真正的唐卡画师必须首先具备高尚的品格。

Tashi Tsering, the last chief painter in old Tibet, made the following comments on *thangkas*: 'Murals and *thangkas* are objects that believers worship, so we shouldn't see them as goods awaiting buyers. Painting shows our reverence and tribute toward the Buddha, and it's not for expressing any secular interests. Hence, having a lofty personality is a prerequisite for a real *thangka* painter.'

活在信仰中

Live in Faith

尼姑次成拉姆曾讲述她磕长头的故事：开始觉得很累，一天只能磕100个，两个月后每天能磕3000个，就这样磕了五年。谈到死亡，次成拉姆说："我不害怕死，我只害怕死了之后不能读佛经了，多在信仰中生活一天也是幸运的。"

Buddhist nun Tsultrim Lhamo tells this story of her prostration: 'At first I felt very tired, and I could only prostrate a hundred times a day. However, two months later, I could do it three thousand times a day, and I have been doing it for five years now.' When talking about death, she says, 'I do not fear death; I only fear that I cannot continue reading scriptures after I die, so I am lucky as long as I have one more day to live in faith.'

评论

精神·信仰
Spirituality and Faith

传递哈达
Passing *Hada*

西藏的法会上人山人海，大家个个都想给活佛献哈达，怎么办呢？于是人们就自觉地依次向前传递哈达，于是哈达如游龙般涌向活佛，源源不断。这种高度默契的配合，大概只有怀着同样的信念和热忱的人们才能够做到。

A religious ceremony in Tibet is packed with people. Everyone wants to present a *hada* to the living Buddha. How should they do it? People voluntarily start to pass forward *hadas* in turns. *Hadas* flock to the Buddha continuously like a swimming dragon. Perhaps only people with the same faith and passion can perform such a highly tacit cooperation.

磕长头的要领
The Essentials of Prostration

到了西藏，到处可以看到磕长头的身影。磕长头时双手合十，要分别在头、口、心的位置停留片刻，这是为了提醒自己，头不要胡思乱想，要虔诚而专注；口不要胡言乱语，要温暖而善良；心不要傲慢，要平静而谦卑。

When you arrive in Tibet, you can see prostrating figures everywhere. When prostrating, two hands are folded and held upon the head, mouth, and heart respectively for a moment. This is to remind yourself: do not have random thoughts in the head, you should be devout and dedicated; do not rave with the mouth, you should be mild and benevolent; do not have an arrogant heart, you should be calm and modest.

摄影：车刚

微观西藏
TIBET: FAST & FURIOUS

摄影：聂晓阳

母亲的清晨
Mother's Mornings

西藏人次吉：母亲的每一天都在溢满檀香味的佛堂中开始。当清晨的第一缕阳光射进阿妈的佛堂时，阿妈早已在佛前供奉了当天第一碗清水，点上藏香，续上新的酥油灯，然后站立着面向佛龛磕拜，一次又一次，直到阿妈心里定下的那个数字达到为止。在阿妈的心里，礼佛必须付出百分之一百的真诚和恭敬。

Tseji, a Tibetan says, 'Every day my mother starts in a prayer hall filled with the scent of sandalwood. By the time the first ray of sunshine has entered the hall, my mother has already presented the day's first bowl of fresh water, lit incense, refilled the butter lamp, and knelt in front of the Buddha niche again and again till she thinks the Buddha is satisfied. In my mother's heart, this ritual must be performed with full sincerity and gratitude.'

宽容
Tolerance

盛噶仁波切讲过这样一个故事：有一对夫妇，他们的儿子成绩很好，却被嫉妒他的一个同学杀害了。得知杀人者因将在监狱中度过漫长的时间而失去了活下去的信心，被害孩子的父母将他认作儿子，鼓励他好好服刑，早日回归社会。

Singa Rinpoche once told this story: a couple once had a son who was a top student. Later their son was murdered by one of his classmates out of envy. The murderer spent a lengthy time in jail. He lost the courage to live, yet the couple adopted him as their son and encouraged him to serve his sentence well.

精神·信仰
Spirituality and Faith

摩顶
Head-Touching Blessing

十世班禅大师圆寂前,在扎什伦布寺接连三天从早到晚为信徒摩顶。摩顶五万多人之后,班禅大师的手都抬不起来了,却仍然坚持为后面的信徒继续摩顶。信徒们有的扶老携幼、日夜排队等候,有的重病在身,被家人抬着送来。班禅大师每一次伸出的手掌都带给他们温暖,甚至生的希望。

Before the 10th Panchen Lama passed away, he performed the head-touching ritual for Buddhist believers continuously for three days. After blessing more than 50,000 people, he could barely lift his hand, but he still insisted on blessing the rest of the believers. Some devotees brought along the whole family, waiting in line day and night; some had serious diseases and were carried by their families. Every time, the Panchen's dedicated outstretched hand gave them warmth and hope of life.

快乐来自内心
Happiness Comes from the Heart

西藏有个谚语:即使再清澈的水,如果在一个杯子里不停地摇晃,它都不会清澈;即使再浑浊的水,如果静静地放着,也自然会变得清澈。有位活佛说,我们的心也是如此,只有给它时间去沉淀,才会变得清静自在,"我们往往以为通过外界的满足才能得到快乐,却忽略了真正的快乐其实就在自己内心"。

A proverb from Tibet: no matter how clear the water is, if it is ceaselessly shaken in a cup, it will not look clear anymore; no matter how muddy the water is, if it is kept still, it will gradually become clear. A living Buddha once remarked, 'Our hearts are the same — only after we give them time to contemplate can they become pure and free. We often assume we can gain happiness through outside gratifications, so we normally neglect the real happiness that lies just in our hearts.'

评论

微观西藏
TIBET: FAST & FURIOUS

失窃之后
After Being Robbed

藏族学者德庆卓嘎讲过这样一个故事：有一个藏民家里被盗了，他居然不生气，心想：可能是我上辈子欠了人家的债，现在小偷把他的钱都拿走了，太好了！我还清账了，轻松了！可能恶劣的自然条件给了西藏人更多的苦难，但他们依然有办法使自己同样或更加幸福。

Dechen Drolkar, a Tibetan scholar, tells a story about a Tibetan whose home was visited by a thief. Surprisingly, the homeowner wasn't even angry. He thought, 'Perhaps my last incarnation owed the thief debts. Now the thief has taken all his money back. Great! I've cleared my debts; I feel at ease now!' The harsh natural conditions make Tibetans suffer more than others, but they have their own ways to be just as happy as others and even happier.

公交"历险"
Bus 'Adventure'

一个朋友说，他曾在拉萨体验公交车，任意上了一车，到了城外，天黑下来，路边没了行人也没有路灯，心里开始发毛：终点在哪？有无回程车？司机师傅看出了他的害怕，不但让他随车返回，还特意停车让他欣赏郊外特别明亮的月亮。

A friend said that he once experienced an interesting bus trip in Lhasa. He randomly jumped on a bus. When the bus went out of Lhasa, the sky was growing dark, and he couldn't see pedestrians or street lights along the roads. He started to panic: 'Where is the destination? Is there a return bus?' The driver saw his fear and offered to let him return on his bus. He even stopped, so they could enjoy the especially bright moon that night on the way back.

评论

精神·信仰
Spirituality and Faith

摄影：觉果

孩子与佛
Children and Buddha

西藏作家德庆卓嘎说：有人日进斗金苦哈哈，有人一碗糌粑乐呵呵，为什么？对今生欲望太多所以不容易满足，对来世不抱信仰所以急功近利，对幸福过于渴望所以忽视当下，对痛苦过于惧怕所以不能承担。人应该向孩子学习怎么得到快乐，孩子和佛一样，都只活在当下，不为失去而烦恼，也不为得到而贪婪。

Tibetan writer Dechen Drolkar says that some people feel bitter even though they are rolling in dough; others smile with only a bowl of *tsampa*. Why? Maybe they desire so much that they will not easily be content, or they do not embrace the beliefs of an afterlife so they expect quick successes. Perhaps they are so eager for future happiness that they neglect the present, or they are too afraid of bearing pains. People should learn how to be happy from children. Children and Buddha are alike: they all live in the present; never worry about losses, and they are never greedy for gains.

微观西藏
TIBET: FAST & FURIOUS

为欺骗者祈祷
Praying for Cheaters

寺庙里的酥油灯要靠不断地添加酥油才能长明不灭。有的香客贪图便宜，买假的酥油送到庙里来。假酥油点燃时会产生黑烟熏染壁画和佛像，还可能会令灯熄灭。但依然有备受其扰的僧人祈祷说："希望他们死后不会因为欺骗而下地狱。"

Butter lamps can only be kept burning by adding yak butter constantly. Some worshippers once wanted to save money and brought fake butter to the temple. This fake butter produced black smoke when lit, corrupting the murals and Buddha statues and even extinguishing the lamp. However, there were still monks bothered by the smoke praying for them, 'We hope they won't go to hell after dying for this deception.'

善取不如善舍
Abandoning Is Better than Taking

画家韩书力在神山圣湖间采风，得到最大的艺术心得就是"舍"，也就是做减法。正是在这些被舍弃的空间里才浮现出他真正深层次的自我意识与境界，他把这个总结为：善取不如善舍。只有舍弃，平和与简约，才能在心灵层面去触摸西藏。

Painter Han Shuli has obtained inspiration from Tibet's sacred mountains and holy lakes. His biggest harvest was one word: 'abandonment', or doing abstractions. It was abandonment that awarded him with a real and deeper sense of self. Han summarized it thus: 'Abandoning is better than taking. Only after abandonment can one see placidness and conciseness, and touch Tibet spiritually in its simplicity.'

评论

精神・信仰
Spirituality and Faith

洞里的遁世者
The Recluse in the Cave

作家白玛娜珍曾忆起在山洞里的一位遁世者:"那是初夏的某个正午,她低头坐在一张破旧的木椅上,头发全白了,凌乱地盖在前额。潮湿的岩壁上挂满了渗出的水珠,白晃晃的太阳被堵在了岩洞外。虽然这里海拔高达 4300 米,但常年总有朝佛的人带着药品、糌粑和蜡烛来看望住在洞里的遁世者。"

Writer Pema Nadron recalls a recluse she once encountered in a cave: 'It was at noon in early summer; she was sitting on a shabby wooden chair with her head down. Her hair was all white and hung messily over her forehead. Water droplets oozed out of the wet rocks and covered the cave walls. The dazzling sunlight was kept outside. Although the altitude there was 4,300 meters, people came to worship Buddha all year round. They would bring medicine, *tsampa* and candles to visit the recluses in the caves.'

磕头朝圣的程序
Procedures of Prostration

有作家这样记录磕长头朝圣的程序:傍晚结束时,向四方磕头,拜见此地诸神,说今晚我将暂栖于此,请求保护;向来的方向磕三个头,答谢神灵与万物;向前方磕三个头,告示明天将要打扰的地方神;最后向前方鞠躬三次。次日早饭后,再步行到昨晚做记号的地方,合掌诵经,继续进发。

A writer recorded the procedures of prostration like this: 'To end a day of prostrations, you have to prostrate in all directions, telling the gods, "I'll rest here tonight, please protect me." Then you need to prostrate three times in the direction from which you have come to thank the gods and all things along the path. You also need to prostrate three times in the forward direction, informing the gods, "I'm going to bother you tomorrow." Last, you need to bow three times. The next day, you should go back to the place where you stopped the previous day and recite scriptures with hands clasped before you start a new day of prostrations.'

微观西藏
TIBET: FAST & FURIOUS

苦难
Hardship

一位游客到西藏的一个贫困村，感叹当地生活艰苦，条件不及拉萨。但当地的一位姑娘却说："我们有电，比邻村强百倍了。"

A tourist visited a poor village in Tibet and sighed about the hardships of local life and its downfalls compared with Lhasa. Nevertheless, a local girl said, 'We have electricity. It's much better here than in our neighboring villages.'

劳动和享受
Work and Enjoyment

看藏民唱歌跳舞很开心，看他们劳动更开心。他们说："干活时唱歌就不觉得累了，而且干得又快又好。"难怪有人说，看他们边唱歌边劳动，就会觉得在这个很多人都把劳动当作受苦的时代，这些把劳动和享受完美结合起来的人，尤其令人感佩。

Watching Tibetans sing and dance is a very delightful thing, and seeing them working is even more so. They say, 'If I sing as I work, then I won't feel tired, and the work can be finished nice and quick.' No wonder some people say when they see Tibetans singing while working, they really admire them. In this era when many consider labor as suffering, Tibetans are one of the few who have combined work and enjoyment perfectly. How admirable they are.

摄影：汤志明

精神·信仰
Spirituality and Faith

耐心等待
Waiting Patiently

一位纪录片导演曾注意到,有次她在江孜郊区乘坐中巴,仅仅35分钟的车程,走了三个半小时——中间有人下车到附近村子办事,汽车就会停下来等,似乎没有人介意,也没有人着急。大家从袍子里掏出杯子,从暖壶或塑料瓶里倒出青稞酒,悠然自得,"在他们眼里,时间不是金钱,生活就是享受当下"。

A documentary director recounts: once she was on board a minibus in the suburbs of Gyangze County, and a normally thirty-five minute ride lasted three-and-a-half hours — the bus would stop and wait while people got off to run errands in nearby villages. It appeared as if no one minded, and no one was anxious. People brought out cups from their robes, and poured out barley wine from thermoses or plastic bottles. Everyone seemed light-hearted and content. 'In their eyes, time is not money; living is just to enjoy the present moment.'

因果不虚
Karma Is Not Empty

据说西藏历史上曾有一个大官,他曾三次下令把境内老百姓的财产平均分配,把富人的财物分给穷人。但是过了一段时间,他发现原来穷的依然变穷,富的依然变富。最后他明白了:因果报应是无法控制的,上辈子造的业,不管怎么样今生都必须承受。

It is said that in Tibetan history there was a high-ranking official who three times ordered the equal division of citizens' properties under his charge, giving rich men's money to poor ones. Yet after a while he found that those who were poor initially stayed in poverty all the same, and those who were rich before became rich again. In the end he saw that karma could not be controlled. What people had done in their previous incarnations must be paid for in their current lives.

评论

微观西藏
TIBET: FAST & FURIOUS

灵魂像风
The Soul Is Like Wind

灵魂是什么样子的？《灵魂像风》的作者马丽华在谈到书名时说："我一步步走向了乡村世界的深处，走进西藏人观念和精神的核心，走进人们的灵魂中去。西藏人说，灵魂像风。于是我便刹那间心生灵感，把这个短语用作书名。"

What is the soul like? When talking about the title of the book *The Soul Is Like the Wind*, author Ma Lihua explains, 'Step by step I walked into the depths of the countryside, then into the core of the Tibetans' concepts and spirit, and finally into their souls. The Tibetans say the soul is like the wind, which instantly gave me the inspiration for titling this book.'

王菲的逻辑
Faye Wong's Logic

李亚鹏曾到西藏做慈善，高寒缺氧，气候恶劣，使他的西藏行非常艰辛。后来，有人问他太太王菲："你担心他吗？"王菲说："心疼，但不担心。他去做那么好的事情，一定会平安，不必担心。"

Li Yapeng, a Chinese actor, once went to Tibet to do charity. The oxygen deficiency and the bad climate made his journey extremely difficult. Later, someone asked his wife, the famous Chinese singer Faye Wong, 'Did you worry about him?' Wong answered, 'My heart ached because of his difficulties, but I didn't worry about him. He went there to do such a good thing, so he would surely be safe. I didn't need to worry.'

摄影：觉果

精神・信仰
Spirituality and Faith

不喧嚣的高原
The Muted Plateau

藏族作家扎西达娃曾说：我们是一个喜欢在宁静状态下思索的民族，喇嘛们静坐于幽暗的佛灯下思索佛陀的教诲，老人们坐在门槛上晒着太阳思索来世的景象……学者们盘腿坐在浩如烟海的经典古书前惊叹祖先的伟大……江河沉默、群山沉默，这是一个没有喧嚣的高原，一切都在宁静中冥想思索。

Tibetan writer Tashi Dawa once said, 'We are a people that enjoy quiet reflection. Lamas quietly sit under the light of a Buddha lamp pondering the teachings of the Buddha, and elders bathe in sunlight imagining their afterlives. Scholars kneel down in front of a sea of classic scriptures, stunned by the wisdom of their ancestors. Rivers flow in silence, and mountains fence out noise. It's a placid plateau, where everything is lost in contemplation.'

言施，心施，颜施
Gifts of Words, Hearts, and Facial Expressions

西藏人认为布施并不局限于金钱。当一个人处在困境中你对他说安慰、鼓励的话，这就是"言施"；你宽容攻击你的人，你认为他们是可怜之人而非可恨之人，这就是"心施"；你每天都保持微笑，而不是遇到一点事就怒目相视，这就是"颜施"。

Tibetans believe that giving alms is not limited to money. When someone is in a difficult situation, you can comfort and encourage them with the gift of words. When you forgive someone who has attacked you, and pity rather than hate them, this is a gift from your heart. When you smile all day and do not display anger when offended, this is a gift of your facial expressions.

评论

215

微观西藏
TIBET: FAST & FURIOUS

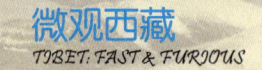

忘掉自己，才是真慈悲
Forgetting Oneself is the Real Mercy

有位西藏的喇嘛说：总有人在施舍钱给乞丐时犹豫，想着他是不是职业乞丐？自己施舍了钱会有怎样的福报？有时钱都施舍出去了，心里却还放不下，让本来应该带来快乐的施舍却带来了痛苦。对很多西藏人来说，给予就是得到，一颗清净的心就是从"舍"开始的。

A Tibetan lama once said, 'Some people always hesitate when they give money to beggars, wondering whether they are professional beggars (people who use begging as an occupation) or what rewards they can receive after giving their money. Sometimes, even after they have given the money, they still cannot get over it, turning a happy gift of charity into a painful experience.' For most Tibetans, giving is gaining, and their inner peace starts from 'abandonment'.

不要把钱看得太重
Don't Worship Money

一位僧人曾这样表述他们的金钱观：在寺院里，钱没有那么大的魔力，我们喇嘛之间并不把钱看得那么重要，相互之间如果借了钱，可以还，也可以不还。钱这个东西，不能一点没有，但也不能太多，太多了胆子会越来越大，使人走火入魔。如果退后一步，对钱的认识就会进入另外一种境界。

A monk once articulated his views on money thus: 'In the monastery, money doesn't have the magical power it possesses elsewhere, and between us monks it's not that important. If we borrow money from each other, we can pay it back, and we can also choose not to. Money isn't something you can be without, but it's not good to have too much, either. Too much money makes you daring and risk-loving. As a result, your personality will change and you'll go down a bad path. If you take a step back, your understanding of money will enter another realm.'

评论

精神·信仰
Spirituality and Faith

摄影：聂晓阳

静得下来的民族
Ethnic Group Able to Quiet Down

作家扎西达娃说："藏族是个一有机会就坐下来的好静的民族。比如一个草原牧人经过艰辛跋涉来到拉萨后，能一连几个星期寄宿在亲戚家，坐着念经，坐着冥想。"这种生活方式似乎也注定了藏族隐忍而活泼的气质。

Writer Tashi Dawa says, 'Tibetan people sit and enjoy silence whenever they get the chance. For example, after a Tibetan herdsman gets worn out by the long and difficult journey to Lhasa, he can lodge with relatives for weeks and do nothing but chant scriptures and sit in meditation.' Such a lifestyle seems to have determined Tibetans' bearing and lively personalities.

善良的护法神
Kind Guardian Deities

在西藏有很多护法神虽造像凶猛、狰狞恐怖，但信徒仍然去朝拜以获其护佑。藏族人认为这些护法神只是对妖魔凶狠，对百姓却很慈祥。他们用善良虔诚的心，希望在这些护法神的佑护下，可以避免任何灾难。

Although many statues of guardian deities look ferocious and dreadful, believers still worship them to gain their protection. When facing these statues, Tibetans believe these guardian deities are only fierce toward demons, but benign to common people. The Tibetans sincerely hope that they can avoid disasters under the protection of these guardian deities.

微观西藏
TIBET: FAST & FURIOUS

一只名叫爷爷的狗
A Dog Named 'Grandpa'

有位活佛曾遇到一只很老的流浪狗，活佛不仅收养了它，还给它取了个名字，叫"爷爷"。他每天说："爷爷，过来。爷爷，晚安。"听上去很可笑，但他相信"这辈子它是一条狗，可能在十万辈子前它是我爷爷。"

A living Buddha once bumped into a very old stray dog, and he not only cared for it, but also gave it a name — 'Grandpa'. Every day he would say, 'Grandpa, come here', and 'Grandpa, good night'. It sounded ridiculous, but he believed: 'In this life he is a dog, but in one of his previous lives he might have been my grandfather.'

杀生禁忌
Taboo Against Killing

西藏人最大的禁忌是杀生。受戒的僧人在这方面更加严格，他们每年夏天都要尽量避免出门，以防踩、死正在孵化的幼虫。西藏僧人并不都吃素，但他们绝不亲手宰杀，而是由专门的屠夫来进行，宰杀时，僧人们还要念专门的经文以减轻动物的痛苦。

The biggest taboo for Tibetans is killing living things. Monks are especially stringent about this. They hardly go outside during the summer in order to avoid stepping on hatching larvae. Although not all Tibetan monks are vegetarians, they never kill animals themselves. Instead, a professional butcher comes to slaughter the animals while the monks recite special scriptures to ease the pain of the killing.

摄影：车刚

精神·信仰
Spirituality and Faith

一个转经者的故事
A Story of Prayer

小说家次仁罗布讲过这样一个故事：年扎老人梦见去世的妻子在地狱里还没能转世，为使亡妻的灵魂早日得到解脱，每天清晨老人便去转经，因为转经时"人与神是最接近的，人心也会变得纯净澄澈"。对信仰的虔诚使老人感到能够活着是何等的幸事，因为有机会为爱人、为自己救赎罪孽。

Novelist Tsering Norbu tells this story: An old man dreamed his deceased wife was stuck in the underworld, unable to be reincarnated. In order to extricate her, he spun prayer wheels every day, as in prayer 'the common and the divine come together, and one's heart will achieve pure clarity'. Devout faith made the old man feel that being alive was such a blessing, as he was able to practice redemption for his beloved and for himself.

乘愿再来的活佛
Reincarnated Living Buddha

在西藏，很多孕妇和家人都会焚香顶礼神佛，希望投胎腹内的生命前世是一个纯粹的佛教徒，甚至是一位活佛。在他们的观念中，活佛本来已经脱离轮回，应该生活在极乐世界，只是为了教化众生解脱苦难，才重返人间，与普通人一样经历生生死死的过程。

In Tibet, many pregnant women and their families burn incense and worship deities to pray that the baby's previous reincarnation was a pure Buddhist, or even a living Buddha. In their beliefs, living Buddhas have already broken away from *samsara* and should live in nirvana (a state of complete happiness and peace); they only come back to Earth and experience the same birth and death as humans do for the purpose of preaching their enlightenment, so that ordinary people can free themselves from pain and suffering.

评论

微观西藏
TIBET: FAST & FURIOUS

拒绝暴富
Rejecting Unexpected Wealth

大昭寺僧人尼玛次仁说："假如我有机会发财致富，或变成一个大官，可以突然地享受物质生活，我会拒绝这样做。我会说，不，因为我还有来世。为了在我的后世能够长期幸福，我不能盲目地接受这一时的欢乐。"

Nyima Tsering, a monk in Jokhang Temple, says, 'If I suddenly had the chance to get rich or become a high-ranking official, and I could enjoy a luxurious material life, I would refuse to do so. I would say no because I have an afterlife. For my long-term happiness, I'd rather not accept this temporary pleasure blindly.'

梦幻意识
Talented at Fantasy

有作家曾这样描述道："比较起其他民族来，藏族人更多具备了形象思维和梦幻意识。他们的不讲推理的直觉主义哲学，富有神秘主义色彩的心灵感应，有如艺术家的浪漫与形象性的思维方式，更甚于汉民族。幻想与梦是藏民族真实生活中一个不能缺少的部分。"

Some authors have put it this way: 'Compared with people of other cultures, Tibetans are more evolved in image thinking and talented at spinning fantasy. They do not follow reasoning, but intuition, and they believe in mysterious telepathy. This romantic and imaginative way of thinking is hardly seen in Han people. Fantasies and dreams are an indispensable part of the lives of Tibetan people.'

摄影：车刚

精神・信仰
Spirituality and Faith

从无常中学会平常心
Gaining Inner Peace from Impermanence

说起"无常",怕是没有人比西藏人有更多的体会了。这里阴晴无常,在最原始的环境下,人们的收成、福祸,都要依靠老天的安排。但他们似乎更容易有一颗平常心,对待得失更加淡然。就像六世达赖喇嘛仓央嘉措所说,"高贵的终归衰微,聚集的终于离分。"

When it comes to 'impermanence', nobody has more intimate experience than Tibetans. The weather in Tibet has always been uncertain. In the primitive conditions of the past, people's harvests and fortunes depended totally on heaven. Tibetans seem to gain inner peace more easily and take gains and losses more lightly. Just as the sixth Dalai Lama Tsangyang Gyatso said, 'What is noble will become obscure, and what is congregated will be separated.'

上进心
The Spirit of Progress

有人问,西藏人在物质方面很容易满足,这是不是不求上进?有活佛说:"上进心使你不断地实现你的价值。但被欲望带到深渊的人,就像一个猎人一样,眼睛只会盯着前方,忙碌一生,只为了去填满一个无底洞,这不是智慧,而是愚昧。"

Someone once asked, 'Tibetans are easily satisfied materially. Is that because they are not industrious?' A living Buddha answered, 'The spirit of progress should make you realize your worth continually. However, those who have been brought to the abyss by material desires become hunter-like, with eyes staring straight ahead, living only to fill up a bottomless hole of desire. This is not wisdom, but folly.'

评论

微观西藏
TIBET: FAST & FURIOUS

因果的故事
The Story of Karma

在太阳下，你将放大镜置于干燥的牛粪上，它便会起火。我们不能说火苗存在于牛粪中、太阳中或放大镜中，但将这些对象合在一起时，就会产生火苗，因为它们符合了燃烧的条件。这就像因果报应一样，西藏人相信因果，所以他们往往能更冷静地看待所谓的"好事"，也能更坦然地接受厄运。

Dry cow dung will burn if you put a magnifying glass over it in sunlight. We cannot say that cow dung, sun, or the magnifying glass contain fire, but when you put these objects together, fire will emerge since they already satisfy the conditions for a fire to start. This is a good example of karma. Tibetans believe in karma, so they tend to be more sober in evaluating those so-called good things and accept any suffering in their lives more easily.

修行与道场
Cultivation and Rites

有高僧说，芸芸众生，有慧根的人毕竟太少，怎么帮助更多的人消除贪、嗔、痴三种烦恼的根源呢？藏传佛教的做法是在一开始通过金碧辉煌的布坛和神秘的法器，吸引人们接近佛法，但随着修行的层次越高，布坛和仪式就会越简单，到最后甚至被认为"大不敬"的厕所都可以做修行的道场。

An eminent monk once said, 'Only a few people have the roots of wisdom after all, so how can we help more people get rid of the three troubles of greed, anger, and ignorance? The Tibetan Buddhist solution is to first attract people toward dharma through the splendid and magnificent *butsudan* (Buddhist altar) and mysterious instruments. As people's level of practice gets higher, the rites will become simpler. In the end, even a restroom, which is considered a profane place, can be used as a place for rites.'

评论

精神·信仰
Spirituality and Faith

摄影：车刚

来不及孤独
No Time for Loneliness

藏画大师尼玛泽仁：你看布达拉宫在蓝天下的巍峨气势和藏民们鲜艳的服饰，这说明人们对自身存在的意识是非常强烈的，更说明他们精神世界的饱满。在茫茫大草原上，长达数月看不见一个生人，与日月星辰为伴，身边的一草一木都被视为相同的生命，他们来不及孤独。

Tibetan painter Nyima Zeren says, 'Look at the towering vigor of the Potala Palace under the blue sky and the brightly-colored clothes of Tibetans. They indicate the people's acute awareness of self-existence, and display the abundance of their spiritual world. Tibetans live on the vast grassland without meeting a single stranger for months, but in the company of the sun, the moon, and the stars, they see every living thing as part of life, and they have no time to feel lonely.'

去世时的心境
The State of Mind Prior to Death

根据藏传佛教的理论，人死亡前的念头和情绪，对于下世的转生会有决定性的影响。普通人临死的时候，对自我更加执着，人活着时最熟悉的情绪就会首先显露出来。如果去世时处于善的心境，就会改善下一世；如果去世时慌乱痛苦，就会对转世产生不好的影响。

According to the theory of Tibetan Buddhism, the ideas and emotions people have before they die have a decisive influence on their reincarnation. When dying, people normally concentrate more on themselves, and the emotions they were most familiar with in their lives will emerge first. If their hearts are in a state of kindness when they die, their afterlife will be improved; but if they are in pain and panic, their reincarnation will be undermined.

微观西藏
TIBET: FAST & FURIOUS

摄影：车刚

快乐靠心

Happiness Stems from the Heart

强巴顿珠是一位普通的拉萨企业家，他说，为什么有人去歌厅、舞厅找乐，反而觉得更没意思？那是因为快乐是靠心感受的，只有让心恢复简单纯净才能有真正的快乐。"像歌厅那种地方，本来就充满了欲望、诱惑和各种不好的情绪，虽然一个人能获得一时的刺激，但内心却因此更加混浊动荡。"

Champa Dondrup, an ordinary Lhasa entrepreneur, says, 'Why do some people feel bored after going to a cabaret or dance club for fun? Because happiness is felt with one's heart. The only way to feel real happiness is to make the heart simple and clean. Places like cabarets are filled with lusts, temptations, and negative emotions. Although one may be ignited by temporary excitement, his or her inner peace will turn into chaos afterwards.'

精神·信仰
Spirituality and Faith

烦恼之源
The Root of Annoyance

在很多藏传佛教的高僧大德看来，人的自私欲是万恶之本，也是烦恼之源。而利他心是摆脱烦恼求得解脱的根本之路。寂天菩萨说：这个世界不管还有什么样的快乐，都来自希望别人快乐；这个世界不管有什么样的痛苦，都来自希望自己快乐。所以有人说：头脑和心就是寺庙，善心就是最大的哲学。

Many eminent Tibetan Buddhist monks think that human selfishness is the source of all evils and annoyance, and altruism is the fundamental way to get rid of annoyance. Shantideva (an eighth-century Indian Buddhist scholar) said, 'No matter what kind of happiness there is in this world, it will always stem from helping others gain happiness; no matter what kind of pain there is in this world, it will always originate in hoping to gain happiness for oneself. So some people say: the brain and the heart are temples, and kindness is the most important philosophy.'

安分
Abidance

在西藏，安分是一种美德。面对比自己地位高和更有钱的人，人们会认为那是别人前世善行的福报，不但不会仇富，而且还会用吐舌头挠耳朵摸脑袋等动作来表示敬意和羡慕。在他们看来，一个人如果不顾因果的安排而急于改变自己的现状，就会每天在争斗、不满和失落中度过，那是一种双倍的惩罚。

In Tibet, abidance is a virtue. People with higher positions or more money are regarded as having been rewarded for their previous lives. People are not angry with them; instead, they show respect and admiration by sticking out their tongues, scratching their ears, touching their heads and so on. In their eyes, if one is eager to change his current status while neglecting the arrangement of karma, he will live every day of his life in struggle, anger, and despair. That is a double punishment.

评论

微观西藏
TIBET: FAST & FURIOUS

护念
Protection of Thoughts

在藏民的宗教观念里，一个人不做恶事固然重要，不起坏的心念更重要，这就是所谓的"身语意"同修。在他们看来，即使没有付诸行动，但一个恶的想法或念头也会带来内心的污染，让人空虚焦躁、心智下降，更容易做出错误的事情，带来恶果和烦恼。

According to Tibetans' religious beliefs, it is certainly important not to do evil things, but it's even more important not to have bad intentions. This is called a balanced practice of body, speech, and mind. In their view, a bad thought can contaminate one's inner world even though it has not turned into a real action yet. It will make a person anxious, empty, silly, and do wrong things more easily, bringing bad results and worries.

磕长头背后
The Meaning of Prostration

西藏人一生都在磕长头，这背后有什么寓意呢？一位藏族母亲告诉孩子："每个人的内心都有一种傲慢，这种情绪会影响人们对事物的评判，造成误差，所以人要不断对抗自己的傲慢，不断修正自己的言行，这其中的一个修行办法，就是令自己全身匍匐在地。"

Tibetans spend their whole lives prostrating. So what is the meaning of it? A Tibetan mother answered this by telling her child, 'There is always a kind of arrogance in people's mind, and it will influence you when you make judgments, or even lead you to do the wrong thing. So we need to keep fighting against that arrogance and correct our behavior. One way to achieve this is to practice prostrations.'

摄影：觉果

精神・信仰
Spirituality and Faith

"再来人"
'Reborn People'

在藏传佛教看来，一个悟道成佛的人最值得尊敬的地方，是他还愿意重返俗世救苦救难，所以"活佛"在藏语中本源的意思，就是"再来人"。一个活佛的前世和转世，虽然动机和目标是一致的，但他们并不是完全相同的人。转世者要根据具体的情况，适应当世人的"业"，以便更好地帮助他们。

In Tibetan Buddhism the most respected people are those who have gained enlightenment and become a Buddha, and still want to go back to the earthly world to relieve people's misery — so the meaning of 'Living Buddha' in Tibetan is 'reborn person'. No incarnation of the Living Buddha is the same, although they have the same motivation and purpose. Reincarnations will adapt to the world according to specific circumstances in order to better help others.

轮回
Samsara

在西藏有一个基本的观念，那就是"轮回"。人们相信，生命不只有一辈子，人去世之后还会有下一辈子、下下辈子以及未来无数辈子，生命不息，轮回不止。有人说，如果相信人生是"一锤子买卖"，人将更加以短期利益为目标，追求现世的享乐；而如果相信来世，人的生命观、价值观和世界观将全然改变。

Samsara is a fundamental concept among Tibetans. People believe that there is not just one life: there is the afterlife, the afterlife of the afterlife, and infinite future lives. Reincarnation and life never stop. Some people say that the belief in a 'one-time deal' life will make a person focus more on short-term goals and pursue pleasures in the current life; the belief in an afterlife can dramatically change people's philosophy, values, and views about the world.

评论

微观西藏
TIBET: FAST & FURIOUS

人身最宝贵
The Body Is Most Precious

在藏传佛教看来，一个人最大的"财宝"是什么？是自己转世为人的"人身"。一个人的出生之所以值得庆祝，是因为虽然生老病死本身都是苦，但一个人在世界上托生为人，也意味着有机会进行自利利他的佛法修行，从而有机会证悟得道。父母的生育之恩，不是让自己享乐，而是给自己一个脱离轮回的机会。

What is the most precious treasure for a Tibetan Buddhist? It is the human body one uses for his or her incarnation into the current life. The idea that one's birth is worth celebrating expresses the view that although birth, senility, illness, and death are all painful in life, once you are reborn as a human, you have the chance to practice Buddhism as a human being, which offers the chance of enlightenment. The gift from your parents should not lead you into a life of pleasure, but give you a chance to break away from *samsara*.

真正的敌人
The Real Enemy

有位西藏高僧说，佛教称斩除烦恼者为"阿罗汉"，意思即"战胜者"，说明烦恼才是真正的敌人，战胜烦恼才是真正的英雄。可惜的是，人们往往不顾死活地和仇敌拼命，而对真正的敌人——烦恼，却不怎么花力气去"战斗"。

An eminent Tibetan monk says that Buddhism calls someone who gets rid of worries an *arahat*, which means 'victor'. It indicates that worries are the real enemy. The real hero is the person capable of fighting off those worries. Unfortunately, people usually fight external enemies at the risk of their lives, but never 'fight' desperately against their real enemy — worries.

评论

精神・信仰
Spirituality and Faith

宿命标记
Mark of Fate

据说，怀着某种强烈愿望转世的人，身上会有某种神秘的宿命标记。如果前世足够虔诚，转世后一降生，这个标记就会立即炙烤着他或她的心，驱赶着他或她去找到自己的使命。

It is said that when people with strong wishes are reincarnated, they will have some kind of mysterious mark of fate on their bodies. If they were devout enough in their previous lives, this mark will fire their hearts and drive them to find their mission in this life right after they are born.

五体投地
Prostration

走在西藏的公路上，你会看到路边有磕长头的藏民，他们用身体丈量大地，用手指数过云彩，像爬梯子一样爬过陡峭的山崖，像读经书一样掀过平坦的草原，他们的目标只有一个：朝圣到拉萨。有作家说："他们相信只有五体投地才能表达最虔诚最深切的情感和愿望。"

In Tibet, you may see Tibetans prostrating on the side of the roads; using their bodies to measure the earth, using their fingers to count the clouds, climbing steep cliffs as if climbing ladders, and flipping through the flat grassland as if it were a scripture scroll. They all have the same objective: a pilgrimage to Lhasa. One writer says, 'They believe that only by fully casting their body to the ground can they express their deepest and most devout emotions and wishes.'

摄影：车刚

微观西藏
TIBET: FAST & FURIOUS

本尊
Yidam

在藏传佛教中，每个修行者都可根据自己的情况选择相应的"本尊"，不同的本尊是为了适应不同性格的人修行的需要。藏密的本尊佛像，有的寂静，有的愤怒，有的慈祥，有的狰狞，全部依人的心性而塑造，面对佛像就是面对自己的心，借幻修真，帮助人通过修行，从里到外都得到净化。

In Tibetan Buddhism, every Buddhist can choose a corresponding *yidam*, or personal deity, according to their own circumstances. People use different *yidams* depending on their needs of cultivation. The *yidam* figures in Esoteric Tibetan Buddhism have various external expressions. Some are quiet; some are angry; some are kind; some are ferocious. All of them are created based on people's dispositions. Facing an image of Buddha is like facing one's own heart. People nourish themselves with illusions and receive complete purification through this process.

藏密
Esoteric Buddhism

"藏密"的"密"，在于每个上师对修持方法都有自己的体悟，其绝招秘不示人，只能在单一的师傅和单一的弟子之间传承。倘若没有师傅的允许，任何人不得把学到的东西传授给别人，也不可以轻易显示所练就的"神通"。所以对密宗信徒来说，最重要的是找到自己信任的上师，否则根本不得其门而入。

The 'esoteric' part of Esoteric Tibetan Buddhism is that every master has a unique experience of cultivation methods, and their methods are never shown to others except their sole disciple. Without a master's permission, no one can pass on to someone else what has been learned, or easily show the 'magical powers' that have been acquired. The most important thing for Esoteric Buddhist disciples is to find a guru they can trust, otherwise they cannot even have the chance to learn the basics.

精神·信仰
Spirituality and Faith

横向长头
Horizontal Prostration

在西藏，有些虔诚的朝圣者觉得，磕纵向的长头仍不足以表达虔诚，于是就磕用身体宽度丈量朝圣之路的"横向长头"。有人说，在陡峭的山路上，这样的磕头简直就像杂技一样惊险。可是，朝圣者不以为苦，面容祥和坚毅，他们身上，洋溢着坚定的内心所赐予的力量和幸福。

In Tibet, devout pilgrims think prostrating vertically is not enough to express their devoutness, so they make horizontal prostrations, measuring the path of pilgrimage with their bodies' length. Some people say that doing so on steep mountain roads is as breathtaking as doing acrobatics. However, pilgrims don't take this as a hardship. Their faces look peaceful and firm, and their bodies pour out power and happiness from their resolute hearts.

放生羊
Released Sheep

《西藏文学》副主编次仁罗布讲过一个真实的故事：一位藏族老汉忽然觉得一头对他咩咩叫的羊是自己去世妻子的转世，于是买下来，天天带它到八廓街转经，以便她来世再投胎做人。这种羊穿耳后叫放生羊，谁也不能再伤害了。后来老汉生病，羊依旧天天自己去八廓街转经。

Norbu Tsering, the deputy editor-in-chief of *Tibet Literature*, tells this true story: an old man suddenly felt that a sheep bleating at him was the reincarnation of his deceased wife. He bought the sheep and circumambulated with her at Barkhor Street every day so that she could be reincarnated as a human in her next life. The ears of this kind of sheep were pierced to indicate that the sheep was freed and no one should hurt her anymore. Later the old man fell ill, but the sheep still circumambulated by herself every day.

评论

酥油灯节
Butter Lamp Festival

每年的藏历正月十五是酥油灯节，拉萨人会制作几层楼高的脚手架，将酥油做成各种图案的灯挂在上面。但这只是一个晚上的奢华，虽然耗费艺术家几个月的心血，但当第一束阳光照耀大地的时候，所有东西都要不留任何痕迹。这个节日的宗教意义，正是在于让世人深刻领会人生无常，不过昙花一现。

The fifteenth of the first month in the Tibetan calendar is the Butter Lamp Festival. People in Lhasa make scaffolds several floors high on which to hang many variously patterned butter lamps, but this is only a one-night luxury. Though this has taken artists months to prepare, when the first ray of sunshine touches the ground, no traces should be left. The religious meaning of this festival is to tell people that life changes like the weather and is just like a flash in the pan.

长远思维
Long-Term Thinking

在藏传佛教看来，一个人的死亡并不是生命的结束，而是生命重新转世的开始。就如人不会把一辈子的存款都花在一顿饭上一样，因为未来还有千万世，所以来世比今生更加重要。这种长远的观点深刻影响了藏传佛教信徒的生活方式。他们总是能够有更加长远的视角：无论今生如何，总还可以希望下辈子比今生更好。

According to Tibetan Buddhism, death is not the end of life; on the contrary, it is the beginning of an afterlife in reincarnation. Just as a person would not spend the savings of his or her whole life on one meal, the future life is more important than this life, since there can be millions of reincarnations in the future. Such long-term perspective has profoundly influenced the lifestyle of Tibetan Buddhist believers. They always have a long-term view: no matter how this life is, they can always hope that the next life will be better than this one.

评论

精神·信仰
Spirituality and Faith

摄影：车刚

活佛之死
Death of Living Buddhas

很多人都会有这样的疑问：活佛怎么会"逝世"呢？藏传佛教认为，活佛像常人一样以死亡示人，就是要通过这一形式告诉众人，佛与世人没有什么两样，佛是觉悟了的众生，众生是未觉悟的佛，只要按照佛法精修，最终就能解脱成佛。

Many people have such a doubt: why would a living Buddha 'die'? Tibetan Buddhism believes that a living Buddha dies just like an ordinary person, because he wants to show that there is no difference between a living Buddha and common people. A Buddha is an enlightened human being, and a human being is a Buddha that hasn't awoken yet. Everyone can break away from *samsara* and become a Buddha eventually, as long as he or she practices Buddhism seriously.

所谓神通
Magical Powers

一位高僧曾说，在西藏，一位真正的密宗上师，绝不会为了炫耀的目的显示神通，不会猜你最近发生了什么，不会答应保佑自己的信徒得财得官，不会四处驱邪捉鬼，不摆排场故作高深……在高僧看来，一个信徒如果只对灵异之事感兴趣，实际已经误入歧途，上师匡正还唯恐不及呢。

An eminent Tibetan monk says that in Tibet real Esoteric Buddhist masters will never show off their magical powers. They will not tell you what has happened to you recently, nor promise their disciples that they will get rich and powerful, nor drive out evil spirits, capture ghosts, or pretend to be profound. In their perspective, it is bad enough for a disciple to focus on myths, so they always waste no time correcting the misbehavior of a disciple.

全村都会为他骄傲
The Pride of a Whole Village

朝圣对于藏传佛教信徒来说，不仅是一种功德的积累，更是一种人生心愿。很多人终其一生，最大的愿望就是能去拉萨朝圣。在这些朝圣者的身后，他的亲友默默地拉着车、赶着羊，那是为朝圣者提供后勤服务的流动的家。如果一个地方出了位曾磕长头去过拉萨的朝圣者，整个村子的人都会感到骄傲。

A pilgrimage for Tibetan Buddhists is not only an accumulation of merits and virtues, but also a wish for life. For many people, the biggest aspiration is to go on a pilgrimage to Lhasa. Behind these pilgrims, their relatives and friends pull carts and herd sheep to provide a mobile home in support. If a pilgrim reaches Lhasa in prostration, the whole village will be proud of him or her.

评论

精神·信仰
Spirituality and Faith

无私的祈祷
Selfless Prayers

藏族学者德庆卓嘎说，西藏人朝佛、祈祷的时候，他首先要祈祷的是：六道众生得幸福，世界众国享和平。他很少说我现在遇到什么问题，请菩萨帮我解决，不会。"你不信的话可以随便问任何人，也可以在八廓街听——这里的人都懂的，只有你真心为别人，最后才能成就自己。"

Tibetan scholar Dechen Drolkar remarks, 'During a Tibetan's pilgrimage and prayer, the first thing he or she prays for is happiness for the six realms of existence*, and peace for all countries of the world. A Tibetan will not say what troubles he or she is facing right now and plead for solutions from the bodhisattva. No, never. If you don't believe this you can ask any Tibetan or you can just listen on Barkhor Street — all people here know, in the end you can realize your potential only when you genuinely care for others.'

* In Buddhism, there are six paths into *samsara* (i.e. the endless cycle of birth, suffering, death, and rebirth). These six paths form the six realms of existence, which include god, people, animals, hell, *asuras* and hungry ghosts.

恩怨情仇
Kindness and Hatred

很多西藏的高僧都会讲述这样的故事：有位圣者化缘，看到一个村妇怀抱小孩，给小孩喂鱼肉，不时抛石头打一只嚼鱼骨头的母狗。圣者不禁失笑，原来村妇怀中的小孩，前生是杀害自己的仇家；她喂食小孩的那条鱼前生是她的丈夫，而她用石头打的那只母狗，前生则是她的母亲。圣者说：这就是世间的恩怨情仇。

Many eminent Tibetan monks like to tell this story: when a sage begged alms, he saw a village woman with a baby in her arms feeding the baby a fish, and occasionally throwing rocks at a female dog that was chewing on fish bones. The sage could not help laughing, because the baby the village woman was carrying was the enemy that killed her in her previous life, while the fish that woman used to feed the baby with was her previous husband, and the female dog used to be her mother. The sage mused, 'These are the gratitudes and resentments, kindnesses and hatreds in this world.'

微观西藏
TIBET: FAST & FURIOUS

摄影：车刚

朝圣到拉萨
Pilgrimage to Lhasa

作家马丽华这样描述她碰到的一个朝圣部落：罗布桑布上一辈人中有几位老人磕着头到过拉萨，这使他们荣耀一生。罗布桑布和亲友也组成了朝圣队，父亲磕头，母亲做后勤，历时一年一月零三天到达拉萨。一年里，每位磕头人磨穿牛皮做的围裙不止八张，用坏木质手套不计其数，上路时的十五头牛也所剩无几。

Writer Ma Lihua describes her encounter with a tribe of pilgrims: 'A few elders from Norbu Sambu's family had reached Lhasa doing prostrations, and this honored them for the rest of their lives. Sambu also organized a pilgrimage team with friends and family. His father did prostrations, and his mother was responsible for logistical support. They arrived in Lhasa after one year, one month and three days. In this year, every person that did prostrations had worn out more than eight leather aprons as well as countless wooden gloves, and the fifteen cattle they took with them were almost all gone.'

惩罚
Punishment

在西藏有这样一个说法：如果有人作恶后逃走，人们可以不必去追赶，因为"善有善报，恶有恶报，不在今生，必在来世"。可不是吗，背负着罪恶感和对来世的恐惧，就是对人最大的惩罚了。

Tibet has a saying: if one escapes after committing evils, people need not chase him or her, because 'good begets good, evil leads to evil, if not in this life, then he or she will pay in another life.' No doubt, no punishment is greater than carrying guilt and fear into afterlife.

精神 · 信仰
Spirituality and Faith

花钱最多的地方
Where to Spend the Most Money

藏族学者平措次仁：大部分西藏人一生中花钱最多的地方，就是朝佛和捐给寺庙，或者施舍给别人。对西藏人来说，施舍就像存钱一样，这辈子施舍出去，下辈子就会得到好报。而且，当你施舍的时候，最好不要抱有什么目的，不求回报，这样积累的功德更多。

Tibetan scholar Phuntsok Tsering says that most Tibetans spend the largest amount of their money on paying respects to Buddha, on contributions to temples or giving alms to others. For Tibetans, charity is like savings. They believe you will be rewarded in the afterlife if you have given alms in this life. Moreover, it is best not to have any intention of gaining rewards in return when you are doing charity, since you can accumulate more merits and virtues without anything attached.

在路上
On the Road

小说家范稳塑造了阿拉西朝圣的故事：他用7年时间去拉萨朝佛，一路磕长头，走过仇人的侮辱，走过险恶的雪山森林，走过瘟疫蔓延的村庄，失去所有亲人，经历了常人不能忍受的身体和精神的双重折磨。他对宗教的虔诚，对仇人的悲悯，对折磨的坚忍，印证了信仰不在别处，就在信仰者通往它的路上。

Storywriter Fan Wen created a story of pilgrimage. In this story, the hero Alaxi spends seven years going to Lhasa on pilgrimage. He prostrates along his journey, bearing insults from his enemies. He walks through sinister snow mountains and forests, and passes villages struck by plagues. He has lost all relatives and has experienced double torture in his body and spirit unbearable to ordinary people. His devoutness to his beliefs, sympathy for his enemies, and perseverance in the face of torture confirm that faith lies nowhere but on the way the believers take.

评论

微观西藏
TIBET: FAST & FURIOUS

菩萨
Bodhisattvas

藏传佛教把那些自己证悟得道之后、发愿重返人间拯救众生的圣人叫"菩萨"。在西藏，所有帮助人类进步的伟人，西藏人听到他们的名字，就会叫他们"菩萨"，认为他们是为了解脱众生苦难来做世人榜样的。人们认为这些伟人的去世，只不过是去"休息"一下，还会转世回来继续完成使命的。

Those who are willing to go back to the mundane world and help the masses after reaching enlightenment are called *bodhisattvas* in Tibetan Buddhism. In Tibet, people call anyone who has helped them progress a *bodhisattva*. Tibetans think these people come to this world to relieve people's sufferings and to set a good example for others. They also believe that these great people die just to take a rest, and they will reincarnate to accomplish their missions.

留下来的东西
Things Left Behind

藏语把身体叫"留下来的东西"，意思是说，如果今生像一场旅行，身体只不过是我们的"行李"。西藏人每当说这个词的时候，就等于在提醒自己，我们只是旅客而已，暂时住在此生和此身，因此他们并不以全部时间和精力改善这些临时的外在环境，让心分散。如果够吃、够住、够穿，就满足了。

The body is called 'things left behind' in Tibetan, which means that if the present life is like a trip, the body is just 'luggage'. Every time Tibetans speak this word, it reminds them that they are just travelers living temporarily in this body for this life, so they will not spend all their time and energy to make their temporary living environment better, thus preventing the distraction of their hearts. People should feel satisfied as long as they have enough food, enough living space and enough clothes.

评论

精神·信仰
Spirituality and Faith

跳崖成佛
Becoming Buddha after Jumping off a Cliff

藏族学者平措扎西曾讲过一个故事：有个屠夫想杀绵羊，中途去解手，羊用蹄子把屠刀埋起来。屠夫发现后，心生怜悯和罪恶，悔恨之下从悬崖跳下，结果顿悟成佛。这一切被一个在山洞修行的喇嘛看到，怀着嫉妒之心，也从悬崖跳下，结果摔死了。原来屠夫跳崖成佛，只是因为在那一刻，他的心变纯净了。

Tibetan scholar Puncog Zhaxi once told a story about a butcher who wanted to kill a sheep. When the butcher went to answer nature's call, the sheep buried his knife with its hoof. After the butcher found out, he felt sympathetic and guilty, so he jumped off a cliff in regret. In the end, he attained sudden enlightenment and became a Buddha. A lama doing retreat in a cave saw this scene and jumped down in jealousy, but he died. The reason why the butcher became a Buddha was that at the moment he jumped off the cliff, his heart became purer than ever.

婴儿观佛殿
Buddha Hall in a Baby's Eyes

西藏人对快乐有一个比喻：婴儿观佛殿。有位高僧说，西藏的佛殿，大都金碧辉煌，婴儿在里面目迷神往，对什么东西都很好奇。他会很自然地对辉煌的佛殿进行观赏和享受，不会闭上眼睛逃避，更不会毁灭它们。但是他们幼稚的心扉，对此种种却绝无留恋，更不懂得起什么欲望。这就是修行者的境界。

Tibetans have a metaphor for happiness: a baby looking at the Buddha hall. One eminent monk says that most Tibetan Buddha halls are magnificent, so babies are dazzled and become curious about everything inside. They will spontaneously watch and enjoy the beauty of the halls. They won't close their eyes to prevaricate or even have thoughts of destroying them. However, their childish hearts will not have any reluctance to leave everything, nor do they have any desires. This is exactly like people with high levels of spiritual cultivation.

微观西藏
TIBET: FAST & FURIOUS

摄影：李建平

佛会不会把妈妈还给他？
Will Buddha Give Back His Mother?

《西藏梦想地》中写到一个真实的故事：一个5岁的孩子跟妈妈从四川阿坝出发，磕等身长头去亚东。途中妈妈病逝，临终告诉孩子坚持到亚东的东嘎寺就能见到佛。四年多后，孩子仍带着梦想磕头跋涉在路上。每晚，他都问同路的人，到了东嘎寺后，佛会不会把妈妈还给他？

Dreamland in Tibet records a true story about a five-year-old boy and his mother. They set out for Yadong, Tibet, from Aba, Sichuan, prostrating along their journey. On the way, his mother dies of a disease, but tells him that he will see the Buddha if he can make it to Dungkar Monastery in Yadong. After more than four years, the boy was still prostrating and trekking toward his dream. Every night, he would ask fellow travelers, 'Will the Buddha give back my mother when I arrive?'

孩子与糖
A Boy and Candy

在亚东附近的帕里镇，一位作家拿糖给一个一路磕长头至此的孩子。由于自小就踏上了漫漫朝圣路，孩子不知道糖是什么。当他知道糖是一种好吃的东西时，问道："这东西我能给佛吃吗？"作家泪流满面。

In the town of Phari near Yadong, a writer gave candy to a boy who had prostrated there. Since the boy had set out on this pilgrimage in childhood, he did not know what candy was. When he eventually understood that candy is something delicious, he asked, 'Can I give this to the Buddha to eat?' The writer burst into tears.

精神・信仰
Spirituality and Faith

穷人乐子多
The Poor Have More Fun

丹增塔克是一名普通的藏医，他说：藏族人喜欢说"穷人乐子多"，我行医走过很多地方，发现自然环境比较偏远的地方，人们更多的是把今天过好就行了，生活很简单，没有太多的想法，也就不会有太大的压力。我觉得这些艰苦地方的人，应该给很多有钱人当生活的老师。

Tenzin Take is an ordinary Tibetan doctor. He says, 'Tibetans like to say, "The poor have more fun." I have been to many places in my work and found that in remote places, people are more likely to focus on today. Their lives are simple without many thoughts, so they also have little pressure. I think these people living in poor places should be teachers of life for many rich individuals.'

众生平等
Equality of All Beings

藏族学者平措次仁：比如说遇到一场灾难，现在只剩下一碗饭，一般的藏族人会给自己的孩子还是会平均分给邻居的孩子？当然是平均的，因为西藏文化不强调众生的分别，别人家的孩子也许上辈子或者下辈子就是自己的孩子。

Tibetan scholar Phuntsok Tsering: 'Let's say there is a catastrophe right now, and only one bowl of food is left. Would ordinary Tibetans give the food to their own children or distribute it equally between their children and the neighbors? They would probably choose the latter, since Tibetan culture doesn't stress the differences between beings. Kids of your neighbors can be your kids in their past or future reincarnations.'

评论

微观西藏
TIBET: FAST & FURIOUS

虔诚
Devoutness

第一次看到朝圣者一边行走，一边五体投地、磕等身长头时，人们的眼里常会噙满泪水。他们风餐露宿、蓬头垢面、转山转水、日夜兼程，用肉身丈量艰辛的信仰之路，孤独而充盈。这时人们往往会羡慕这种超越时间和生命的执着、虔诚和苦行，渴望对大地全身心的匍匐和信任。

Seeing pilgrims prostrating as they walk, people's eyes will brim with tears. They eat in the wind, and sleep in the dew. With disheveled hair and dusty faces, they plod through mountains and waters, and press forward day and night, measuring the arduous path of faith with their body. They are lonely but replete. Those who watch them tend to envy their persistence and devoutness which transcend time and life. They will desire to be immersed in the prostration and trust toward Earth, and yearn to acquire a kind of guide, redemption, and harbor for their souls.

磕头朝圣的规矩
Rules for Prostration

有作家讲到磕头朝圣的规矩，每天自上路起，只准念经，不准讲话，遇到非讲的时候，要先念经以求宽恕；途中遇河，要目测河距，涉水而过后补磕；下山时因为有惯性，下了山要补磕相应距离；在雪深过膝的雪山，就拿绳子丈量过，到拉萨后补磕。

A writer wrote about the rules of prostration: 'Every day after you set out, you can only recite scriptures, without any other utterance. If you have to speak to others, you need to recite scriptures first to ask for forgiveness. When crossing a river, you have to measure the distance with your eyes, and make up this distance of prostration after going across. Because of the downward momentum while going downhill, you also have to make up the prostrations at the foot of the mountain. On mountains covered with snow deeper than to the knee, you have to measure the uncovered distance with a rope, and make it up when you come to Lhasa.'

评论

逸闻·趣谈
Cool Stories

微观西藏
TIBET: FAST & FURIOUS

"八角街"误会
The Misunderstanding of 'Eight-Cornered Street'

很多人看到"八角街"会望文生义，以为是条有八个"角"的街，实际上这是一个误会。八角街，就是八廓街。因为在拉萨的四川人很多，他们的方言中，"廓"与"角"的发音相近，就把藏语"barkhor"音译成带方言味儿的"八角街"了。

When many people see 八角街 (literally eight-cornered street), they take it literally and think it is actually a street with eight corners. In fact, this is a beautiful misunderstanding. 八角街 is the same as 八廓街 (Barkhor Street). Since there are many people from Sichuan in Lhasa, in the Sichuan dialect, the pronunciation of 角 is similar to that of 廓. Thus, the original Barkhor Street, thanks to dialect pronunciation, became 'Eight-Cornered Street'.

令人又敬又畏的灶神
The Respected and Revered Kitchen God

过去，西藏流行对灶神的崇拜。传说她是女性神，负责掌管家庭、财产，也守护生命。每提起她，人们总是毕恭毕敬，平时要供祭，搬家时首先要给"灶神移位"。不过家庭主妇们对她有些微词，说她心胸比针尖还小，脾气比巫婆还怪，家里所有麻烦事都是她在使坏，当然了，她们也只敢在心里腹诽一下。

In the past, the worship of the kitchen deity used to be popular in Tibet. Legends described her as a goddess in charge of home affairs and finances, while also protecting life. People are extremely deferential whenever she is mentioned, and frequently make offerings to her. Before moving house, a ceremony is held to move her 'place'. However, housewives also have some things to say about her — she is said to be unpredictable and short-tempered, and she is blamed for all the troubles in a house. Of course, everyone has to vent their discontent via veiled criticism.

评论

摄影：车刚

乞丐村
Beggar Village

藏医丹增塔克说：西藏过去有个村子曾经遭灾，没有吃的，一些男人就去当强盗。后来有个活佛劝说他们当强盗是害人害己，还不如去要饭，既能让自己吃饱，还能帮助施舍者积累功德，于是每年特定时候全村出外乞讨一段时间，便成了当地的传统。

The Tibetan doctor Tenzin Take says, 'A Tibetan village once had a disaster. Without food, some men became robbers. Later, a living Buddha told them that robbing harmed both themselves and others. He advised that even begging is better than robbing, since it would not only help them feed themselves, but also let the giver accumulate better karma. Consequently, the whole village would leave and beg for a period at a particular time, which developed into a local tradition.'

关帝庙
Temple of Guan Yu

拉萨有座无人不晓的关帝庙，是乾隆年间修建的。在寻常藏族百姓的观念中，常常把关云长看成藏族英雄格萨尔王的化身。有意思的是，《格萨尔王》这部藏族著名的英雄史诗也被汉族学者们形象地称为《藏三国》。

Lhasa has the well-known Guan Yu Temple, built during the flourishing Qing Dynasty. (Guan Yu was a famous general during the Three Kingdoms period in China.) In the eyes of average Tibetans, Guan Yu is usually seen as the incarnation of the famous Tibetan hero King Gesar. Interestingly, *The Epic of King Gesar* is also termed *The Tibetan Three Kingdoms* by Han scholars.

微观西藏
TIBET: FAST & FURIOUS

夸奖
Giving Compliments

在西藏，不能随便夸奖别人。有位作家说他曾夸奖一个漂亮的小姑娘，结果她母亲生气地拉走了这个小姑娘。原来，她认为夸奖会招来鬼神的嫉妒，导致生病招灾。

In Tibet, you cannot compliment others as you would elsewhere. A writer said he once complimented a pretty little girl, but her mother angrily dragged the girl away. As a matter of fact, her mother thought compliments would bring ghosts' jealousy and lead to illness and trouble.

敬畏玛尼石
Revering *Mani* Stones

在西藏，玛尼石的内容通常是佛菩萨像、护法神、经书摘抄等，但是有的人也会刻上他们的忏悔。他们如果不慎踩死一只青蛙，就会挑选良辰吉日念经后请人将其形象刻在玛尼石上，旁边刻六字真言，并在背面刻：为杀生赎罪，向佛致敬。所以，面对这样的玛尼石，人们会从心底升起更多对生命的敬畏。

In Tibet, *mani* stones often feature buddhas, bodhisattvas, guardian deities, and excerpts from scriptures, but some people also engrave them with their repentance. For example, if a Tibetan accidentally steps on a frog, he might choose an auspicious day, recite scriptures, and invite a carver to carve the frog's figure on a *mani* stone with the six-syllable mantra *om mani padme hum* next to it. On the back of the stone they would inscribe, 'To atone for killing, to pay tribute to the Buddha.' Hence, when facing such *mani* stones, a sense of reverence toward life will rise from the bottom of people's hearts.

摄影：聂晓阳

逸闻·趣谈
Cool Stories

不喝就挨扎
Don't Drink, Get Pricked

西藏人特别能喝酒,他们常自酿青稞酒,逢年过节最好的礼物便是整箱的啤酒。几乎没有西藏人不喝酒,对于那些拒绝对饮的人,他们都准备了小针,扎一下以示惩罚。入藏拍摄纪录片的书云就因为滴酒不沾,被扎了不少回。

Tibetans are heavy drinkers. They often produce barley wines at home. The best gift on holidays is a whole case of beer. Almost all Tibetans drink. Those who refuse to drink are pricked with a small needle as a token of punishment. When Shu Yun entered Tibet to film her documentary, she was pricked many times for not having any alcohol.

拐弯抹角
Beating Around the Bush

一个生活在国外的藏族女孩在博客里写道:人们很难从一个藏族老人那里得到对一个问题的直接回答。比如问家庭住址,你可能会得到这样的答案:"我家挨着卖面包的女士家,不是一般面包,是特别的黄面包。还挨着另一位女士家,就是寺庙旁那条路右侧的女士……"

A Tibetan girl living abroad maintains a blog, and she writes that sometimes it can be impossible to get a straightforward answer out of an elderly Tibetan. If you try to ask an elderly Tibetan his address, you will most likely get an answer that is close to this: 'The place is right next to the lady that sells bread, not just any bread, but a kind of special yellow bread, and next to another lady, whose home stands on the right side of the road by the temple...'

评论

微观西藏
TIBET: FAST & FURIOUS

强盗歌
Robbers' Songs

西藏人爱唱歌，劳动有劳动歌，谈恋爱有爱情歌，仪式典礼上有赞颂歌，喝酒时有劝酒歌，高僧大德有传道歌，就连强盗也有"强盗歌"。藏族民俗学家德庆卓嘎曾在藏北草原搜集到不少《盗侠歌》，其中一首写道："我骑在马上无忧无虑，宝座上头人也比不上我；我漂泊无定浪迹天涯，蓝天下大地便是我家。"

Tibetans love singing. They sing labor songs when they are working, love songs when they are in love, songs of praise at ceremonies, and toast songs when they are drinking. Eminent monks have preaching songs, and even robbers have 'robbers' songs'. Tibetan folklorist Dechen Drolkar has collected many 'songs for chivalrous robbers', and this is one of them: 'I am carefree on the horse, even better than a chief on a throne; I wander around the world, and all lands under the blue sky are my home.'

喜马拉雅挑夫
Himalayan Porters

夏尔巴人以"喜马拉雅山挑夫"著称于世。他们天生耐高寒，抗缺氧，无氧登顶珠峰人数最多，几乎是这个领域的国际神话。夏尔巴人的血红蛋白浓度高于常人，肺活量也大得惊人。一位西方记者曾经开玩笑说，夏尔巴人长着专门用于登山的第三片肺叶。

The Sherpa people are known as 'Himalayan porters'. They have a preternatural resistance to the cold and lack of oxygen at high altitudes. Among those who have reached the summit of Mt. Qomolangma without the use of supplementary oxygen, the Sherpa people are the largest group, practically making an international legend in the field of mountaineering. Sherpas have a higher concentration of hemoglobin (which helps transport oxygen in the body) than ordinary people, and their lung power is astonishingly large. A Western reporter once joked that Sherpas have a third lung lobe specially designated to mountaineering.

评论

逸闻·趣谈
Cool Stories

摄影：觉果

扎个藏式小辫
Tibetan-style Plaits

在西藏，不少家长给孩子取名"扎桑"（好头发），就是为了讨个好口彩，让孩子有头好头发。西藏传统观念相信，如果把出生时的头发一直蓄到老，就会带来福气。现在，很多游客也喜欢顶着一头藏式小辫儿，以此来过把"西藏瘾"。

In Tibet, many parents name their children Tasang ('good hair') just for its auspiciousness so that their children can grow a headful of good hair. Traditional Tibetans believe if they keep their hair from birth until they become old, it will bring them good fortune. Nowadays, many tourists also like to experience the Tibetan hairstyle to satisfy their 'Tibetan addiction'.

胳膊与脸
Arms and Faces

西藏女人给人印象深刻的是舞动的长袖，而男人则是一条赤裸的臂膀。有作家讲过这样一个故事：有年冬天，在藏南谷地上，被冻得发抖的英国游客问一位从风雪中走来的西藏男人："你把胳膊放在外面，不冷吗？"西藏男人微微一笑，说："你的脸也在外面，你冷不冷呢？"

Tibetan women often impress people with their long waving sleeves, while Tibetan men impress with their bare arms. In wintertime, in a valley of southern Tibet, a shivering British tourist asked a Tibetan man who was walking through the wind and snow, 'You don't cover your arms. Don't you feel cold?' The Tibetan smiled and answered, 'Your face is also bare. Do you feel cold?'

微观西藏
TIBET: FAST & FURIOUS

高原红
Rosy Cheeks

"高原红，美丽的高原红。煮了又煮的酥油茶，还是当年那样浓。"这首歌朗朗上口，但是很多人不知道，这脸颊部位丰富、增生的毛细血管形成的"高原红"才是藏族人为什么能在低氧环境下正常生活的秘密所在。因为藏族人体内氧的运输能力超群，他们有着丰富的毛细血管网，能把血液四通八达地运送到所有细胞。

'Rosy cheeks, beautiful rosy cheeks. The repeatedly brewed butter tea still tastes as strong as it used to.' This song is melodious and popular, but few people know that Tibetans' bodies have a superior capacity to transport oxygen. Tibetans have a rich net of capillaries that can carry blood efficiently to all of the cells in their bodies. Their rosy cheeks caused by the rich and proliferous capillaries are the secret that enables Tibetans to live normally with low levels of oxygen.

"它"在忏悔
'It' Is in Repentance

在西藏经常能看到刻着小狗小羊和一行咒文的玛尼石，意思是属狗属羊的人犯了错，别人不知，但天知地知佛知，所以寝食难安，就请人刻这样的玛尼石，含蓄表达自己下不为例的意愿，还有烟鬼酒徒为表戒烟戒酒的决心，也刻这种玛尼石。

In Tibet you can often see *mani* stones engraved with dogs or sheep and a line of a mantra. This means that some people born in the year of the dog or sheep did something wrong, and others didn't know. Nevertheless, heaven, the earth, and Buddha all knew. Thinking of these would torture the wrongdoers' hearts day in and day out. Hence, they ask craftsmen to make these *mani* stones to euphemistically express their resolve not to repeat such deeds again. Likewise, when heavy smokers or drinkers want to express their determination to give up smoking or drinking, they also make such *mani* stones.

评论

逸闻·趣谈
Cool Stories

用瓢敬酒的门巴族人
Monpas Use a Gourd Ladle for Toasts

有作家曾到墨脱门巴族人家做客，晚饭后，他们开始喝酒。主人敬酒是一次一瓢，那种瓢大得人一只手都很难端住。作家很快喝醉了。在送他回去的路上，主人按照门巴族的习俗逢人就炫耀：他们把客人给灌醉了。

A writer once visited a Monpa family in Mêdog County, and they started drinking after dinner. Every time the host proposed a toast, he would hand him a gourd ladle filled with liquor. The ladle was so big that one could hardly hold it. The writer soon got drunk. After sending him back, the host bragged to the people he met that he had gotten his guest drunk.

雪山"冰激凌"
Snow Mountain 'Ice Cream Cone'

电影《转山》里，骑行入藏的晓川指着远方的雪山说："你看那雪山，像不像一座大的冰激凌？这种色泽……加 175ml 牛奶，再加 225ml 的奶油，再加两勺糖一起搅拌才出得来……还得再加香草才可以。"

In the film *Kora*, Xiao Chuan cycles into Tibet and remarks, while pointing to the remote snow mountains, 'Look at that snow mountain. Doesn't it look like a big ice cream cone? This kind of color and luster... you can only get that by adding 175ml of milk plus 225ml of cream, two spoons of sugar, and then stir... you also need to add some vanilla.'

摄影：聂晓阳

微观西藏
TIBET: FAST & FURIOUS

摄影：聂晓阳

牦牛像少女

Yaks Resemble Young Girls

美国人龙安志说："雪顿节时，牦牛被当作美女来打扮，角上挂着哈达，毛上系着花朵，背上搭着饰有狮、龙图形的座毯，像去约会的少女。藏民花十天时间用象征地、水、火、风、空的五种颜色把牦牛打扮得五彩缤纷。"威武的牦牛在节日里露出娇艳的一面，似乎也让我们看到了坚韧的藏民族有颗柔软的心。

Laurence Brahm, an American, says, 'During Shoton Festival, yaks are dressed up as pretty girls. People put *hadas* on their horns, tie flowers onto their fur, and cover their backs with cushions decorated in patterns of lions and dragons. They look just like young girls going on a date. Tibetans usually spend ten days decorating yaks with the five colors representing earth, water, fire, wind and sky respectively.' The mighty yaks show their tender and beautiful sides during this festival, and they symbolize the soft hearts of the tenacious Tibetans.

逸闻·趣谈
Cool Stories

一首老歌
An Old Song

民俗学家廖东凡在他的书里记载了西藏一首关于尼姑的老歌:"在所有的狗里,最自由的是野狗;虽然没有早饭晚饭,但也没有铁链拴着颈脖。在所有的女人里,最自由的是尼姑;虽然没有头饰胸饰,但也不用侍候丈夫公婆。"这首歌也反映了崇尚"众生平等"的西藏传统观念。

Folklorist Liao Dongfan records this old Tibetan song about nuns in his book: 'Among all dogs, the wild ones are the freest. Although they go without breakfast or dinner, neither do they have chains on their necks. Among all women, nuns are the freest. Although they have no headwear or plastrons, neither do they need to attend to husbands or parents-in-law.' This song also reflects the traditional Tibetan idea that advocates the concept of 'equality of all beings'.

西藏人的名字
Tibetan Names

西藏人有两种常见的名字,一种用出生当天的星期几来命名,另一种就是吉祥用语,比如次仁——长寿;顿珠——如意等。讲究一些的人家要请僧人取带有宗教色彩的名字,比如卓玛——仙女;卓嘎——度母;多吉——金刚等。也有的为了好养活,给孩子取名为其加——狗屎。

There are two common ways for Tibetans to choose their names: using the day of the week on which they were born, or using auspicious expressions, such as 'Tsering' (long life), and 'Dondrup' (as one wishes). Some families ask monks to give their babies a religious name. For instance, 'Drolma' means 'fairy'; 'Drolkar' is Tara (a bodhisattva); and 'Dorje' is *vajra* (the firmness and power of spirit). In the hope that their baby can survive easily, some parents name their child 'Chikya', which means 'dog shit'.

评论

微观西藏
TIBET: FAST & FURIOUS

布达拉宫前的大象
Elephants Below Potala Palace

大象本是热带地区的动物,可是在高寒的拉萨,过去却曾经居住着一公一母两头大象。每天,牧象人把它们牵到布达拉宫前的草地上吃草,然后赶着它们绕布达拉宫转个"孜廓"。这时,大象还会面朝布达拉宫行礼。很少有西藏人见过大象,更别说这样通人性的大象,所以人们把它们视为神物,称呼时都会用敬语。

Elephants are tropical animals. However, an elephant couple used to live in high and frigid Lhasa. Every day, elephant tenders would herd them into the grassland below the Potala Palace. Then they took the elephants around the Potala Palace to practice circumambulation. At this point, the elephants would turn their faces toward the Potala Palace and salute it. Few Tibetans had ever seen elephants, not to mention elephants behaving like humans. Therefore, people regarded them as supernatural creatures, and used honorific terms to address them.

甜茶馆的绰号
Nicknames of Sweet Tea Houses

藏族人是起绰号的能手,就连日常去的甜茶馆都有自己的绰号。有一家被人叫作"华丽鼻涕"的茶馆是因为装修华丽而甜茶却淡得像清鼻涕一样。还有一间茶馆,由于最早开始尝试晚上营业,而得名"猫头鹰茶馆"。"漏底茶馆"的名字传开,则是因为开张头一天卖的藏包子就露馅儿了。

Tibetans are experts at giving nicknames. They even nickname the sweet tea houses they often go to. One teahouse is called 'Luxury Snot' because the tea the shop serves is as light as clear snot and it is luxuriously decorated. Another one is named 'Owl Teahouse' because it was the first teahouse that attempted opening at night. The name of 'Leaking Teahouse' spread because the Tibetan-style steamed buns sold in the shop leaked on its opening day.

评论

摄影：觉果

聪明的黑颈鹤
Smart Black-Necked Cranes

几乎跑遍西藏的著名画家余友心先生有这样的亲身经历：黑颈鹤看到外地人老远就飞走了，看到当地人却一动不动。也许这就是它们能在这片恶劣的自然环境中繁衍生息的秘诀。

The famous painter Yu Youxin, who has been to most places in Tibet, had this personal experience: black-necked cranes would fly away when they saw non-local visitors in the distance, but they would stay at the same spot if they saw local people. Perhaps that is one of the secrets enabling them to thrive under the harsh natural environment.

魔湖
The Demon Lake

一般来说，藏族人往往将散落在青藏高原的湖泊视作神湖，可是，神湖也有"善恶"之分，人们相信大部分神湖能为他们带来福德，若喝了湖水，甚至可消除掉身上的疾病。但在藏北羌塘的扎布曲，有个即使到了冬天也不会冰封的小湖，当地人称它是"魔湖"，相传谁的影子投入到湖塘中，谁就会被湖魔吞掉。

Generally speaking, Tibetans designate many of the lakes spread around the Qinghai-Tibet Plateau as holy lakes. However, despite their holiness, some have turned into 'good' and 'bad' lakes over time. People believe that most of the lakes will bring them good fortune, and drinking water from these lakes can cure disease. However, in Tsapoqu of Changtang in Northern Tibet, there is a lake that does not freeze even during the winter. It is called 'Demon Lake' by the local people. It is said that if your shadow falls upon the lake, you will be swallowed by the demon of the lake.

微观西藏
TIBET: FAST & FURIOUS

摄影：觉果

能穿的都穿上
Wear All You Can

画家昂桑介绍说，藏女喜欢戴很大的玉石和绿松石项链，特别是康巴妇女，她们会把自己所有能戴的、能穿的都戴上、穿上。在重大节日里，有的人戴的、穿的太多，路都走不动了，要几个人把她抬到台上。她们表达了藏族人民内心的感情，那便是把最美的东西展现给别人。

Painter Ang Sang says, 'Tibetan women, especially Khampa women, love wearing big necklaces of jade and turquoise. The Khampa women usually put on everything they are able to wear.' At large festivals, if someone wears too much to walk, others will carry her to the platform. These women display Tibetans' inner emotions: showing the most beautiful things to others.

逸闻·趣谈
Cool Stories

本命年的"水萝卜"
'Water Radish' During One's Zodiac Year

在西藏,本命年被认为是一个敏感的年份。有人讲了这样一个故事:从前拉萨有规矩,本命年不得吃鱼,如若发现,就被用鱼钩钩住嘴唇,在八廓街游街一圈,以示惩处。但是一些正逢本命年的人仍然想吃禁果,走街串巷的卖鱼人迎合这一心理,叫卖时只喊"卖水萝卜"。

In Tibet, one's zodiac year (every twelfth year from the year one was born) is considered to be sensitive. There is a story: in the past, there was a rule that forbade people to eat fish during their zodiac years. If anyone was found to have violated the rule, he or she would be punished by being paraded on Barkhor Street with lips clamped shut by a fishhook. However, some people in their zodiac years still wanted to eat fish, thus fish sellers who peddled their wares would cry 'water radish' to cater to this need.

被姑娘抱上马
Put on a Horse by a Girl

有人讲了一个故事,一个内地来的人在乡间骑马,因缺氧总爬不到马背上。一位藏族姑娘走过来,轻松地将他抱起来放在马背上,嫣然一笑,然后离去。时隔多年,这人都在惊讶那姑娘抱男人像抱婴儿一样的力量和她敢于抱陌生男人的勇气。

Someone told a story about a man from the mainland who wanted to ride a horse in the countryside. Due to oxygen deficiency, he couldn't get on the back of the horse. A Tibetan girl came, picked him up easily and dropped him onto the horse's back. With a sweet smile, she left. Years have passed and the man is still amazed by the power of the girl who picked him up as if he were a child, as well as by her courage to carry a male stranger.

评论

在高原上烧开水
Boiling Water on the Plateau

西藏阿里的开水只有60度左右，而且烧到这个温度也要等个40来分钟。作家毕淑敏说，40多年前她在阿里用烧菜的大铁锅煮水，一帮人拿着各种容器等着水开。但是"一看三不开"。碰上一个性急的人把锅盖揭开，大家就只能再多等两分钟了。最后，那水"就好像是被人们焦灼的目光烧开的"。

Water boils at about 60℃ in Ngari, and you have to wait over forty minutes for the water to get to that temperature. Writer Bi Shumin said that when she was in Ngari forty years ago, they used a big iron cooking pot to boil water. A group of people holding all sorts of containers waited around the pot for the water to boil, but it was a truly restless wait. Someone impatiently opened the pot cover to have a look, then everyone had to wait two more minutes. At last, the water 'seemed to be boiling because of the burning stares from the people's anxious eyes.'

惊人的茶消费量
Astonishing Tea Consumption

藏族人有"三日无茶就会病"的说法。茶不仅能提神，抵抗高原寒冷，还能帮助爱吃肉的藏民消化。因此，茶的消耗量是很惊人的。西藏最大的茶锅在大昭寺，过去拉萨举行传召法会时，要同时为三万名僧人供茶。一上茶，几百个茶务僧人就要扛着大茶壶，穿梭于一排排僧人之间，场面蔚为壮观。

Tibetans often say, 'A person will get ill in three days without tea.' Tea not only brightens their spirits and helps fight off the cold weather of the plateau, but also enables them digest the meat they love to eat. Therefore, the volume of tea consumption is astonishing. The biggest tea pot in Tibet is located in Jokhang Temple. In the past, when the Great Prayer Festival took place in Lhasa, tea was offered to 30,000 monks. At tea time, hundreds of 'tea monks' held large tea pots on their shoulders and served rows after rows of monks, presenting a spectacular sight.

逸闻·趣谈
Cool Stories

爱美的康巴人
Khampas Care about Looks

画家薛继业说，康巴人身材魁梧，头缠红色或者黑色的丝线，他们每个人都自以为傲，认为自己是最帅的。薛继业还讲了这样一个听来的笑话，说康巴汉子泡温泉，就怕"脱光衣服、解散头发之后，人家不知道自己是康巴人"。

Painter Xue Jiye describes Khampas as people who are 'tall and strong, with red or black silk thread binding their hair together. Everyone is proud of themselves and thinks they are the most beautiful creation ever.' Xue also tells a story he once heard: when a Khampa man was bathing in a hot spring, he was worried that 'once he took off his clothing and let down his hair, nobody would recognize that he was a Khampa.'

爱情花
Flower of Love

格桑花是高原的象征，花开八瓣，随处可见，普通得很。然而西藏却有一个很美的传说：不管是谁，只要找到了八瓣格桑花，就找到了幸福。有位影星在微博里秀了她得到的一束来自远方的格桑花，立即引发了一片热潮：千里迢迢从西藏采摘格桑花，再捧到恋人手中。

The *kelsang* flower is the symbol of the plateau. It is a quite ordinary flower with eight petals and can be seen all over Tibet. However, there is a beautiful legend in Tibet: if someone has found an eight-petaled *kelsang* flower, it signifies that he or she has found happiness. One movie star showed off on her blog a bundle of beautiful *kelsang* flowers she had received from a distant place. This instantly led to a craze of going all the way to Tibet just to fetch *kelsang* flowers and handing them to loved ones.

评论

微观西藏
TIBET: FAST & FURIOUS

摄影：车刚

做菜，是种权力
The Power of Cooking

20世纪70年代，作家色波到墨脱出差，一位门巴族妇女留他在家吃饭。女人把饭做好，却要等丈夫回来做菜。因为菜肴很珍贵，所以由谁做菜就成了权力的象征。门巴族人吃饭是每人用一个小碗盛自己的菜，所以在物质匮乏的墨脱，掌勺分菜的权力也就必然落在了男人手中。

In the 1970s, writer Sebo went on business to Mêdog County. A Monpa woman persuaded him to eat dinner at her home. The woman cooked rice, but she had to wait for her husband to come home to prepare the vegetables and meat. As vegetables and meat were extremely valuable, then the privilege of cooking them became a symbol of power. Every Monpa used a small bowl to hold their dishes. In an era when goods were in short supply, the power to fill the bowls with delicious food fell in the hands of men.

"阴间通道"
'Hell Channel'

纳木错湖畔有一个著名的"阴间通道"，传说它可以测量人的业障多少。积德行善的人，再胖也能穿得过；反之，有些人不论怎么挣扎，也不能从通道中挤出去，还会引得洞口外面的人哈哈大笑。

Next to Lake Namtso is the famous 'Hell Channel', which is said to be capable of measuring people's karma. Nice people, no matter how chubby they are, will manage to get through. In contrast, not so nice people, no matter how hard they struggle, will never get through the crowded channel, which will make visitors outside the channel burst into laughter.

逸闻・趣谈
Cool Stories

"盐语"
'Salt Language'

作家扎西达娃讲，过去每年冬春之交，西藏北部的藏民就赶着上百只或更多的牦牛去盐湖驮盐，用来交换粮食。盐人们从离开帐篷踏上驮盐路的那一刻起，他们之间就开始用一种很奇特的语言交流，据说这种语言是为了取悦盐湖女神，外人称之为"盐语"。

Writer Tashi Dawa recounts that in the past, between the end of winter and the beginning of spring, locals from the north of Tibet would drive hundreds of yaks toward the salt lakes. The yaks were used to carry salt back to trade for grain. From the moment the locals left their tents and began the journey of carrying salt, they would start to use an unusual language to communicate with each other. It is said this language would please the goddess of the salt lakes. Outsiders call it 'salt language'.

另类拯救
Another Type of Rescue

民俗学家廖东凡忆起在羊卓雍湖畔遇到过的一支队伍：大伙儿抬着一只被打死但被装饰得很漂亮的狼，挨个村庄地演出。当地人认为，打狼并非作孽，而是积善，是帮助狼早日结束罪恶的生命，使它的灵魂得到超度，所以他们还将狼打扮得漂漂亮亮的，体体面面地送它出发。

Liao Dongfan, a folklorist, recalls a hunting squad he came across by the Lake Yamdrok. They carried a beautifully decorated wolf they had killed in a procession around the villages. The local people believed that killing a wolf was not committing a sin, but accumulating merits. It was to help the wolf end its evil life sooner and release its soul from purgatory. So they also decorated the wolf beautifully to send it off with dignity.

评论

微观西藏
TIBET: FAST & FURIOUS

别有风情的扎扎服饰
Distinctive 'Zaza' Clothing

山南地区流行"扎扎服",即反穿的氆氇,传说与文成公主有关。一说是公主有次与扎扎地方的百姓饮酒作乐,敬酒的人将公主的衣服弄湿了,她就把氆氇反穿过来,别有一番风情,扎扎服饰得以流行。还有人说,由于松赞干布英年早逝,文成公主常反穿着氆氇,怀念夫君,被扎扎妇女看到了,便纷纷效仿。

The popular *zaza* clothing in Lhoka (Shannan) is made from *pulu* cloth* with the underside out. It is related in legend to Princess Wencheng. It is said when the princess first drank and partied with the local people, someone spilled a drink on her clothes when proposing a toast, and so she turned it inside out, making it stylish and popular. Others say when Songtsan Gambo died an early death, the princess turned her clothes inside out as a sign of mourning her husband, and local women followed suit when they saw her dressed in this way.

* A kind of handmade wool for clothes and blankets, it is also presented as a gift during rites.

僧人运动会
The Sports Games of the Monks

西藏有一类特殊的僧人,不读经、不坐禅,而是舞刀弄棍、尚武好斗。这些刀枪不离身的"武僧"叫作"陀陀",他们往往担任寺庙里的苦力杂役,比如熬茶、背水、分粥……有时也担任警卫。大寺院之间举行的体育对抗赛就是由陀陀唱主角的运动会,这些参赛"运动员"会充分施展拳脚,比赛精彩激烈。

There are a special type of monks in Tibet, who neither chant the Buddhist scriptures, nor do they sit in meditation. They are bellicose warriors who are skilled in playing with swords and sticks. These monks never walk around without weapons. They are called *dhatas*. They are often the ones who do the hard labor in temples, such as brewing tea, carrying water, and handing out porridge. Sometimes they also act as security guards. *Dhatas* play the leading role in sports games between large temples. These athletes put their martial arts and skills to good use, ensuring an intense and splendid competition.

逸闻·趣谈
Cool Stories

西藏庄园里的四大名著
The Four Great Classical Novels in a Tibetan Manor

江孜郊外的帕拉庄园是西藏保存最完好的旧时贵族豪宅。1959年以前，西藏赫赫有名的大贵族帕拉·扎西旺久就生活在这里。如今，在这座已经成为旅游景点的奢华庄园里，游人们惊讶地发现：汉式雕花门洞与藏式木门并存，而且门上还雕绘着中国四大古典名著里的故事。

At Phalha Manor in the Gyangze countryside stands the best-preserved manor of the old Tibetan nobility. Prior to 1959, the well-known Tibetan noble Phalha Tashi Wangchuk resided here. Today, this luxurious manor has become a popular tourist spot. Travelers often realize with surprise that Han-style engraved doors and Tibetan-style wooden doors coexist. In addition, even stories from China's Four Great Classic Novels are found carved on them.

神秘的古墓群
The Mysterious Tombs

在盛行天葬的西藏，拉孜方圆数平方公里的庞大古墓群显得尤为突出。古墓群有古墓135座，距今已逾千年。它的墓主人究竟是谁？有没有陪葬品？为什么在久远的过去，这里的丧葬习俗跟今天如此不同？没人说得清，也没有找到任何史料记载。

Tibet is known for the practice of celestial burials, so a large ancient tomb group in Lhatse County, measuring several square kilometers, seems quite out of place. It has 135 ancient tombs, some more than a thousand years old. Who are their owners? Are there any artifacts buried with them? Why were the funerary practices in the distant past so different from those of today? No one can say for certain, and no one has ever found any relevant historical records.

评论

微观西藏
TIBET: FAST & FURIOUS

摄影：觉果

牦牛的秘密
The Secret of the Yaks

牦牛多生活在海拔 3000 米以上的高原，耐饥寒能负重，善渡险路激流，有"高原之舟"之称。近期科学家们研究发现，牦牛特有的三个基因可令其更好地适应高海拔的缺氧状态，另外五个基因则使其从食物中最大程度地获取能量。

Most yaks live on plateaus more than 3,000 meters above sea level. They can withstand cold weather and hunger, and are good at carrying heavy burdens and crossing perilous ground and water — thus they are known as the 'Ships of the Highlands'. Recently, scientists have discovered that yaks have three special genes that allow them to better adapt to the thin air at high altitudes, and another five genes that allow them to absorb as much energy from food as possible.

车牌号
License Plate Numbers

西藏的车牌很好记。有人戏谈：首府拉萨是老大，自然是藏 A；昌都的康巴汉子生性豪爽，爱喝啤酒（beer），是藏 B；字母 D 长得像大肚子孕妇，人丁兴旺的日喀则就是藏 D。

Tibetan license plates are very easy to remember. The capital Lhasa is the boss, so its license plate is naturally '藏 A' (藏 is the Chinese abbreviation for the Tibet Autonomous Region). The Khampas from Qamdo are expansive in nature and love beer, thus they are '藏 B'. The letter 'D' looks like a big-bellied pregnant woman, thus Xigaze, the region with the most population, is '藏 D'.

女人节
Women's Day

总以为拉萨是一个神圣庄严的地方，没想到也有一个有趣的节日：女人节。这天女人们可以随便使性子，可以随便向男人要钱，不能不给。一个单位的女同胞，这天连要带"抢"的钱多达上千，晚上大家一起HAPPY。不过，朋友说，也有小气的男人在这天躲起来。

I always thought Lhasa was a sacred and solemn place, but quite unexpectedly I discovered an amusing holiday: Women's Day. On this day women can be capricious. They can casually ask money from men, who cannot refuse. The female workers in a workplace can collect up to a thousand yuan by asking, or even 'robbing', on this day. In the evening they go partying and celebrating. Nevertheless, as a friend told me, there are some stingy men who hide themselves on this day.

男人节
Men's Day

西藏不仅有女人节，还有男人节。据作家马丽华记述，过去在阿里的科加村，每年2月11到15日，男人们都要过男人节。他们聚集在科加寺门口的小广场上，喝酒看藏戏，享受坐在垫子上的特别待遇。而往常执掌家事的女人只能为他们把壶倒酒。

Tibet not only has a Women's Day but also a Men's Day. Author Ma Lihua records that in the past, every year from January 11 to 15, men would celebrate Men's Day in the Khorchak Village of Ngari. They would gather at the small plaza in front of the gate of the Khorchak Monastery, drink liquor, and watch Tibetan Opera, enjoying the special treatment of being seated on cushions. Their women, who were usually in charge of the family, could only pour drinks for them.

微观西藏
TIBET: FAST & FURIOUS

西藏情结
Tibetan Romance

有记者访问作家海岩时，才发现尽管他从未到过西藏，却常为笔下人物设定去西藏的情节。《玉观音》中杨瑞带着安心的玉观音到西藏朝拜；《五星大饭店》结尾，金志爱独自去了西藏……海岩说："一个人在追求心灵的变化、升华、安定时，就会选择远离尘嚣。在这种心态下，就会去西藏。"

When a reporter was interviewing author Hai Yan, he discovered that Hai Yan had never been to Tibet, but had simply penned tales for his characters associated with Tibet. In *The Jade Goddess of Mercy*, Yang Rui carries An Xin's jade goddess statue to Tibet for worship. At the end of *The Five Star Hotel*, Jin Zhi'ai goes alone to Tibet. Hai Yan said, 'When people seek spiritual change, sublimation, and tranquility, they need to get away from bustle and distractions. Then Tibet is the place to go.'

古老的天文历算
Astrology

西藏每年的传统历书都由藏医院主管天文历算的人员测算发布，不仅发布藏历日期，还预报来年是否风调雨顺，连每日的凶吉都一一标明。据说西藏的历书曾预报了1986年间当地的三次地震，连大体时间和方位都准确。一位院长还遗憾地说，若不是人手少，他们还能"报出震中"。

Traditional Tibetan calendars, including addenda, are issued annually by astrologers at the Hospital of Tibetan Medicine. They not only mark important Tibetan calendar dates, but also predict if the weather is propitious, with auspicious and unlucky days being specified. It is said that in 1986 the three major earthquakes were predicted, with the times at which they occurred as well as more or less accurate locations. A head of the hospital said regretfully that if they had had more hands, they'd have been able to 'predict the epicenters'.

评论

逸闻·趣谈
Cool Stories

摄影：聂晓阳

神仙眷侣
Divine Couples

西藏的神山圣湖都是成双成对的——念青唐古拉与纳木错、冈底斯与玛旁雍错、达尔果山与当惹雍错、西亚尔山与俄亚尔湖等。当地人借助想象的翅膀，为神灵们编出婚丧嫁娶、生儿育女的故事，创作了人与神交错的丰富的精神世界。

The holy mountains and lakes in Tibet are all in pairs — Nyainqen Tanglha and Lake Namtso, Gangdise and Lake Manasarovar, Mount Dargo and Lake Tangra Yutso, Xiyer Hill and Lake Eyar. The local people have created great spiritual realms with their imaginations, and enliven them with stories of funerals, weddings, and raising children, as well as those of dynamic interactions between the common people and the divine.

牦牛妈妈
The Mother Yak

"驴友"阿发讲了这样一个故事：有次在去林芝的路上，遇到一群牦牛，司机不停地按喇叭，几只小牦牛就是不肯离开公路。突然一只牦牛妈妈从草地上飞也似的冲上公路，用自己的身体挡住汽车，眼睛瞪着司机，任它的孩子们在车前嬉戏。司机毫无办法，只有耐心地停车等待。

Backpacker Afa told this story: once, when he was on his way to Nyingchi, he came across a herd of yaks. The driver kept honking, but several young yaks wouldn't leave the road. Suddenly, a mother yak dashed into the road, blocked the car with its body and stared at the driver. Her children went on playing in front of the car. The driver could do nothing but wait patiently.

267

微观西藏
TIBET: FAST & FURIOUS

善良的店员
A Kind Clerk

画家黄扎吉：我有一个藏族学生，她去打工卖服装，她知道进价是多少，所以每次有牧区来买衣服的人问她多少钱，她说80，然后又会偷偷和牧民说，你别买，这个进价只有20元。她没有办法把进价只有20元这个事藏在心里不说出来，那样的话她会很痛苦。结果是她被辞退了。

Painter Huang Zhaji says, 'I have a Tibetan student who worked as a clothing seller. She knew the buying prices, and when somebody from a pasturing area asked her how much certain clothing was, she would first say eighty, and then secretly tell the herdsman that he should not buy it since its buying price was only twenty. She couldn't hide the buying price in her heart, because it would make her feel pain. In the end, she was fired.'

奇妙的毛驴节
The Donkey Festival

过去，毛驴是西藏很多地方的主要驮畜，干着最繁重的活儿。为此，泽当地区专门有毛驴节。这一天，毛驴们被卸下脖套和木鞍，被邀请喝青稞酒，吃酥油茶，而农人们则要套上驴的脖套，学着驴的姿势，用嘴巴直接舔盆中的糌粑，还要学驴的姿态奔跑打滚，而自由的驴呢则乱蹦乱跳，人欢驴舞，热闹之极。

In the past, donkeys were the main beast of burden in many regions of Tibet, and they did the most onerous work. For this reason, in the Tsethang region, there is a special festival for donkeys. On this day, donkeys are freed of their collars and wooden saddles, and invited to drink barley liquor and butter tea. The farmers wear donkey collars and mime donkey postures, lapping up roasted barley flour from a pot, running and rolling around as donkeys do. Meanwhile, the donkeys jump around freely themselves — it is quite a sight.

评论

逃犯的西藏感受
A Fugitive in Tibet

有作家讲过一个故事：一个犯人逃到西藏四年，后来耐不住内心的煎熬回到家乡被逮捕。他对审讯人说，西藏的阳光太强烈，像火焰一样燃烧着自己的心，每次抬头都睁不开眼睛，于是每日间只能低头走路。

An author told this story: a criminal fled to Tibet, but eventually he was unable to bear the moral suffering that tortured his heart and he returned to his hometown after four years, where he was then arrested. He told interrogators that the sun in Tibet was too bright, burning his heart like a torch. Whenever he raised his head he could not open his eyes, and each day he could only walk with his head lowered.

摄影：车刚

微观西藏
TIBET: FAST & FURIOUS

藏书楼
Tibetan Libraries

藏域有自己的藏书楼，且浩瀚不亚于中原。这些藏书一般深锁于名寺之中，萨迦寺便因三千多部的珍贵藏书而知名。其中更有 20 部贝叶经，是镇寺之宝。贝叶经是用金粉把经文书写在贝多罗树叶上，极为罕见。据说曾有一位学者走遍印度，也所获无几，看到萨迦寺 20 部、近 4000 页贝叶经后不禁啧啧称奇。

Tibetan libraries have extensive collections that are comparable to those of the mainland. These books are usually locked up in well-known monasteries, with the Sakya Monastery having a collection of more than three thousand items. Among these works are twenty *pattras*, which are highly treasured by the monastery. A *pattra* is a rare kind of sutra written in powdered gold on palm leaves. It is said that a scholar once traveled all over India but saw very few of them, so the over four thousand pages of *pattras* treasured by Sakya left him awestruck.

"雪人"
The 'Yeti'

在人迹罕至的喜马拉雅山麓地区，最富神秘色彩的传说大概要算"雪人"了。在西藏的一些经书和史志上都有对雪人的记载，有人把它和尼斯湖水怪、UFO、百慕大三角区一起被列为"世界四大自然之谜"。据说 1960 年，中国人第一次登顶珠穆朗玛峰期间，登山队帐篷周围就时常出现一串串神秘的脚印。

In the inaccessible regions of the Himalayan foothills, the most outlandish legend is that of the 'yeti', or snowman. In a number of Tibetan scriptures and historical accounts, the existence of the yeti was vigorously affirmed, and it has been termed one of the four great mysteries of the earth besides the Loch Ness Monster, UFOs and the Bermuda Triangle. In 1960, when the Chinese team first summitted Qomolangma, the climbers found a set of huge freakish footprints around their tents.

评论

逸闻·趣谈
Cool Stories

西藏"桃花源"
'Peach Blossom Spring' in Tibet

昌都八宿县来古村被认为是西藏版的桃花源，是中国最美的村庄之一。村子附近的然乌湖下游山峰连成绝壁，湖水从唯一一个狭口流出，把这一带和外界隔绝。据说多年前，一位村妇不小心将一小捆麦穗掉在水里，冲到外面被一位年轻人发现，出于好奇他带着一群小伙子跋山涉水，才发现了这个村庄。

Leku village of Baxoi County in Qamdo is regarded as the Tibetan 'Peach Blossom Spring' *. It is one of the most beautiful villages in China. The escarpment downstream of Lake Rawok forms adjacent cliffs, and the lake water can only flow out through a narrow point, isolating this area from the outside. It is said that many years ago a village woman accidentally dropped a bundle of wheat ears into the lake. This bundle floated out of the lake and was found by a young man. Out of curiosity, he gathered a group of friends and traveled a long distance. In the end, they discovered this village.

* A fable by poet Tao Yuanming in 421 A.D. about the chance discovery of an ethereal utopia, where people led an ideal existence in harmony with nature, unaware of the outside world for centuries. Now this phrase is used to describe an unspoiled wilderness of great beauty.

布达拉宫传奇
The Legend of Potala Palace

对许多人来说，他们去西藏的理由就是布达拉宫。布达拉宫主楼13层，高178米，按颜色分为红宫和白宫两部分。据说，宫殿东墙是由拉萨一带的石匠完成的，墙角尖若刀斧；西墙由日喀则一带的石匠完成，讲求圆滑。传说，从东墙上扔下一只羊，到墙底羊被劈成两半；从西墙上扔下一个鸡蛋，滚到下面也完好无损。

For many people, the Potala Palace is the only reason to come to Tibet. The main building of the Palace is 178 meters high with thirteen floors. It is divided into a red palace and a white palace according to the wall colors. It is said the east walls of the palace were built by stonemasons around Lhasa, so the corners of the walls were made sharp like a knife, while the west walls were built by stonemasons from around Xigaze, who preferred rounded edges. Hence a story goes that if you drop a sheep from the east walls, it will be cut in half when it reaches the ground; if you drop an egg from the west walls, it will roll down intact.

微观西藏
TIBET: FAST & FURIOUS

摄影：车刚

吃羊羔的"黑狼"
The 'Black Wolves' and the Lambs

藏地牧民有一种习惯，养老了的牛、羊和牧羊狗要放生，任其自生自灭。有记者曾讲过这样一个故事：在昂仁县的一个村里，出现了两只"黑狼"专吃小羊羔，后来才发现，其实那"黑狼"就是牧民放生的牧羊狗，饿极了专捉小羊羔吃。

The shepherds of Tibet have a custom: when a cow, sheep, or sheepdog grows old, it is released to die on its own. A reporter once told this story: in a village in Ngamring, two black wolves were found to eat small lambs regularly. Later it was discovered that the two 'black wolves' were actually sheepdogs. They were feeding on young lambs because they were starving.

评论

逸闻·趣谈
Cool Stories

不能随便许愿
Don't Make Promises Carelessly

长期在西藏工作的记者宁世群说：与小喇嘛相处，你不能随便许愿，答应的事就一定要办到。有一次他答应天德林寺一个小喇嘛，给他看《西藏考古》一书，后来工作忙，把这事完全忘在脑后了。一年后他再去天德林寺，受到了众僧冷遇，方知喇嘛们把他看成了说谎的人。后来他赶紧托人把书捎去，才得到谅解。

Ning Shiqun, a veteran reporter who worked for a long time in Tibet, says that when you interact with young lamas, you can't make promises without keeping them. He once promised a young lama in the Tiandelin Monastery to lend him the book *Archaeology in Tibet*, but later he was busy with his work and forgot about the promise completely. A year later he went to the monastery and was cold-shouldered by all of the lamas. He realized quickly that he was seen as a liar. He lost no time arranging for the book to be brought to the young lama, at which point he was forgiven.

婴儿性别先保密
Keep Your Baby's Sex Secret

西藏一些地方的民俗认为妇女分娩会给全家带来不洁，所以这期间全家人不能外出，也不让别人进家门。他们相信婴儿刚出生的几天，有一种恶神会把刚生的男孩变成女孩，所以要在7天后请喇嘛举行仪式，才能向外界正式公开婴儿的性别。人们相信，举行了这种仪式，才能保证婴儿及其全家平平安安。

People in some regions of Tibet believe that a woman's childbirth can bring uncleanness to the whole family. So, during this time, family members are not allowed outside and nobody is allowed into the house. They believe that during the first days after a child has been born, evil spirits will turn a boy into a girl. So they invite lamas seven days after the birth to perform rites, at which time they will also announce the sex of the child publically. Some people believe that the child's and family's safety can only be guaranteed once these rites have been performed.

防君子不防小人
It Can Only Stop Gentlemen

有"驴友"发现很多藏式小院的大门,即使从里面插上门栓,从外面也可以打开。原来,大门上有一个特殊的木制圆球,和门栓固定在一起,如果将圆球往右边拧,门栓就关上了;如果往左边拧,门栓就打开了。这种从里面和外面都可以控制的门栓,恐怕就是人们常说的"防君子不防小人"吧。

Some backpackers found that the gates of Tibetan yards can be opened from outside even if they have been bolted from the inside. As a matter of fact, there is a special wood ball on the gate that is fixed with the bolt. If the ball is turned to the right, the door is bolted; if it is turned to the left, the door can be opened. Consequently, people from either inside or outside are able to turn the bolt of a gate. This is probably why people often say, 'It can only stop gentlemen, but not villains.'

摄影:聂晓阳

山、湖皆有灵
Spirituality of Mountains and Lakes

西藏人似乎总是小心翼翼，很少抱怨，也许怕抱怨会激怒神灵。他们相信山、湖都是神灵的魂魄居所，就像肉体都是灵魂寄居的地方一样。比如，藏北最著名的传说都与纳木错湖和念青唐古拉山有关，而且它们是一对"夫妻"。人们相信，在它们的本命年转山转湖，会给同样属相的朝圣者带来格外的好运。

Tibetans are always cautious and seldom complain because they worry that their gripes may infuriate the deities. For them, mountains and lakes are the homes for deities' souls, just as the body is the home for a human's soul. For example, the most famous tales in northern Tibet are about a 'married couple' — Lake Namtso and Nyenchen Tanglha Mountains. People believe circumambulating in the year of the mountains' and lakes' zodiac will bring special good luck to pilgrims of the same zodiac year.

专情的黑颈鹤
Faithful Black-Necked Cranes

世界上四分之三的黑颈鹤在西藏越冬，在林周县还有一个专门的黑颈鹤保护区。据说黑颈鹤很有灵性，情感专一，如果配偶死了，有的孤鹤会守在尸体旁不吃不喝，活活饿死。当地老人传说，黑颈鹤南迁那天，如果是晴天，失去爱人的黑颈鹤飞过湖面，看到自己的倒影，总以为是已逝的恋人，就会飞扑下去。

Three quarters of the world's black-necked cranes spend the winter in Tibet. There's a special reserve in Lhünzhub County for them. It is said that black-necked cranes are intelligent and faithful. If their spouses pass away, some of the lonely cranes will stay by the bodies until they themselves die from starvation. The local elders told such a legend: on the day when black-necked cranes migrate to the south, if it is sunny, those who have lost their spouses will swoop down into the water when they see their reflections in the lake, thinking they have seen their deceased lovers again.

评论

微观西藏
TIBET: FAST & FURIOUS

摄影：车刚

献哈达的故事
A Story about Hadas

哈达在西藏的消费量惊人，这是因为在庆典上，哈达要献给每一个需要祝贺的人和物。作家平措扎西讲过这样一个故事：他的一位朋友去为一处新建房贺喜，因为新房是旅馆，有六十多间房间，前去贺喜的人为每间房都挂上一条哈达，再加上为主人敬献的哈达，一个人总共献出去的哈达就将近七十条。

The consumption of *hadas* in Tibet is stunningly high for the reason that in each celebration, *hadas* should be presented to every person or object that deserves a blessing. Writer Phuntsok Tashi tells this story: one of his friends went to celebrate the construction of a new building. Since the new building was a hotel with more than sixty rooms, people who went there had to present one *hada* to each room. Consequently, including those given to the hosts, each congratulator had to offer nearly seventy *hadas*.

评论

逸闻·趣谈
Cool Stories

"去西藏"的别样含义
Special Implications of 'Going to Tibet'

作家尼玛达娃说：19世纪西方社会出现了一种时尚，当不能确定某人的下落时，人们就习惯性地说他去了西藏。在小说《空中楼阁的冒险》中，福尔摩斯解释他瀑布逃生后的去向时说："我在西藏旅行了两年，在那里以访问拉萨来消遣，并且与喇嘛首领度过了一些日子。"

Tibetan author Nyima Dawa says that western society developed a fashion in the nineteenth century of assuming that someone lost must have gone to Tibet. In the novel *Castles in the Sky*, Sherlock Holmes explains his whereabouts after escaping from a waterfall: 'I traveled in Tibet for two years, stayed Lhasa for leisure, and spent some time with the leading lamas.'

良辰吉日
Lucky Dates

西藏人很随性，他们会成倍地增加吉利的日子，删去不吉利的日子。比如可能藏历中会有两个连着的二月二日，却找不到二月四日。据说西藏人结婚，新娘必须在凌晨4点前嫁出去，因为一天中最初的几个小时被看作是最吉利的。

Tibetans are freewheeling. They tend to add lucky days in multiples and delete unlucky dates. For instance, there might be two February seconds in a row on a Tibetan calendar, but no February fourth. Moreover, since the first few hours of a day are considered to be lucky, in a Tibetan wedding the bride has to be married before four in the morning.

藏袍
Tibetan Robes

传统藏装的主要特点是肥腰、长袖、大襟、长袍，白天天热时可以脱下外衣袖子，或干脆露出一边臂膀以图凉快，把袖子束在腰间，显得豁达潇洒，到了晚上，宽敞的袖袍又可以当被子，一物多用。

Traditional Tibetan costumes feature a big waistline, long sleeves, a large front, and a long robe. When it gets hot in the day, you can take off the sleeves of the outer clothing or just put one arm in the air to cool off. After doing that you can tie the sleeves on your waist to appear more natural. At night, you can also use these big sleeves as a quilt. It's a multipurpose dress.

微观西藏
TIBET: FAST & FURIOUS

受欢迎的白颜色
Popular Color White

在西藏，白色代表的是力量和尊贵。过去有些穷人为了省钱，不给小孩献哈达，但必须用白色糌粑在肩头点一下以表祝福；过去妇女在祭神时，头上要缠一撮白羊毛表示恭敬；以前用鞭刑惩罚犯人时，只要在受刑人屁股上放上哈达，就表示要替他说情。

In Tibet, the color white represents power and nobility. Formerly, poor people could not afford *hadas* (usually white traditional silk ceremonial scarves symbolizing purity and compassion) to present to children; therefore, they would pinch some white *tsampa* and touch the children's shoulders to show their good wishes. In the past, when worshipping gods, women had to wrap a clump of white wool around their heads to show their respect. If someone wanted to plead for a convict who was going to be caned, then he or she just needed to put a *hada* on the buttocks of the convict.

银屏下的祈祷
Prayer Before Screen

据说过去西藏刚刚能看到电影的时候，有一次扎什伦布寺组织看电影，喇嘛们看到影片中打仗死了很多人，居然自发地念起经来，为那些死去的生灵诵经超度。有一位高僧曾问阿底峡尊者，慈悲心该如何生起？尊者回答：就像爱自己的孩子一样爱一切众生。

It is said that in the past, when Tibetans had just started to watch movies, the lamas in Tashilhunpo Monastery were assembled for a film-watching event. When they saw many people being killed in a battle on the screen, they started reciting scriptures spontaneously to release the souls from purgatory. One eminent monk once asked the Venerable Atisa*, 'How should one cultivate mercy?' Atisa's answer was, 'Love everyone just as your own child.'

* Atisa (982—1054), a Buddhist teacher and a major figure, established a new lineage of Tibetan Buddhism.

评论

逸闻·趣谈
Cool Stories

摄影：觉果

帮典
Bangdian

"帮典"是极具特色的藏族妇女服饰。这种用五彩丝线或毛线手工织成的色彩亮丽的横条围裙，虽然在不同地区图案有所差别，但统一的规定是只有已婚女士才能佩戴。旅游者杨猫来到一家出售藏服的特色商店买"帮典"，店主惊讶地望着她，她忙指着身边的儿子说，"婚了婚了，连孩子都有了。"

Bangdian is a very distinctive kind of clothing for Tibetan women. It is a vibrantly colored, horizontally striped apron made by hand from threads of silk or wool in five different colors. Although the design varies in different regions, a unanimous stipulation states that only married women can wear this apron. A tourist named Cat Yang once went to a specialty shop that sold Tibetan costumes to buy a *bangdian*. The shopkeeper looked at her in surprise, so she pointed to her son who stood beside her, 'Well, I'm married, and I've even had a child.'

参考文献 | References

巴荒《阳光与荒野的诱惑》，东方出版社，1997年。
白玛娜珍《拉萨红尘》，西藏人民出版社，2002年。
白玛娜珍《西藏的月光》，重庆出版社，2002年。
白玉芬《藏族风俗文化》，西藏人民出版社，2007年。
毕淑敏《西藏，面冰十年》，北京十月文艺出版社，2011年。
边巴次仁《拉萨河畔的洗澡盛会》，《中国三峡》2009年第4期。
曹水群《西藏饮食文化资源的特点及其旅游开发》，《云南财经大学学报（社会科学版）》2010年第2期。
陈丹青《高原遗存的梦痕》，《文汇报》2010年4月18日。
陈坤《突然就走到了西藏》，华东师范大学出版社，2012年。
陈立明、曹晓燕《西藏民俗文化》，中国藏学出版社，2010年。
多识仁波切《爱心中爆发的智慧》，国际文化出版公司，2010年。
杜文娟、刘伟《阿里阿里》，江苏文艺出版社，2012年。
顾胜祥《雪域情思——回忆我的援藏岁月》，《秘书工作》2008年第10期。
何奕霖《阿来小说中的西藏地域文化书写》，《北方文学》2011年10月刊。
胡小伟《"大地"上信仰的旗帜》，《安徽文学》2008年第3期。
加央西热《盐湖的传说及驼队的遭遇》，《西藏行吟——西藏诗歌散文选》，中国藏学出版社，2007年。
兰仁巴大师《心传录——一位西藏著名修行者的笔记》，甘肃民族出版社，2006年。
李澍晔、刘燕华《八廓街58个男背包客的内心独白》，中国民主法制出版社，2011年。
李文韬《西藏支教日记》，清华大学出版社，2011年。
刘垚《西藏登山学校成立十周年 尼玛次仁守望雪山》，《北京晚报》2009年7月6日。
廖东凡《藏地风俗》，中国藏学出版社，2008年。
廖东凡《节庆四季》，中国藏学出版社，2008年。
廖东凡《灵山圣境》，中国藏学出版社，2008年。
廖东凡《雪域众神》，中国藏学出版社，2008年。
廖东凡《雪域西藏风情录》，西藏人民出版社，1998年。
廖东凡等《漫游西藏》，西藏人民出版社，1998年。
凌仕江《你知西藏的天有多蓝》，《环境导报》1998年第15期。
凌仕江《西藏的天堂时光》，地震出版社，2007年。
凌仕江《说好了一起去西藏》，中共中央党校出版社，2008年。
凌仕江《西藏时间》，当代中国出版社，2011年。
刘沙《西藏梦想地》，上海文艺出版社，2009年。
龙安志《寻找香格里拉——中国西部之行》，新世界出版社，2008年。
卢小飞《西藏的女儿——60年60人口述实录》，中国藏学出版社，2011年。
马丽华《藏北游历》，中国藏学出版社，2007年。
马丽华《藏东红山脉》，中国藏学出版社，2007年。
马丽华《灵魂像风》，中国藏学出版社，2007年。
马丽华《西行阿里》，中国藏学出版社，2007年。

马丽华《风化成典：西藏文史故事十五讲》，中国藏学出版社，2009 年。

南怀瑾《禅与生命的认知》，东方出版社，2009 年。

尼玛达娃《西藏，改变一生的旅行》，汕头大学出版社，2011 年。

聂晓阳《与仓央嘉措一起修行》，华夏出版社，2011 年。

宁世群《藏传佛教僧侣生活》，青海人民出版社，1998 年。

裴闯、拉巴、季明《藏民族姓氏的变化》，《西藏日报》2005 年 8 月 31 日。

彭西梅《〈系在皮绳扣上的魂〉中人物解析》，《井冈山学院学报》2008 年第 1 期。

平措扎西《世俗西藏》，作家出版社，2005 年。

桑杰端智《藏文化与藏族人》，甘肃民族出版社，2009 年。

桑吉扎西《当关羽遇上格萨尔》，《中国宗教》2010 年第 3 期。

色波《你在何方行吟》，四川文艺出版社，2002 年。

索甲仁波切《西藏生死之书》，中国社会科学出版社、青海人民出版社，1999 年。

沙漠驼铃《醉在拉萨》，《商业文化》2010 年第 3 期。

沈宗濂、柳陞祺《西藏与西藏人》，中国藏学出版社，2006 年。

盛噶仁波切《我就是这样一个活佛》，江苏文艺出版社，2008 年。

书云《西藏一年》，北京十月文艺出版社，2009 年。

宋步明《玛尼石》，《宿迁日报》2009 年 12 月 6 日。

谈锡永《密宗百问》，华夏出版社，2008 年。

汪曾祺《国风文丛·西藏卷：雪域佛光》，中国对外翻译出版公司，1996 年。

王敏《西藏：走出香格里拉的神话》，《社会观察》2011 年第 9 期。

王尧、陈庆英《西藏历史文化辞典》，西藏人民出版社、浙江人民出版社，1998 年。

《西藏文学丛书》编委会《西藏行吟——西藏诗歌散文选》，中国藏学出版社，2007 年。

向庸《以珠峰为禅》，新星出版社，2010 年。

邢肃芝［洛桑珍珠］口述，张健飞、杨念群笔述《雪域求法记》，生活·读书·新知三联书店，2008 年。

许敏《马原：西藏把我点燃》，《新世纪周刊》2006 年 5 月 8 号刊。

杨嘉铭、赵心愚、杨环《西藏建筑的历史文化》，青海人民出版社，2003 年。

杨君《藏族为中华文明做出了重大贡献》，《中国宗教》2007 年第 12 期。

雨程程《走进青藏高原之五——印象拉萨》，《中外建筑》2012 年第 2 期。

张婷《干杯，西藏！》，《凤凰周刊》2006 年第 22 期。

张祖文《看着你开花——告诉你一个真实的西藏》，印刷工业出版社，2011 年。

子文《苍茫西藏》，中国工人出版社，2009 年。

《中国西藏》《中国藏学》《西藏旅游》《西藏文学》《西藏人文地理》，2007—2012 年。

| 后 记 |

在编写这本书的过程中,我们在走访之余,研读了四百多篇论文,细看了一百多本有关书籍,翻阅了大量的杂志。应该说,这本书是站在诸多前辈学人和作者的肩膀上。在此,我首先要向这些长期以来默默耕耘西藏、传播西藏的各界人士表示感谢,并向他们致以深深的敬意。

我还要感谢商务印书馆,尤其是感谢商务印书馆副总编辑周洪波先生和总编室主任刘祚臣先生。周洪波先生还亲自前往西藏调研,并参与了本书所有重要的讨论,全程鼎力呵护和支撑每一个成书环节。可以说,没有他的勇气、智慧和坚持,就不会有这本书的问世。

感谢好友郑红兵,他用一块"如母石"的缘分帮我真正走上探寻雪域精神世界的旅程。也感谢我的朋友强沫先生、John Conner 教授、Gerald Kato 教授、Dan Boylan 先生、郭颖颐(Dr. Kwok)教授、王在喆博士、Walter Chang 先生、Vernon Ching 先生、Frances Goo 女士以及 Richard & Clarita Kaapuni 夫妇等,和他们的多次讨论坚定了我人生下半场致力于"信仰研究和写作"的信念。尤其要感谢的是 James Patton 先生和 Julia Chu 女士,在美丽的夏威夷,有几个月的时间,我每周至少有两天会去他们家拜访,在他们风景宜人的半山雅居里,我们不仅享受美食和咖啡,而且每次都会有七八个小时的热烈讨论,讨论的中心话题就是西藏。在北京访问期间,Patton 先生还特意抽出两天时间和我讨论本书构想,并为本书贡献了英文书名。

感谢本书的责任编辑储丹丹,如果不是她卓越的组织工作和流程服务,本书的诞生不会这么顺利。感谢肖淼晨,作为我的助理她做了大量工作,夜以继日,勤奋敬业。也感谢本书项目组的同事胡继平、蔡长虹、吕海春、倪咏娟、胡逸君、周驰、何毓玲、钟鸣、王冰等,和他们的合作不但富有成效,而且十分愉快。

钟声先生自始至终关心本书进展,刘萱女士带给我们很多启发,旦增伦珠、刘伟、廉湘民、严文斌、陆俭明、张稷、袁舫、钱厚生、朱英璜、谭宏凯、张永青、丁逸旻、朱宏立、邵玉进、魏武、余友心、韩书力、车刚、吴雨初、觉果、廖琴、德庆卓嘎、次仁罗布、丹增塔克、黄扎吉、平措次仁、多吉占堆、强巴顿珠、卓锋、刘长江、曾晓东、多穷等师友也先后为本书贡献了他们的思想、建议和各种形式的支持,在此一并表示诚挚的谢意。

感谢我的年轻朋友杨惠妍、陈翀夫妇,他们委托我在北京市红十字基金会设立专项基金,救助一批急需帮助的西藏先天性心脏病患儿,不但深化了我的"藏缘",更使我有机会和那些纯朴的西藏孩子和他们的家长亲密接触,同哭同笑,把自己的心和他们的融为一体。

当然,要感谢的人还有很多,但最郑重的感谢要献给西藏,这方离天最近的土地和纯朴善良的人民。愿所有人都能从我们挂一漏万的"微观"中有所受益。

聂晓阳
2012 年 9 月

Afterword

During the preparation of this book, in addition to all the interviews, we studied over four hundred essays, read more than a hundred relevant books, and browsed a large number of magazine articles. We should say that this book stands on the shoulders of many predecessor scholars and authors. So I would first like to express my appreciation and pay my respects to them.

I would also like to thank the Commercial Press, especially the Deputy Editor-in-Chief Zhou Hongbo and the Director of the Chief Editor's Office, Liu Zuochen. Mr. Zhou personally led a group to Tibet for interviews and attended all critical discussions of this book, helping and supporting every stage of the publication. I can say that without his courage, intelligence, and persistence, this book would not have been published.

I want to thank my friend Zheng Hongbing. He helped me set off on the journey of discovering the spiritual world of this snow-covered plateau with the inspiration of a 'Tibet Mother-Stone'. I also want to thank Mr. Qiang Mo, Prof. John Conner, Prof. Gerald Kato, Mr. Dan Boylan, Dr. Kwok, Dr. Wang Zaizhe, Mr. Walter Chang, Mr. Vernon Ching, Ms. Frances Goo, and Mr. and Mrs. Kaapuni. The discussions I had with them on many occasions steadied my determination on faith-related writing. I particularly want to thank Mr. James Patton and Ms. Julia Chu. During several months in beautiful Hawaii, I would spend at least two days every week in their hillside home. We would not only enjoy delicious food and coffee, but also have vibrant discussions about Tibet. Mr. Patton also contributed an English title for this book.

I want to express my thanks to the executive editor of this book, Chu Dandan. Without her remarkable work with regards to organization and workflow, the preparation of this book would not have run as smoothly as it did. I also want to thank my assistant Xiao Miaochen. She has diligently and dedicatedly done a large amount of work around the clock. My appreciation also goes to Hu Jiping, Cai Changhong, Lyu Haichun, Ni Yongjuan, Hu Yijun, Zhou Chi, He Yuling, Zhong Ming, Wang Bing and others that had contributed to this project. The cooperation with this team was not only productive, but also delightful.

Zhong Sheng guided the progress of this book from beginning to end, while Liu Xuan gave us many ideas. Tenzin Lhundrup, Liu Wei, Lian Xiangmin, Yan Wenbin, Lu Jianming, Zhang Ji, Yuan Fang, Qian Housheng, Zhu Yinghuang, Tan Hongkai, Zhang Yongqing, Ding Yimin, Zhu Hongli, Shao Yujin, Wei Wu, Yu Youxin, Han Shuli, Che Gang, Wu Yuchu, Jogod, Liao Qin, Dechen Drolkar, Tsering Norbu, Tenzin Take, Huang Zhaji, Phuntsok Tsering, Champa Dondrup, Zhuo Feng, Liu Changjiang, Zeng Xiaodong, Doje Zhamdu, Doqung and other friends also contributed their thoughts, advice, and support in various ways, and I would like to express my sincere appreciation to them.

I want to say thanks to my friends Yang Huiyan and Chen Chong. The young couple entrusted me with establishing a special fund at the Beijing Red Cross Foundation to help those who have congenital heart disease in Tibet. This not only deepened my attachment to Tibet, but also gave me a chance to have a close contact with a number of Tibetan children and their parents. I cried and laughed with them, knitting together my heart and theirs.

Of course, there are still many other names that need to be mentioned. However, the most earnest appreciation goes to Tibet, a land that is closest to sky, and to the kind Tibetans. I sincerely hope everyone can learn something from this book.

Nie Xiaoyang
September, 2012

图书在版编目(CIP)数据

微观西藏:汉英版:汉英对照/聂晓阳主编.—北京：商务印书馆，2012(2018.9重印)
(微观中国)
ISBN 978-7-100-09474-0

I.①微… II.①聂… III.①西藏—概况—汉、英 IV.①K927.5

中国版本图书馆 CIP 数据核字(2012)第 218732 号

权利保留，侵权必究。

微 观 西 藏
(汉英版)

Tibet: Fast & Furious

聂晓阳　主编

商 务 印 书 馆 出 版
(北京王府井大街 36 号　邮政编码 100710)
商 务 印 书 馆 发 行
北京中科印刷有限公司印刷
ISBN 978-7-100-09474-0

2012 年 9 月第 1 版　开本 787×1092　1/16
2018 年 9 月北京第 2 次印刷　印张 18¼
定价：68.00 元